D1078845

NEW PERSPEC
ON BULLYING

NEW PERSPECTIVES ON BULLYING

Helen Cowie and Dawn Jennifer

McGraw Hill

Open University Press

Open University Press
McGraw-Hill Education
McGraw-Hill House
Shoppenhangers Road
Maidenhead
Berkshire
England
SL6 2QL

email: enquiries@openup.co.uk
world wide web: www.openup.co.uk

and Two Penn Plaza, New York, NY 10121—2289, USA

A catalogue record of this book is available from the British Library

ISBN-10: 0-33-522247-7 (pb) 0-33-522243-9 (hb)
ISBN-13: 978-0-33-5222476 (pb) 978-0-33-5222438 (hb)

Typeset by Kerrypress, Luton, Bedfordshire
Printed and bound in the UK by Bell and Bain Ltd, Glasgow

The McGraw-Hill Companies

In memory of Isabel (HC)

To Tony (DJ)

CONTENTS

Acknowledgements   IX

List of figures   X

List of tables   XI

1 Knowledge about school bullying   1

2 The whole-school approach   23

3 Working with the relationship to help the bullied pupil   40

4 Working with the relationship to change bullying behaviour   53

5 Working with the relationship to help the whole class   67

6 Peers helping peers   85

7 The role of narrative in counteracting bullying   104

8 Creating a supportive environment   117

References   132

Subject and author index   155

ACKNOWLEDGEMENTS

The authors would like to thank the following people for their contributions to the writing of this book: Soledad Andrès, Tony Daly, Milagros Escobar Espejo, Stefania Ferrazzuolo, Sonia Sharp, Julie Shaughnessy, Cathy Warren, Siân Williams and World Health Organization.

We would like to thank Taylor and Francis (UK) Journals (http:www.informa-world.com) for permission to reproduce Figures 3 and 4 from Cowie, H. and Sharp, S. (1992) 'Students themselves tackle the problem of school bullying', *Pastoral Care in Education*, 10(4): 31–37 as Figures 5.1 and 5.2.

Tables

1.1 Protective factors of bullying   20
5.1 Developing effective groups   75

Figures

1.1 Ecological model for understanding school bullying   19
2.1 A relational model for addressing school bullying   34
5.1 Why? Why? diagram   77
5.2 How? How? diagram   79
6.1 Forms of peer support   86
8.1 Knowledge about school bullying   119

1 KNOWLEDGE ABOUT SCHOOL BULLYING

Chapter overview

Teachers have a reasonable knowledge about the nature of school bullying, particularly physical forms. However, even though they recognize it as an issue, they often underestimate the seriousness of relational bullying and its negative impact on the victim. Furthermore, many teachers lack the knowledge, skills and confidence with which to recognize and challenge bullying.

This chapter focuses on the essential aspects of school bullying that experienced teachers and teachers in training will need to be aware of in order to address the issue. We identify the different forms that bullying takes–physical, verbal, relational and cyber–and highlight some individual differences that might be used as a reason for bullying, such as, race, religion or culture, disability, sexual orientation and gender. We explore participant roles in school bullying including bullies and their assistants, victims and their defenders, bully–victims and bystanders. We examine the risk factors for bullying, drawing upon examples identified by research on school bullying and youth offending and highlight protective factors that might help to safeguard children and young people from involvement in bullying.

The essential aspects of school bullying

Issues of definition

While there has been a growing worldwide interest in school bullying among practitioners, researchers, and parents and carers over the past 25 years, there is currently no consensus regarding its definition, with variations widespread in the literature and numerous discussion and review papers published on the subject (e.g. Arora 1996; Naylor et al. 2006; Smith et al. 2002; Underwood et al. 2001). Nevertheless, there is general agreement regarding the key characteristics that constitute bullying. These include the deliberate intention to harm another individual; repetition of the bullying behaviour over time; and an imbalance of power, such that the victim has difficulty defending him- or herself effectively (e.g. Olweus 1991; Smith and Morita 1999). Not all researchers are in agreement with these key criteria, however. For example, a minority believe that an aggressive behaviour does not have to be repeated over time to be considered bullying (e.g. Stephenson and Smith 1989).

A commonly used definition for research purposes is one proposed by Olweus (1994). He defines school bullying as a subset of aggressive behaviour with certain specific characteristics such that 'a person is being bullied or victimized when he or she is exposed, repeatedly and over time, to negative actions on the part of one or more other students' (Olweus 1994: 1173). He further states that 'there is a good deal of bullying without violence (e.g. bullying by words, gestures, intentional exclusion from the group) and, likewise,... there is a good deal of violence that cannot be characterized as bullying (e.g. an occasional fight in the playground)' (Olweus 1999: 12). There appears to be general agreement that the terms 'bullying' and 'violence' overlap, and that the accepted understanding of bullying is that it is a particularly destructive form of aggression (Slee 2003).

A review of the literature suggests that teachers and pupils hold much broader definitions of bullying than those used by researchers, particularly younger children (e.g. Guerin and Hennessy 2002; Smith et al.1999). For example, in a questionnaire survey of 225 teachers and 1820 secondary school pupils, which sought to investigate definitions of bullying, Naylor et al. (2006) found that only 18 per cent of teachers and 8 per cent of pupils included repetition of bullying behaviour in their responses. Furthermore, only 25 per cent of teachers and 4 per cent of pupils included intention to harm, and while nearly three-quarters of teachers invoked the imbalance of power criterion in their definitions, only 40 per cent of pupils did so.

Indeed, research findings suggest an age trend in children's definitions of bullying with changes in how they define the term as they get older (Naylor et al. 2006; Smith et al. 1999; Smith et al. 2002). The results of a study that explored the definitions of 166 primary schoolchildren, with a modal age of 12, suggested that repetition and intention might not be the most important defining characteristics of bullying (Guerin and Hennessy 2002). Semi-structured interviews revealed that the majority of pupils believed that intent was not necessary for a particular behaviour to be defined as bullying. In terms of repetition, nearly half of all participants perceived that behaviours occurring once or twice constituted bullying; moreover, just over half reported that behaviours did not have to be repeated over time to be considered bullying. Indeed, using a pictorial questionnaire with 6- and -7-year-olds, Smith and Levan (1995) found that children's definitions of bullying included occasional or one-off episodes of fighting and aggressive behaviour. Furthermore, in an interview study of 159 partici-pants ranging in age from 5 to 29, younger children were significantly less likely to mention the imbalance of power criterion (Smith et al. 1999). Whereas 12 per cent of 9- to -10-year-olds mentioned an imbalance of power when defining bullying, 30 per cent of 15 to 16-year-olds mentioned this characteristic.

Physical, verbal and relational bullying

Early research into bullying focused on aggressive physical behaviour in boys, in part because physical aggression is more easily observable and of a form that is stereotypi-cally male (Underwood et al. 2001). In the 1980s and 1990s, however, research recognized other forms of bullying including verbal and psychological (e.g., Farrington 1993). Björkqvist, Lagerspetz and Kaukianen (1992) distinguished between direct physical, direct verbal and indirect aggression. *Direct physical* aggression includes such behaviours as pushing, hitting, punching or kicking. *Direct verbal* aggression may take the form of yelling abuse at another, name-calling, using insulting expressions or making verbal threats. *Indirect aggression*, sometimes referred to as social aggression (Cairns et al. 1989) or relational aggression (Crick and Grotpeter 1995), as the term implies, uses less direct forms of aggressive behaviour such as spreading malicious rumours about another, excluding a person from the group, or disclosing another's secrets to a third person (Björkqvist, Lagerspetz and Österman 1992). Given that these terms are used inter-changeably in the literature, we will do the same in this book.

Research with teachers suggests that relational bullying is perceived as less severe than other forms of bullying (Hazler et al. 2001). For example, in a study to compare preservice teachers' responses to physical, verbal and relational bullying scenarios, participants rated relational bullying as less serious than other forms of bullying (Bauman and Del Rio 2006). Furthermore, they expressed the least empathy for victims of relational bullying, were least likely to intervene in incidences of relational bullying, and proposed the least severe actions towards bullies involved in relational bullying than those engaged in physical or verbal forms (Bauman and Del Rio 2006).

This finding is consistent with the results of research with inservice teachers. In a recent study of primary, middle and high school teachers in Australia, Ellis and Shute (2007) found that physical bullying (spitting on someone) was rated as significantly more serious than verbal bullying (name-calling), which, in turn, was rated as significantly more serious than relational bullying (giving dirty looks). For incidents which teachers rated as less serious (giving dirty looks), relatively high numbers of teachers considered it best to let students sort it out for themselves, perceiving it as too minor to bother with and more influenced by whether they had time to deal with it. Gender differences were also apparent, with male teachers more likely to ignore dirty looks and rating name-calling as less serious than female teachers did. In order that harm to pupils can be reduced, the authors concluded that it is important that information about the detrimental effects of all types of bullying are disseminated to teachers and policy makers. To this end, Box 1.1 presents a summary of the negative consequences of bullying to pupils. (For further discussion, see Chapter 3.)

Box 1.1   Negative consequences of school bullying to pupils

There is ample evidence that illustrates the possible detrimental effects of bullying and other aggressive behaviour upon schoolchildren (e.g. Hawker and Boulton 2000; Rigby 2003). In their meta-analysis of 20 years' research, Hawker and Boulton (2000) found that victimization was most strongly associated with depression, and moderately associated with loneliness, and low social and global self-esteem. Bullies are more likely to experience social-psychological adjustment problems such as depression, loneliness and social isolation (Coie and Dodge 1998; Crick and Grotpeter 1995) and are at increased risk of bullying and offending as adults (Farrington 1995; Olweus 1991). Indeed, recent research suggests that engagement in school bullying is part of a more general violent and aggressive behaviour pattern. Specifically, bullying in school is strongly linked to violent behaviour and weapon-carrying on the streets (Andershed et al. 2001), and a significant predictor of later gang membership (Holmes and Brandenburg-Ayres 1998).

Although there is a dearth of literature on the effects of bullying on the peer group generally, the majority of pupils in a Canadian study reported that bullying was distressing (Harachi et al. 1999). This concurs with findings from a study that evaluated the effectiveness of peer support systems in challenging school bullying, which suggested that many pupils who had not actually used the system nevertheless appreciated the provision of the service to protect their safety, suggesting that they had felt unsafe before the system was introduced (Cowie 1998). Research into bullying in the workplace also supports the notion that bullying has an impact on the wider social group, with observers, as well as victims, experiencing their work environment more negatively than non-observers do (Jennifer 2000).

Nevertheless, previous research with pre-, infant, junior and secondary school teachers suggested that the majority felt a responsibility to prevent bullying in the classroom and in the playground (Boulton 1997). However, regardless of the length of service, participants expressed a lack of confidence in their ability to deal with bullying and 87 per cent said that they wanted more training (Boulton 1997). Indeed, research with trainee teachers found that the majority of participants were in favour of teacher training that incorporated activities on how to prevent bullying (Nicolaides et al. 2002).

Similarly, research suggests that children and young people consider relational aggression as less severe than other forms of bullying. An American study that investigated elementary children's moral reasoning about physical and relational aggression found that fourth and fifth graders tended to rate physical aggression (e.g. hitting a peer) as more wrong and harmful than relational aggression (e.g. excluding a peer from one's group of friends) (Murray-Close et al. 2006). In addition, girls tended to judge aggression in general as more wrong than boys did, and were more likely to believe that relational behaviours were harmful for the victim. Indeed, interviews with children and young people ranging in age from 8 to 16 revealed that while physical aspects of behaviour entered definitions of bullying at all ages, the youngest pupils aged 5 to 6 were less likely to define bullying in terms of verbal or indirect bullying behaviour (Smith et al. 1999). Examples of verbal bullying became more frequent in the later primary years, and examples of indirect bullying became more frequent at secondary school age.

To complicate matters even further, indirect aggression has been divided into subtypes. There has been much research into reactive (e.g. an angry or defensive response to provocation) and proactive aggression (e.g. to obtain a desired goal)

(Crick and Dodge 1996; Salmivalli and Nieminen 2002). Most research has focused on reactive forms of bullying and aggression whereby aggressive behaviours under investigation are a response to provocation employed to express anger and cause harm (Underwood et al. 2001). On the other hand, as has been previously suggested, aggression might be employed for more proactive reasons, for example, 'to attain status with particular peers or for the entertainment value of manipulating others' relationships or self-esteem' (Underwood et al. 2001: 253). Research in Australia, which supports this possibility, has found that adolescent girls mention alleviating boredom, creating excitement and managing peer relationships as major motivations for using indirect aggressive behaviours (Owens et al. 2000). Box 1.2 presents an example of a recent study that explored children's pictorial and narrative representations of their bullying experiences that identified sadistic aspects of bullying not currently captured in the existing subtypes of aggression. (See more on this study in Chapter 7.)

Box 1.2 Children's pictorial and narrative representations of bullying experiences

Bosacki et al. (2006) carried out an interview study in Canada with 82 children aged 8 to 12 that required participants to draw and narrate stories of 'someone being bullied'. In response to open-ended questions about the characters portrayed in the children's drawings, comments on bullies' motives for bullying concur with previously identified concepts of instrumental and reactive aggression (Crick and Dodge 1996; Salmivalli and Nieminen 2002). Other psychological motives that the children ascribed to the bully, however, were not consistent with existing subtypes of bullying and aggression; that is children mentioned sadistic motives, such as wanting to make the victim sad (70 per cent). Indeed, the bully was portrayed as smiling in 78 per cent of children's drawings of a bullying situation and when asked what the bully in their drawing might be feeling, 50 per cent of participants mentioned positive feelings, such as happy or glad. In addition, the majority of drawings (93 per cent) depicted only two participants; that is the bully and the victim, suggesting that children did not share adult researchers' claims that bullying is a social process that extends beyond the bully/victim dyad (Pepler et al. 1999; Salmivalli 2001a). The drawings did reflect, however, the notion of a power imbalance, with the majority of bullies portrayed as larger than the victims were. This finding contrasts with the results of a questionnaire study carried out by Naylor et al. (2006) which suggested that 13 to 14-year-old pupils were more likely than 11 to 12-year-old pupils to refer to an imbalance of power (Naylor et al. 2006).

It is difficult to be certain about the incidence of school bullying since, in addition to issues of definition, there is currently no systematic collection of school bullying statistics. Nevertheless, large-scale studies indicate that school bullying is a reality for many young people in the United Kingdom (UK) (e.g. Glover et al. 2000; Whitney and Smith 1993). Research conducted in 2006, in which 2132 pupils aged 9 to 14 participated, confirms that bullying is an issue for a substantial number of children and young people (Shaughnessy and Jennifer 2007). The results of this study also inform our understanding of the nature of school bullying in terms of common types of bullying behaviour, who engages in bullying others and the locations where bullying occurs (see Box 1.3).

Box 1.3 The scale and nature of bullying in schools

2132 pupils aged 9 to 14 drawn from 16 schools in a large UK city, including primary and secondary schools, a special school and a Pupil Referral Unit, participated. A self-complete anonymous questionnaire survey was conducted during the autumn term using an adapted version of the *Revised Olweus Bully/Victim Questionnaire* (1996). Results suggested that 40 per cent of primary children and 33 per cent of secondary children had been bullied *'once or twice'* or more in the past two or three months. In terms of bullying others, 25 per cent of primary school children and 31 per cent of secondary pupils reported that they had taken part in bullying others in the past two or three months, with boys significantly more likely to engage in bullying others than girls. Whereas in primary schools the majority of participants reported that bullying was carried out by pupils in the same class, in secondary schools equal numbers of participants reported that bullying was carried out by pupils in a different class and pupils in the same class. At both primary and secondary level, boys were more likely to report being bullied by one boy or several boys, whereas girls were more likely to report being bullied by one girl or several girls. In addition, in secondary schools, girls were more likely to report being bullied by both girls and boys than boys were.

In both primary and secondary schools, the most commonly experienced bullying behaviour took the form of being given dirty looks and having lies told about one. In addition, physical bullying was experienced frequently at primary level. Boys were more likely to experience physical bullying, while girls were more likely to experience indirect forms (i.e. being left out or ignored, having false rumours spread about one, being given dirty looks). The least reported bullying behaviours were nasty messages or pictures by text or mobile phone and nasty mobile phone calls. While the majority of bullying was reported to have occurred on the playground/school field (79 per cent of primary children and 69 per cent of secondary children reported this), 31 per cent of primary children and 49 per cent of secondary children reported that it had occurred in the classroom with the teacher present. In addition, primary pupils reported that bullying had occurred in the classroom with the teacher absent (34 per cent) and in the dining room (31 per cent). Boys were more likely than girls were to be bullied in the toilets. Secondary pupils reported that bullying had occurred in the classroom with the teacher absent (39 per cent), in the hallways/stairwells (34 per cent), in a PE class or the changing rooms/showers (32 per cent) and on the way to and from school (29 per cent). Girls were more likely than boys were to be bullied in the dining room; boys were more likely than girls to experience bullying in a PE class or the changing rooms/showers.

(adapted from Shaughnessy and Jennifer 2007)

While such self-report surveys enlighten us with regard to the incidence and nature of bullying in schools, some researchers have pointed out that the phenomenon cannot be understood without taking into account the social situation in which it takes place (O'Connell et al. 1999; Salmivalli 2001a). Lagerspetz et al. (1982) distinguished two important features of bullying, that is, it is collective in nature and it is based on social relationships in the group. Furthermore, research suggests that certain dimensions of the social group context (negative affect, high aversive behaviour, high activity level, low group cohesion, competitiveness) are related to the occurrence of aggressive behaviours among individual children in the group (DeRosier et al. 1994).

The social group context also has an effect on how children react to aggression between members of the group, for example, siding with the victim, which, in turn, influences the group atmosphere following the aggressive episode. Thus, some researchers have developed peer nomination and evaluation techniques to investigate participant roles in the bullying process (e.g. Björkqvist and Österman 1998; Salmivalli et al. 1996). The results of studies using such techniques suggest that peers play various roles in the bullying episode from providing an audience to becoming actively involved in the interaction between the bully and the victim (O'Connell et al. 1999). For example, the *Participant Role Scale* developed by Salmivalli et al. (1996) involved children evaluating how well each child in their class, including themselves, fits 50 behavioural descriptions of bullying situations (e.g. starts bullying, doesn't do anything) from which the Participant Roles were then derived. Pupils were also requested to identify peers in their class who were being bullied by others (Salmivalli et al. 1996).

In addition to the roles that one might expect to find, that is, *Bullies* and *Victims* as implicitly defined in the Olweus (1991) definition cited above, and those not involved, Salmivalli et al.'s (1996) research has distinguished a further four participant roles. *Assistants* actively participate in the bullying (e.g. through physically restraining a victim) and *Reinforcers* may provide positive feedback to a bully by shouting encouragement. Although *Outsiders* may not be directly involved (i.e. they are unaware of the incident), they may contribute indirectly to a bullying situation merely through silent approval or, possibly unwittingly, by not taking a stance (overt or otherwise) against a bully. Salmivalli (1999) suggests that some of those involved in bullying (e.g. Outsiders), although aware of their passive role and knowing that bullying often requires the intervention of others, may lack the necessary skills to intervene actively. Finally, and as the label suggests, *Defenders* actively defend victims by intervening in the bullying process through, for example, telling an adult or comforting the victim.

A similar procedure has been employed in the UK. Sutton and Smith (1999) used a shortened adaptation of the Participant Role Scale (Salmivalli et al. 1996) with 193 7 to 11-year-olds in England. They found that a participant role could be assigned to 84.5 per cent of the total sample, with 18.1 per cent victims, 14.0 per cent bullies,

5.7 per cent reinforcers, 7.3 per cent assistants, 27.5 per cent defenders, 11.9 per cent outsiders, and 15.5 per cent with no role. In addition, they found that 5.7 per cent of victims had a secondary role of bully, and 8.0 per cent of bullies had a secondary role of victim. Sometimes referred to as provocative or aggressive victims, these individuals display characteristics of both bullies and victims (Griffin and Gross 2004; Smith 2004). The role that a bully–victim takes is context-dependent, such that they may bully in situations where they are in a position of power, whereas in another situation they may be the victim. Moreover, these roles are not necessarily stable and static over time (Ferrazzuolo 2004). For example, a follow-up study designed to compare friendships, behavioural characteristics, victimization experiences and coping strategies of 406 pupils aged 13 to 16 provided information on participant role movement (Smith et al. 2004). Participants were followed up from an earlier study, which enabled the classification of victim profiles on two occasions, two years apart. The classification revealed that of the 204 victims participating in the first study, 58 could be classified as continuing victims, and 146 as escaped victims. Of the 209 non-victims participating in the first study, 175 had never been bullied over the previous two years (non-victims); whereas 34 were currently being bullied (new victims) (the remaining 7 were classified as in-between status and dropped from the analysis). Box 1.4 presents the results of a study which explored children's understanding of the social group context within which school bullying takes place, the results of which suggest that such adult perceptions of participant roles are not that clear-cut.

Box 1.4 Children's understanding of the social group context within which school bullying takes place

In an interview study with 64 Year 6 pupils, facilitated with the use of a hypothetical story of peer bullying using pictorial vignettes, Jennifer (2007) found that in respect of children's representations of each of the bully characters in the hypothetical story, participants identified three key roles. These were leader, assistant and follower or reinforcer, providing evidence of children's understanding of different roles that individuals take in bullying episodes. Each character in the hypothetical story was ascribed with distinct behavioural tendencies by participants. While these behavioural descriptions seem similar to researcher-generated descriptions of the Bully, Assistant of the Bully and Reinforcer of the Bully roles as itemized in the *Participant Role Scale* (Salmivalli et al. 1996), this study represented a distinctive opportunity for children to discuss participant roles in their own voices. As such, a gender difference was apparent, with male and female participants focusing on different forms of bullying behaviour for each of the three characters not previously documented.

In terms of the leader character, participants' representations focused on behaviours that were clearly proactive and leader-like. Furthermore, male participants focused attention on direct physical bullying such as fighting, physical restraint, stealing others' money or belongings, and hurting others, and direct verbal bullying, such as blackmail, teasing, threatening, swearing and shouting. On the other hand, female participants highlighted the leader's direct verbal bullying, such as threatening others, picking on individuals who were perceived to be different, swearing and using rude words, watching and laughing, and indirect bullying, such as ignoring others and social exclusion.

With regard to the assistant character, participants perceived that he or she played a supportive role in terms of offering assistance and encouragement, and providing support by 'tagging along'. In terms of specific bullying behaviours perpetrated by the assistant character, male participants highlighted behaviours such as restraining the victim and threatening others, while female participants focused on making fun of the victim. Furthermore, participants described behaviours such as feeling forced to bully others, obeying the leader and taking the blame for the bullying that clearly suggested that this character experienced the leader's behaviour as dominating and oppressive. Observing that the assistant participated in bullying others out of fear of the leader, specifically a fear of being bullied by him or her, clearly indicated that participants perceived that the assistant experienced the leader's behaviour as threatening and intimidating. In representing the assistant character as dominated by and fearful of the leader, participants' responses in this study extend researchers' knowledge about the nature of the attachments among bullies and what induces assistants to join in, in a primary school-aged sample.

In terms of the follower character, female participants described behaviours that evidently reinforce bullying, such as tagging along, watching, laughing, smiling, smirking and sticking up for the bully. On the other hand, male participants perceived that the follower character experienced the leader's behaviour as the assistant character did, that is, dominating and intimidating through, for example, being forced to take part, obeying the leader and taking the blame. The findings further revealed that participants perceived that the follower character was not much involved in bullying, lending support to the adult notion of a passive bully, that is, a child who participates in bullying others but who does not usually take the initiative (Olweus 1994). The perception that the follower or reinforcer character was minimally involved might be explained in terms of participants not realizing that by exhibiting behaviours such as laughing and watching, followers provide an audience for the bully, which reinforces the bully's behaviour and signals approval of the bullying (O'Connell et al. 1999; Pepler et al. 1999; Salmivalli et al. 1996).

(adapted from Jennifer 2007)

That a gender difference was apparent in the behavioural descriptions for each of the bully characters in the hypothetical story provides evidence from the child's perspective that within the social world of males bullying has a different meaning and purpose compared with that of females (Salmivalli et al. 1998). For males, it might be a question of power, domination and showing off, whereas for females it might have more to do with social relationships and social situations (Salmivalli et al. 1998). That male participants drew attention to direct physical and direct verbal behaviours, and that female participants focused on direct verbal and indirect behaviours, reflects gender differences in the use of different types of bullying identified by previous research. Not only do the results of this study provide evidence for primary schoolchildren's understanding of participant roles in bullying episodes, but also they draw attention to the nature of the bullying behaviour that occurs among members of the bully group. (See Box 8.1 for further details about this study.)

Cyber bullying

More recently, research demonstrates that advances in technology have provided a new means of bullying. Cyber bullying can be defined as a form of covert psychological bullying conveyed through the use of electronic media, such as mobile phones and the internet, that is deliberately intended to harm another (Cowie and Jennifer 2007; Department for Children, Schools and Families (DCSFh 2007a). It includes bullying by text message or mobile phone calling, by instant messenger services and social networking sites, by email, and by images or videos posted on the Internet or mobile phones (Cowie and Jennifer 2007; DCSF 2007a). Cyber bullying differs from other forms of bullying in a number of important ways (Cowie and Jennifer 2007; DCSF 2007a). First, it creates a sense of anonymity and hidden identity that serves to distance the bully from the victim. Second, in contrast to other forms of bullying, cyber bullying reaches a far wider audience at rapid speed. Third, since the victim is accessible in any place and at any time of day or night, cyber bullying transcends boundaries of time, and physical and personal space. Finally, bystanders to cyber bullying can easily become perpetrators, for example, by recording an act of bullying on a mobile phone and circulating it to others. In addition, cyber bullying differs from other forms of bullying in terms of the types of behaviour that bullies engage in. These include threats and intimidation, harassment and stalking, vilification and defamation, such as name-calling and insults, social exclusion or peer rejection, unauthorized publication of private information or images, identity theft, unauthorized access and impersonation, and manipulation, for example, putting pressure on someone to reveal personal information or arrange a face-to-face meeting (DCSF 2007a). Despite these important differences, it should be noted that cyber bullying may form part of a relationship that includes off-line, face-to-face, bullying as well.

In terms of prevalence, to date, few empirical studies have been carried out in the UK to investigate the phenomenon of cyber bullying. Drawing upon research in Canada, an anonymous questionnaire survey of 264 pupils from junior high schools found that 25 per cent of participants had been cyber-bullied (Li 2006). In terms of gender differences, Li (2006) found no significant differences between the proportion of males and females who reported being cyber-bullied. However, consistent with research on what might be termed ordinary bullying, males were more likely to cyber bully others than were females. Among the cyber victims, about 62 per cent were cyber-bullied one to three times and nearly 40 per cent were cyber-bullied more than three times. No significant differences were found with regard to the frequency of being cyber-bullied. This contrasts with the results of a four-year study of over 11000 secondary school pupils conducted in the UK, which identified that every year more young females than young males reported receiving nasty or threatening emails or text messages (Noret and Rivers 2006). The data also highlighted an increase in the receipt of such messages in young females, with incidence rising from nearly 15 per cent in 2002 to just over 21 per cent in 2005. This concurs with the findings of a survey of over 1500 9 to 19-year-olds which found that older children were more likely to experience online bullying, with 11 per cent of 9 to 11-year-olds, 35 per cent of 12 to 15-year-olds and 44 per cent of 16 to 19-year-olds reporting this (Livingston and Bober 2005).

In terms of specific online bullying behaviours that young people have experienced, an Internet-based survey found that of 384 respondents under the age of 18, over half had been ignored by others (60 per cent), half had been disrespected by others (50 per cent), nearly one-third had been called names by others (30 per cent), and one-fifth had been threatened by others (21 per cent), picked on by others (20 per cent), been made fun of by others (19 per cent) and experienced rumours spread by others (19 per cent) (Patchin and Hinduja 2006). Furthermore, the survey revealed that cyber bullying was most prevalent in chat rooms with 22 per cent of cyber victims reporting this, followed by computer text messages (14 per cent) and email (13 per cent) (Patchin and Hinduja 2006). Nevertheless, while advances in technology have offered a new means of bullying, mobile phones and the Internet offer a new means with which to address it. (See Chapter 6 for a discussion on cyber peer support.)

Physical, verbal, relational and cyber forms of bullying can be used to bully others for reasons related to issues of actual or perceived difference (Jennifer 2007; Lahelma 2004). For example, race, religion or culture (Moran et al. 1993; Varma-Joshi et al. 2004); special educational needs (SEN) or disability (Mencap 2007); sexual orientation (Rivers and Cowie 2006; Vicars 2006); and gender (Duncan 1998). The remainder of this section takes a brief look at each of these reasons for bullying, while Case Study 1.1 highlights a young female's view of the causes of bullying.

Case Study 1.1   Annie's Story

In a study that explored children's understanding of bullying in primary school in their own voices, Jennifer (2007) carried out semi-structured interviews with 64 children, aged 10 to 11, using pictorial vignettes depicting a hypothetical story of peer bullying. The pictorial vignettes included scenarios depicting psychologically and physically violent acts performed by one individual or by a group of peers (social exclusion, teasing, physical obstruction, attack on personal possessions, actual damage to personal possessions, group physical attack, coercion, blackmail, social isolation). When Annie was asked what she thought was happening in the hypothetical story from the beginning to the end she said, 'They're bullying this girl because she's in a slight way different to other people, they seem like, in every school you get a bunch of horrible people and they seem like them …she's getting teased and she's having her things taken off her and just, they're being horrible and she doesn't know what to do because she seems like a quiet girl 'cos she's not doing anything about it …they're cutting her hair off, they're trying to get her to steal money just like, and it seems to me they can't be bothered to do anything by themselves so they started doing this because, maybe at the beginning they were nice people, they started doing this because they needed like something and then now they just get pleasure out of it ...they're bullying this girl because she's in a slight way different to other people ...cos people are really different, because maybe sometimes people just don't like them or they don't fit in or they [the bullies] don't think they're right to be part of the popular group and they just put them into this group that's geeky ...in every school you get a bunch of horrible people and they [the bullies] seem like them ...".

Racist bullying

While there is a dearth of research on racist bullying, data extrapolated from a number of studies reveals that children from ethnic minority groups experience indirect bullying of a racist nature (e.g. Moran et al. 1993; Varma-Joshi et al. 2004). For example, in a London-based study that investigated black and white 11-year-olds' views of teasing and fighting in junior schools, of the 175 pupils significantly more black children than white children reported that they had been subjected to teasing because of the colour of their skin, that is, 27 per cent compared with 9 per cent (Mooney et al. 1991). In a study that examined the specific role of ethnicity in the experience of bullying, Moran et al. (1993) interviewed 33 pairs of Asian and white children, matched for gender, age and school. For those children being bullied, no differences by ethnicity were found for where it happened, or the likelihood of seeking help. However, the authors found a significant difference by ethnicity for racist name-calling with one-half of the bullied Asian children, but none of the bullied white children, experiencing name-calling in relation to their colour or race.

Furthermore, small-scale qualitative studies suggest that racist bullying of gypsy traveller children is also an issue. For example, a study of secondary school-aged traveller children in Scotland revealed that all 18 pupils had experienced name-calling in school related to their cultural background (Lloyd and Stead 2001). A three-year phenomenological study that tracked a sample of 44 gypsy traveller children in England from their final term in primary school until the end of Key Stage 4 (aged 14) found that, of those that transferred to secondary school, 80 per cent reported that they had encountered some form of racial abuse, particularly during their first year (Derrington 2005). In addition, six pupils (four boys and two girls) reported experiencing physical attacks in secondary school. The results of both studies suggest that self-exclusion and poor attendance of gypsy traveller children at secondary school are related to bullying (Derrington 2005; Lloyd and Stead 2001).

Disablist bullying

To date there has been relatively little empirical research into disablist bullying. Nevertheless, research reveals that children with a learning disability, are substantially more at risk of being bullied than other children (Martlew and Hodson 1991; Nabuzoka and Smith 1993; Norwich and Kelly 2004). Whitney et al. (1994) carried out an interview study with 186 children aged between 6- and 11-years-old, drawn from three primary schools, to look at bully/victim problems among children with special needs, compared with children of the same age who had no special needs (labelled mainstream children by the researchers). The results revealed that nearly two-thirds of the children with special educational needs reported being bullied, compared with just over one quarter of mainstream children. Children with special educational needs were also more at risk of bullying others, with just under one-third reporting bullying others compared to about one-sixth of mainstream children.

More recently, Norwich and Kelly (2004) examined the views of 101 children with moderate learning difficulties aged 10 to 11 and 13 to 14 regarding their experiences of school in mainstream and special schools. Overall, 83 per cent of the sample reported that they had experienced some form of bullying, with 68 per cent experiencing a mixture of types of bullying, 24 per cent experiencing mainly verbal bullying, 5 per cent experiencing mainly physical bullying and 3 per cent experiencing mainly teasing. About half of the sample (49 per cent) reported that the bullying was related to their learning difficulty. Participants identified the perpetrators of bullying as pupils in their own schools, pupils from other mainstream schools, and neighbours and peers outside school. About half of the sample (52 per cent) reported bullying perpetrated by pupils in their own school, with differences according to age, gender and school type. Mainstream primary girls reported significantly more in-school bullying than special school primary girls (83 per cent compared with 42 per cent), while there was no such difference between mainstream and special schoolboys.

In contrast, mainstream secondary boys reported less in-school bullying than special school secondary boys (17 per cent compared with 70 per cent), while there were no such differences between mainstream secondary girls and special school secondary girls. Pupils in both mainstream and special schools reported bullying by pupils from other mainstream schools. Special school pupils reported significantly more bullying overall by other mainstream pupils than mainstream pupils did (30 per cent compared with 6 per cent). Pupils in special schools reported significantly more bullying by neighbours and peers outside school than mainstream pupils (48 per cent compared with 4 per cent), highlighting the notion of neighbourhood bullying (see Box 1.5).

Box 1.5   Neighbourhood Bullying

In a study that considered the street experiences of a group of urban children living in a large East Midlands town in the UK, Percy-Smith and Matthews' (2001) focused on the issue of neighbourhood bullying in two contrasting urban neighbourhoods, one located in the inner city and one in the suburbs. Semi-structured interviews were carried out with 181 young people aged 10 to 15 on their doorsteps or in their homes, with 24 young people participating in further research activities including child-led neighbourhood tours, child-taken photographs and drawings, and interviews to explore in more depth the issues raised. Throughout the duration of the fieldwork (18 months), regular contact was maintained with young people both on the street and in youth projects, and observations of young people's behaviour, interaction and communication were recorded in field diaries.

The results suggested that 46 per cent of young people in the inner-city neighbourhood and 27 per cent of those in the suburbs reported being bullied within their locality. The authors distinguished four common types of bullying behaviour, predominantly perpetrated by older teenagers. These included 'barging in' whereby older children move in on younger children's games, with the intention to disrupt or take over; 'extortion', whereby children are either threatened or coerced into taking part in some form of antisocial behaviour; 'intimidation', which involved taunts, insults, threats and pushing, often for the entertainment of the perpetrators; and, 'name-calling', most frequently occurring among girls.

Two spatial features emerged from the data. First, bullying was more prevalent in the inner city neighbourhood (57 per cent) compared with the suburban area (42 per cent). Percy-Smith and Matthews (2001) suggest this may relate to the large numbers of young people 'hanging out' on the street within the inner urban area, coupled with a general lack of social opportunity, a closer propinquity of different groups of young people, each with their own microcultures, and a sense of boredom for some, a feature repeatedly identified through informal discussions. On the other hand, the researchers observed that young people in the suburbs had more space in which to meet and to develop their own identities, and were more likely to be supported by their parents in undertaking organized activities in clubs and organizations. Second, while bullying was sporadic, spontaneous and dependent largely on social encounter rather than place, there were particular areas within each neighbourhood where bullying was more common. In both neighbourhoods, these included spaces where different groups of young people were likely to meet away from the gaze of adults, that is, parks (20 per cent inner/36 per cent suburban), local shopping parades (29 per cent inner/10 per cent suburban) and local streets (68 per cent inner/25 per cent suburban).

Of those reporting being bullied, 87 per cent in the inner neighbourhood and 70 per cent in the suburbs mentioned that the perpetrators were older kids or gangs. Whereas boys were only likely to be bullied by other boys, girls reported being bullied by both boys and girls. The results suggest that, in general, girls are less likely to experience neighbourhood bullying than boys are. In the inner city neighbourhood, 36 per cent of girls compared with 64 per cent of boys had experienced being bullied. In the suburban neighbourhood, these figures were 45 per cent compared with 55 per cent, respectively. In parallel with the incidence and nature of school bullying, these findings indicate that boys are more actively involved in neighbourhood bullying than girls are.

The authors conclude that neighbourhood bullying is a significant problem for many young people. They suggest that most instances of neighbourhood bullying are the result of collisions between groups, each with its own microc-ulture, within local encounter spaces where individuals attempt to create and exploit power differentials in order to strengthen their own status and identity.

Homophobic bullying

Studies of lesbian, gay and bisexual adults have revealed that this group of individuals are more likely to experience bullying at school. For example, in a three-year retrospective questionnaire survey of 190 lesbian, gay, bisexual and transgendered adults regarding their experiences of bullying at school, the results suggested that participants' experiences of homophobia were both longterm (mean duration of five years) and systematic (Rivers and Cowie 2006). Furthermore, homophobic bullying was perpetrated by groups of peers, usually all males or groups of males and females, rather than by individuals. The most frequent forms of bullying were verbal in nature, including name-calling (mostly names that were sexual in nature or specifically related to their actual or *perceived* sexual orientation) and being ridiculed in front of others (82 per cent and 71 per cent, respectively) (Rivers and Cowie 2006). A large number of participants also reported indirect bullying, in the form of being teased (58 per cent) and having rumours spread about them (59 per cent). A majority of participants reported physical bullying (60 per cent), and a minority reported being sexually assaulted either by peers or by teachers at school (11 per cent) (Rivers and Cowie 2006). Physical forms of bullying such as hitting and kicking were found to be significantly associated with outdoor locations such as in the school playground or on the way home from school. In contrast, sexual assaults were associated with the changing rooms. Generally, verbal abuse was associated with taking place within the school building, for example, name-calling was significantly associated with locations such as classrooms and changing rooms. Participants who reported indirect bullying also reported being bullied within the school building. Being frightened by a look or stare and rumour-spreading were associated with bullying taking place in corridors, classrooms and changing rooms.

Furthermore, research suggests that children of gay and lesbian parents experi-ence bullying of a homophobic nature (Ray and Gregory 2001). In a small-scale study of 48 children and young people conducted in Australia, Ray and Gregory (2001) found that the experience of being bullied mostly began after Grade 2, with just under half of children in Grades 3 to 6 being bullied, decreasing to one-third of secondary school pupils. The types of bullying experienced by participants included verbal abuse, teasing and joking, and physical and sexual violence. Almost half the participants had experienced teasing or bullying in relation to their parents' sexuality, and large numbers of children were subjected to anti-gay sentiments on a daily basis.

Gender bullying

Based on findings from research into sexual bullying, Duncan (1998) suggests that sexual identity formation during adolescence plays an important role in the kinds of behaviour that are involved in school bullying in general. In a study of sexual bullying in secondary schools, Duncan (1998) undertook single-sex group interviews and participant observation over a period of five years with approximately 100 pupils. During the girls' interviews, the most commonly cited objectionable behaviours were perpetrated by boys although participant observations often featured other girls as active perpetrators. Participants identified a continuum of bullying behaviours ranging from sexual name-calling by boys, to rumour-spreading and destruction of sexual reputations by boys or girls, to sexual assaults perpetrated by gangs of boys, and beating up of girls by cliques of girls motivated by sexual jealousy. The older girls in the sample observed an increased use of sexualized verbal abuse as they progressed through the school, which peaked at around Year 9. Indeed, the interviews with both boys and girls confirmed the observation that girls' developing bodies provided the excuse for sexualized verbal bullying.

While sexual bullying is recognized as one of many expressions of violence predominantly perpetrated by males against women (WOMANKIND Worldwide 2007), gender bullying affects both genders, and can be perpetrated by both genders on opposite and same-gender victims. For example, the sexual bullying of girls by other girls, based upon a social esteemed sexual identity, that is, being a popular girl, has been documented by Duncan (2004). Research also suggests that young men whose socio-sexual identity does not conform to the dominant ideal of masculinity (i.e. macho, 'one of the lads') also experience name-calling, marginalization and abuse based upon gender (Duncan 2006) (for further discussion see Chapter 4). Furthermore, pupils identifying as transgender or experiencing gender variant feelings, that is, individuals who feel that their assigned sex at birth is at odds with their gender identity, also experience gender bullying (Whittle et al. 2007). In an online survey of over 800 transgender people for the Equalities Review, Whittle et al. (2007) found that over half of natal females with a male identity and nearly half of natal males with a female identity had experienced bullying at school. Physical abuse occurred in about a quarter of cases and about a quarter of respondents had been bullied by teachers. While transgender, logically, is a gender issue, the discrimination experienced by transpeople (transphobia) is akin to the homophobic discrimination experienced by lesbian, gay and bisexual people (Lucas 2004).

Bullying as an injury risk factor

As medical practitioners, Laflamme et al. (2002) and Engström et al. (2005) identified an aspect of bullying that had scarcely been investigated before–the effect of an act of victimization on a pupil's likelihood of being injured. They predicted that the emotions of fear, anger or sadness, triggered by an episode of bullying, might lower children's capacity to anticipate and avoid risk through, for example, distraction or lack of concentration. In comparison with non-bullied peers, children who are victimized are more likely to suffer poor health, low self-esteem, unhappiness, anxiety and depression. So, these authors were interested to find out whether bullying at school could trigger a chain of events that led to a lowering of vigilance and attention and resulting in involvement in greater exposure to danger in their environment. Here are some examples as reported by Laflamme et al. (2002: 23–24):

- A 14-year-old girl took part in a snowball fight. She was hit by a schoolmate, lost her balance, fell down and broke her ankle. On the previous day, she was bullied because she was about to change school and so was perceived as having 'let down' one of her friends who then mobilized a group to harass her.
- A 10-year-old girl was on a sports outing with her class and had to take part in a team competition. For one of the activities, she had to vault over a boy who was crouching on all fours. Their team was losing and so she felt under pressure. Another pupil was supposed to help her jump but did not. She missed her jump, fell on her arm and broke it. The day before she had been threatened by a schoolmate who said that she would hit her. She was often bullied about her weight.
- A 14-year-old boy broke his knee during a basketball course at school while demonstrating a move. During break time, the same morning, an older boy had said very nasty things about his mother.
- A 13-year-old girl was cycling to school with some friends when they saw ahead of them a group of young people that often bully their schoolmates. The girls were afraid and decided to take another route to school. The girl rode over a pedestrian crossing without looking and was hit by a car.

In Box 1.6 we report the results of the full study.

Box 1.6. Do episodes of peer victimization trigger physical injury?

This two-year study involved 575 children aged between 10 and 15 years living in Stockholm County. Inclusion criteria for participation in the study were that the children had been hospitalized or called back to hospital for a medical check-up because of a physical injury. Children who had been physically injured during a bullying episode were excluded from the study, as were children who had self-harmed or who had been injured while under the influence of drugs or alcohol. The researchers gathered information through interviews on the children's exposure to peer victimization at school prior to the injury. All interviews were conducted within 10 days of the injury to minimize recall bias. Of the 575 children, 26 per cent reported that they had been bullied at least once during the last school term, 15 per cent had been victimized more than once a week, and 4.4 per cent had been bullied on the day of the injury. A further 14 (2.4 per cent) were bullied by peers within 2 hours of the injury, and 7 (1.2 per cent) within 15 minutes.

The researchers found that being bullied is an injury trigger that especially manifests itself in the short period after the bullying episode. The risk of being injured was 5.5 times higher among children exposed to a bullying episode within 15 minutes before the injury than during periods of no victimization. They also found that the injury risk within 15 minutes after a bullying episode was significantly higher among children who are seldom bullied than among those who reported that they were bullied more than once a week. The injuries sustained by children recently exposed to bullying tended to involve loss of balance (through tripping, falling or missing a step) and difficulty in managing traffic. The researchers suggest that these injuries can be attributed to loss of peripheral vision which would reduce risk anticipation and risk-management. The researchers conclude that, while we know that victims of bullying suffer mental health effects, what is less well known is that there may be short-term negative effects on their physical safety. There are clearly important implications for our knowledge of the ways in which children relate to their environment and the emotional impact on their perceptiveness and attention of distressing experiences.

(Engström et al. 2005: 19–25).

Context

In this book, we understand the multiple causes of school bullying in terms of the interaction of risk factors operating at four different levels thought to contribute to aggressive behaviour, that is, individual, interpersonal, community and society. This idea is illustrated in Figure 1.1 and is based on the World Health Organization's (WHO 1999, 2002) model of how to understand violence.

The first level of the model focuses on the biological and personal history characteristics of the individual that might contribute to the development of bullying behaviour or victimization. For example, early work carried out by Olweus (1980, 1997) with a sample of adolescents ($n = 51$) revealed the importance of a number of factors in the development of an aggressive reaction pattern including the child's temperament. A child with a 'hot-headed' temperament as opposed to a child with a quieter disposition was more likely to develop into an aggressive youngster. Moreover, Olweus (1978, cited in Olweus 1997) found that, in general, typical victims were more anxious and insecure than other pupils. This, combined with low levels of self-esteem and feelings of shame, stupidity and unattractiveness, led Olweus (1997: 176) to label this type of victim *passive/submissive* stating that their behaviour and attitude were 'a signal to others that they are insecure and worthless individuals who will not retaliate if they are attacked or insulted'. On the other hand, *provocative victims* were characterized by a combination of both anxious and aggressive reaction patterns; they could also be regarded as lacking in concentration, suffering from hyperactivity, and displaying irritating behaviour (Olweus 1997).

The second level of the model concentrates on how interpersonal relationships, such as those with peers and family, have the potential to increase the risk for victimization and perpetration of violence in terms of shaping an individual's behaviour. For example, peer friendships can act either as a protective factor against

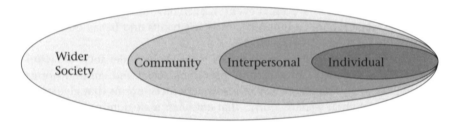

Figure 1.1 Ecological model for understanding school bullying
Source: adapted from WHO (2002).

victimization or as a risk factor for engaging in bullying of others. Pellegrini et al.'s (1999) study with a sample of elementary schoolchildren explored the relationship between the occurrence of victimization and bullying with group affiliation. Their results suggested that having friends and being liked by one's peers acted as protective factors against victimization. On the other hand, research into aggressive behaviour and social networks with 10- and 13-year-olds suggested that aggressive children tended to affiliate with aggressive peers thereby providing mutual support for aggressive behaviours towards others (Cairns et al. 1988). In terms of the family context, in their study of bullying and parenting styles with 238 11 to 14-year-olds, Baldry and Farrington (2000) found that bullies were more likely than non-bullies were to have authoritarian, high punitive and low supportive parents who disagreed with each other. Olweus (1980, 1997) identified a number of other factors in the development of an aggressive reaction pattern in adolescent boys. These included a negative emotional attitude characterized by a lack of warmth and involvement by the primary caregiver during the early years; permissiveness on the part of the primary caregiver for aggressive behaviour by the child; and the use of power-assertive child-rearing methods such as physical punishment and violent emotional outbursts. Olweus (1997: 179) summarizes these findings stating, 'too little love and care and too much "freedom" in childhood are conditions that contribute strongly in the development of an aggressive reaction pattern'. (For further discussion see Chapter 4.)

The third level of the model examines the community contexts in which interpersonal relationships occur, in this case schools and neighbourhoods, and seeks to identify those settings that are associated with an increased risk for violent behaviour, either as a victim or as a perpetrator. Risk factors at this level may include high levels of residential mobility, heterogeneity, high population density, high levels of unemployment, and the local presence of gangs, guns and drug-dealing activity. Thus, specific characteristics of a neighbourhood, such as violent behaviour, weapon-carrying and gang feuds on the streets can permeate school communities to support violent attitudes and behaviours. For instance, a study that addressed possible cross-cultural differences in children's moral appraisals in relation to the task of putting themselves into the role of the bully in a bullying scenario found that children from southern Italy attributed higher attitudes of moral disengagement (i.e. pride and indifference) to themselves in comparison to the Spanish participants (Menesini, Sanchez et al. 2003). These authors suggest that specific characteristics of southern Italy, such as, high unemployment, the strong presence of organized crime, which is almost accepted as a normal event in everyday life, and 'Mafia-like feelings' which often pervade school communities, people's habits and behaviours, can easily support attitudes of moral disengagement.

The fourth level of the ecological model looks at the wider societal factors that influence rates of violence. These include prevailing social and cultural norms that support violence as an acceptable way to resolve conflicts, norms that give priority to parental rights over child welfare, norms that entrench male dominance over women and children, norms that support the use of excessive force by police against citizens, and norms that support political conflict. For instance, it has been suggested that schools tend to perpetuate typically male values, which are in opposition to the development of empathic responses to others (Askew 1989; Carter 2002). As an example, based on a four-year action research project in an all boys' comprehensive, Carter (2002) examined the dynamics of classroom relationships, perceptions of rights and constructions of male identities. Based on her findings she argued that attitudes and behaviours (e.g. aggressive interplay, low-level verbal and emotional harassment, overt racism, open peer criticism) which explicitly espoused competition and masculinity were prevalent and reinforced by implicit practices and subtle encouragement (e.g. minimal help for pupils experiencing problems). Furthermore, there seemed to be a reluctance among the staff to intervene in conflicts (e.g. in the corridors), thereby compounding assumptions of acceptability.

Other societal factors, such as the health, educational, economic and social policies that maintain high levels of economic or social inequality between groups in society, are also included at this level. As an example, a nationwide study carried out in the Republic of Ireland found that in both primary and secondary schools designated as 'disadvantaged' (achieved on the basis of socio-economic and educational indicators such as unemployment levels, housing, medical card holders, and information on basic literacy and numeracy skills), significantly more pupils reported that they had bullied others than did pupils from 'advantaged' schools (O'Moore et al. 1997).

The absence of such risk factors will help to protect children and young people against involvement in crime, drug abuse and antisocial behaviour. In addition, there are a number of protective factors that may help to protect children and young people from bullying, especially those from high-risk backgrounds. Protective factors refer to 'factors that have been consistently associated with good outcomes for children growing up in circumstances where they are, otherwise, heavily exposed to risk' (France and Utting 2005: 80). Such factors are summarized in Table 1.1.

Table 1.1. Protective factors for bullying (taken from Beinart et al. 2002; Farrington 1996; Youth Justice Board 2005).

Individual Characteristics

Female gender

Resilient temperament

A sense of self-efficacy

A positive, outgoing disposition

High intelligence

Interpersonal

A strong sense of attachment with one or both parents, characterized by a stable, warm and affectionate relationship

Parents who maintain a strong interest in their children's education

Opportunities for consultation, shared social activities and positive involvement in family and school life

Parents and teachers who provide effective supervision, clear rules and consistent discipline

Parents, teachers and peers who hold pro-social attitudes and model positive social behaviour

Recognition and due praise within the family and the school

Community

Opportunities to feel positively involved in the life of the school and the local community

Parents, teachers and community leaders who lead by example and hold clearly stated expectations regarding behaviour

Encouragement for all children and young people to fulfil their potential

Wider Society

Healthy social attitudes towards anti-social and criminal behaviour

Learning points

- While there is widespread agreement within the research community that bullying is characterized by three key features, that is, intentionality, repetition and an imbalance of power between perpetrator and victim, teachers and pupils hold much broader definitions.
- School bullying takes different forms, including physical, verbal, relational and cyber. However, both staff and pupils are more likely to view physical bullying as more serious and harmful than other forms of bullying.
- Large-scale studies suggest that school bullying is a daily reality for many children and young people.

- A number of individual differences, such as race, religion or culture, disability, sexual orientation and gender might be used as reasons for bullying others.
- Bullying can be understood in terms of an interaction of risk factors operating at four different levels, that is, individual characteristics, interpersonal relationships, community contexts and wider society.
- Research suggests that both trainee teachers and inservice teachers would like more training to understand, identify and address school bullying.

Resources

Department for Children, Schools and Families (DCSF) (2007) *Safe to Learn: Embedding Anti-bullying Work in Schools*. London: DCSF.

DCSF (2008) Bullying Involving Children with Special Educational Needs and Disabilities: Safe to learn: Embedding Anti-bullying Work in Schools. London: DCSF.

DCSF (2007) *Cyberbullying: Safe to Learn: Embedding Anti-bullying Work in Schools*. London: DCSF.

DCSF (2007) *Homophobic Bullying: Safe to Learn: Embedding Anti-bullying Work in Schools*. London: DCSF.

Spell it out: Tackling homophobia in our schools. London: Stonewall. DVD and teachers' resource. (www.stonewall.org.uk).

Department for Education and Skills (2006). Bullying Around Racism, Religion and Culture. London: DfES.

Web sites

Digizen offers information and advice on recognizing and addressing cyber bullying, including classroom resources and a downloadable film called '*Let's Fight it Together*' (www.digizen.org).

EACH provides training on the legalities concerning sexual orientation and strives to challenge homophobia through education (www.eachaction.org.uk).

Lesbian, Gay, Bisexual and Trans History Month, an annual event every February (www.lgbthistorymonth.org.uk).

MENCAP is the UK's leading learning disability charity working with people with a learning disability and their families and carers (www.mencap.org.uk).

Schools Out works for equality in education for Lesbian, Gay, Bisexual and Transpeople (www.schools-out.org.uk).

Stonewall is an organization which aims to promote a safe learning environment for all by challenging homophobia and homophobic bullying in schools (www.stonewall.org.uk).

WOMANKIND aims to raise awareness and transform attitudes to stop violence against women (www.womankind.org.uk).

Young Voice is a registered charity working on youth participation and engagement, focusing on bullying (www.young-voice.org).

YWCA England and Wales is the leading charity working with young women facing poverty, discrimination or abuse, including those that have been bullied at school or faced violence at home (www.ywca.org.uk).

2 THE WHOLE-SCHOOL APPROACH

Chapter overview

In this chapter, we present a whole-school approach to the prevention and reduction of school bullying as an essential framework within which the elements of an intervention or set of interventions can be carefully coordinated at different levels. The focus of a whole-school approach is on both the school as a formal organization (i.e. the institutional aspects of the school) and the school as a community (i.e. the informal relationships and networks that exist within the school). From this perspective, one of the core principles of a whole-school approach is to not only challenge and address bullying in schools, but also to foster opportunities for democracy, participation and citizenship. We identify a four-stage process for the understanding, reduction and prevention of school bullying, which includes the implementation of a needs analysis. We explore a relational approach that adopts an ecological framework for the prevention and reduction of bullying incidents. Any discussion about the reduction and prevention of school bullying, however, necessitates an understanding of the legal context within which such work takes place. The aim of the first section of this chapter, therefore, is to take a brief look at what the law says that schools should be doing to address school bullying.

Legislation, policy and guidance

Schools have a statutory responsibility to ensure that they have in place an anti-bullying policy and behaviour management practices that satisfy current legislation, including children's rights as set out in the United Nations Convention on the Rights of the Child (UN hcrc 1989) (see below) and government policy, such as the *Every Child Matters* (DfES 2004) framework (see Box 2.1). Furthermore, it is also important to note that while bullying is not a specific criminal offence in the UK (DCSF 2007a), there are criminal laws that can apply with regard to, for example, the carrying of weapons or cyber bullying activities, such as threatening and menacing communications.

Box 2.1 Every Child Matters

The *Every Child Matters* (DfES 2004) framework provides a focus for schools to think about supporting children and young people to grow into respectful, confident and socially and emotionally healthy adults. Children and young people who experience school bullying will not be able to meet the outcomes identified in *Every Child Matters* (DfES 2004). For example, children and young people experiencing bullying at school will not:

Be healthy: Children and young people involved in bullying may not enjoy good physical and mental health and live a healthy lifestyle. For example, victims of bullying often experience anxiety and depression, low self-esteem, and physical and psychosomatic complaints (see Chapter 3). In extreme cases, they may commit suicide (Kaltiala-Heino et al. 1999). Bullies are more likely to experience social-psychological adjustment problems such as depression, loneliness and social isolation (Coie and Dodge 1998; Crick and Grotpeter 1995) (see Chapter 4). In addition, bullying has a negative impact on the wider social group with bystanders experiencing fear, embarrassment and inadequacy, resulting in loss of self-respect for not responding or responding ineffectively to a bullying situation (Hazler 1996b).

Stay safe: Children and young people who bully others are not staying safe since bullies are at increased risk of bullying and offending as adults (Farrington 1995; Olweus 1991). Engagement in school bullying is part of a more general violent and aggressive behaviour pattern, strongly linked to violent behaviour and weapon carrying on the streets (Andershed et al. 2001), and a significant predictor of later gang membership (Holmes and Brandenburg-Ayres 1998).

Enjoy and achieve: Children and young people involved in school bullying may not be able to enjoy their experience of school or achieve their full potential. In a study to investigate the incidence and impact of bullying in 25 secondary schools, Glover et al. (2000) found that bullying and violent behaviour adversely affected pupils' engagement with the learning process. Nearly half of participants found it 'hard to answer in class' and 10 per cent responded that they 'get discouraged'.

Make a positive contribution: Children and young people engaged in bullying may not be positively involved with the school community and wider society. When children and young people feel marginalized and rejected by the group, as in the case of victims, or alienated and disenfranchised from the school community, as in the case of bullies, their capacity to empathize with others is diminished (Malley et al. 2001). Where there is a decreased capacity to empathize with others, children and young people experience a lack of a sense of belonging and disconnectedness, reducing their chances of assuming social responsibility and their ability to contribute positively to the life of the school community.

Achieve economic well-being: Children and young people who experience bullying may be prevented by economic disadvantage from achieving their full potential in life. In a retrospective study of two groups of lesbian, gay and bisexual adults who reported anti-lesbian/gay bullying at school, Rivers (2000) compared one group with a history of school absenteeism with a second group who reported attending school on a regular basis. The findings suggested an association between the experience of bullying and a history of absenteeism, with GCE A-level passes significantly higher among those who reported regular attendance at school, suggesting that those participants who were bullied were likely to leave school earlier with fewer qualifications.

(adapted from DfES 2003)

Governing bodies have a legal responsibility to ensure that '... functions relating to the conduct of the school are exercised with a view to safeguarding and promoting the welfare of children who are pupils at the school' (Section 175, Education Act 2002). The law requires that 'The standard of behaviour which is to be regarded as acceptable at the school shall be determined by the head teacher, so far as it is not determined by the governing body' (Section 61, School Standards and Framework Act 1998). In accordance with the governing body's written statement of general principles, the head teacher will establish measures (e.g. rules, rewards, sanctions) with a view to 'encouraging good behaviour and respect for others on the part of pupils and, in particular, preventing all forms of bullying among pupils' (Section 89, Education and Inspections Act 2006; Section 61, School Standards and Framework Act 1998). Furthermore, the School Standards and Framework Act (1998) states that the measures determined by the head teacher shall be publicized in the form of a written document and circulated within the school and to parents, and attention drawn to the policy at least once per school year to all pupils, parents and carers, and all individuals employed, or providing services, at the school. In addition, the Local Government Act's (Section 104, 2000) amendment of Section 28 of the Local Government Act (1998) indicates that nothing shall deter the head teacher, the governing body, or a teacher from taking steps to prevent all forms of bullying. In addition, the Government's recently launched *Safe to Learn: Embedding Anti-bullying Work in Schools* focuses on:

> the steps they need to go through to create and implement a whole-school anti-bullying policy ...the importance of recording and reporting incidents of bullying ...[the] need to apply disciplinary sanctions ...to work with bullies so that they are held to account for their actions and accept responsibility for the harm they have caused ...and advice on how to address staff training.

(DCSF 2007b: 4)

The essential aspects of the whole-school approach

Bullying has probably always been a common feature of the school experience. In a recent survey, Shaughnessy and Jennifer (2007) found that nearly one-half of primary schoolchildren (40 per cent) and one-third of secondary schoolchildren (33 per cent) had experienced bullying in the past two or three months. In addition, anecdotal evidence suggests that school bullying is a major cause for concern for children and young people in the UK. Since its launch in 1986, ChildLine has helped to provide confidential advice and protection to nearly two million children and young people (2005). For the ninth consecutive year, in the period April 2004 to March 2005, bullying was the single most common reason for children and young people to call the helpline; of 140,000 calls, 23 per cent were regarding bullying. When the recently appointed Children's Commissioner for England held a competition in 2006 inviting children and young people to advise him of what was most important to them, bullying attracted the largest single number of online responses than any other issue (Office of the Children's Commissioner 2006).

Despite the presence of bullying in our schools, we do not have to accept it as an inevitable part of growing up. Since the 1970s, many researchers, practitioners and policy makers have undertaken to understand the causes of school bullying, and the means by which it can be reduced and prevented. The WHO's (2002) *World Report on Violence and Health* recommends a four-stage process for reducing and preventing violence, which moves from problem to solution, and which we have adapted for the understanding, reduction and prevention of school bullying. These are:

- understanding all aspects of school bullying, through the systematic collection of data on the scale and nature of the phenomenon;
- investigating why school bullying occurs–its causes, the risk factors for involvement in bullying incidents, the factors that might be modified through intervention;
- exploring means of preventing school bullying by designing, implementing, monitoring and evaluating interventions
- implementing interventions in a range of settings (e.g. whole-school, classroom, playground), determining their cost-effectiveness and widely disseminating information about them.

In adopting these four recommendations, any understanding and effective management of school bullying necessitates two conditions. First, addressing the issue must be informed by a 'reliable and valid knowledge base' that can be used to inform the principles of management and regulation (Leather et al. 1999: 183). Second, a strategy is required to transform the knowledge base into the design and development of effective policy, procedures and systems, practice and behaviour management structures, and a positive culture and ethos. We have suggested elsewhere that this knowledge base can be achieved through the means of a needs analysis (also known as a self-audit or a self-evaluation) (Cowie and Jennifer 2007). Cowie and Wallace (2000) suggest that a needs analysis provides a school with a structured and impartial means of identifying the needs of a particular group, assessing the availability of resources to meet those needs, and planning and selecting an appropriate intervention or set of interventions. According to Cowie and Jennifer (2007) a needs analysis involves eight steps:

1 collecting information about the setting and the people;
2 identifying the issues;

3 designing a set of shared goals;
4 identifying the resources available;
5 identifying potential difficulties;
6 planning the intervention;
7 promoting and implementing the intervention;
8 monitoring and evaluation.

Our experience of working with schools suggests a number of crucial factors that are central to the success of conducting a needs analysis. These include:

- acceptance of the existence of school bullying;
- visible support and participation from the senior management team;
- the formation of a working group;
- systematic and impartial implementation of a whole-school community needs analysis;
- a relational approach to the planning and implementation of the intervention or set of interventions;
- training in policy and practice;
- ongoing review and evaluation.

Acceptance of the existence of school bullying

A school senior management team that is unaware of the bullying experienced by their children and young people will not yet be sensitive to the need to effect change, although other members of the school community may be aware of the issue, for example, parents and carers, lunchtime supervisors or the school nurse. Essential to the planning and implementation of an anti-bullying programme is the acceptance that school bullying is a matter that requires responsive and reflexive action (Jennifer and Shaughnessy 2005). A school that is sensitive to the bullying experienced by their pupils, acknowledges its existence, takes ownership of its occurrence, confronts the issues that are causing it and begins to recognize some of the negative aspects of not addressing such behaviours, is more able to demonstrate a commitment to change (Cowie et al. 2004). Commitment from the senior management team means more than the presence of a mission statement or an anti-bullying charter; rather it rests upon the visible support and participation from the highest levels within the organization and the involvement of representatives from all sections of the school community.

Visible support and participation from the senior management team

The entire process of developing a whole-school community approach to countering bullying, from the acceptance of the existence of school bullying, through carrying out the needs analysis, to ongoing review and evaluation, can only be achieved with the visible support and participation of the senior management team (Braverman 1999). In the absence of such support from senior management, any initiatives to address school bullying will fail to effect the desired change. For example, a middle-level manager in a mixed comprehensive school was tasked with the implementation of Checkpoints for Schools (Varnava 2000), a self-audit tool to address school bullying and violence, with staff members and Year 7 pupils (Shaughnessy and Jennifer 2004). The attempted implementation of the intervention was unsuccessful. Visible support and participation from the highest levels of the school management were not evident. In addition, the manager identified ineffective communication and collaboration among staff, professional isolation, and the lack of a working group (see below) to facilitate the implementation of the self-audit, as key reasons for its lack of success. The formation of a working group composed of representatives from all sections of the school community, including individuals in leadership positions who are actively involved in decision-making who can guide the group, is the first indication of support. Such a team can only be convened with the direction, support and vision of someone at the top of the organization.

In addition, the management of a needs analysis and subsequent implementation of an intervention or set of interventions requires culture change that can be challenging and, at times, even disturbing (Cowie and Wallace 2000). For example, the participation of children and young people in the development and management of a needs analysis often involves a major change in adults' ways of relating to young people; it requires a view of children and young people as active and competent citizens, which emphasizes the validity and value of their experiences and perspectives. This shift in relating to pupils impacts upon the status ascribed to children and young people, which some adults and young people find disconcerting and threatening; while some are inspired and motivated by this new way of working, others are induced to sabotage the process (Jennifer 2007).

Addressing a process of change requires an understanding of what school culture is. According to Roffey (2000: 12):

> the culture of a school is the impression that it leaves – how people are with each other, what the expectations are in the broader sense, the attitudes and perceptions that prevail, the general demeanour of the people who work there and the consistency and cohesion amongst the workforce.

Hopkins et al. (1994, cited in Angelides and Ainscow 2000) have identified six dimensions related to school context that help to conceptualize culture:

1   *observed behavioural patterns* when teachers interact in a staffroom, such as the language they use and the rituals they establish;
2   the *norms* that evolve in working groups of teachers with regard to lesson planning or monitoring the progress of pupils;
3   the *dominant values* supported by a school, its aims or mission statement;
4   the *philosophy* that, for example, guides the dominant approach to teaching and learning of particular subjects in a school;
5   the *rules of the game* that new teachers have to learn in order to get along in the school or their department;
6   the *feeling or climate* conveyed by the entrance hall to a school, or the way in which pupils' work is or is not displayed.

Roffey (2000) suggests that a significant determinant of change is the power of school culture. She identifies a number of factors within a school culture that underpin positive change including:

- the recognition that it is every individual in the school's responsibility to address bullying;
- the assumption that more can always be achieved and that improvement is continuous;
- a belief in lifelong learning, that is, teachers too are part of the learning culture;
- that it is acceptable to take risks, that is, it is acceptable to fail if trying something new does not work first time;
- the perception that support is available;
- the valuing of diversity among staff and pupils;
- openness and the possibility of discussing differences;
- a sense of celebration and shared humour

(Roffey 2000).

The formation of a working group

A working group needs to be formed, which is composed of individuals representing all sections of the school community, including children and young people (e.g. school council representatives), staff (head teacher, Personal, Social and Health Education (PSHE) coordinator, head of year), non-teaching staff (e.g. school nurse or counsellor, school caretaker, lunchtime supervisors), parents and carers, school governors and representatives from the wider local community (e.g. the Educational Psychologist, the police). Such a composition will improve the working group's ability to motivate different sections and individuals within the whole-school community particularly in the initial stages of the needs analysis (Meuret and Morlaix 2003). Moreover, if the process of engaging in a needs analysis is based upon discussions with all sections of the whole-school community, involvement in the process will increase a sense of 'ownership' and enhance individual commitment to the process of change.

One means of involving children and young people in the working group is through the school council. Jessica Gold, Chief Executive of School Councils UK (www.schoolcouncils.org), notes that many school councils are involved in helping to reduce school bullying. She suggests that school councils can carry out a survey of pupils and staff to help understand the incidence and nature of bullying in and around the school. Once the information has been collected and analysed, the school council can set up an anti-bullying sub-committee, which can consist of council members and other volunteers that can work alongside the working group to explore strategies for moving forward. In a study of children's civil rights based on the UNCRC (1989), the results demonstrated that children and young people cared deeply about being heard and respected (Alderson 1999; 2000). Since school councils are a practical indicator of respect for children's rights, the survey included questions about children and young people's perceptions and views regarding their school councils (see Box 2.2).

Box 2.2   Civil rights in schools and views on school councils

In a survey of pupils' and teachers' views of civil rights, school councils and daily life at school, results suggested that school councils provide a useful method for pupils to contribute to school policy development (Alderson 2000). A questionnaire was completed by 2,272 pupils aged 7 to 17, in Great Britain and Northern Ireland, 58 teachers completed a single sheet teachers' survey, and school visits were carried out to conduct 34 group discussions, each consisting of six pupils. About half of the pupils reported that they had a school council. Of these, pupils who thought their council was effective generally held positive views about their school's social and academic activities, whereas those pupils who claimed their council was ineffective generally had more negative attitudes about their daily life at school. In addition, the survey results showed that a council perceived by students to be tokenistic had as much or more negative impact than having no council.

Visits to the schools demonstrated that teachers' views ranged from perceiving school councils as central to positive activities and relationships in the school, through to perceiving them as negative, that is, school councils were viewed as a formality, as unnecessary, as an extra burden for overstressed staff, or even as a danger to be avoided. Indeed, when teachers perceived school councils as a means of meeting targets and gaining publicity, for example, pupils did not perceive them as useful. One 8-year-old said, 'The council meetings aren't much good because we have to write the newsletter then, and we can't discuss things'. On the other hand, in a school where everyone knew that the council dealt with bullying and discipline problems if the classes could not resolve them, as well as reviewing a budget and planning some of the activities, amenities and policies in the school, pupils and teachers respected and relied on the council.

The results suggested that school councils are more likely to work when linked to other school practices, such as class circle time both before and after school council meetings, when council members could effectively report and feed back between peers and school management. Furthermore, the findings suggested that in schools where staff and pupils worked together through school councils, they could draw on a wider range of insights to solve problems together. The results suggested that when adults respected pupils as morally competent individuals, it was easier for children and young people to respect the adults and one another. Alderson (2000) concluded that school councils helped everyone to enjoy being a member of a positive, worthwhile community in which pupils were valued, and shared ideals and values were considered.

(adapted from Alderson 2000)

The responsibilities of the working group will evolve over time in tandem with the process of the needs analysis. For example, once established, the working group will be responsible for planning and managing the needs analysis, and monitoring and evaluating the intervention (Cowie and Jennifer 2007). However, monitoring and evaluation does not represent the end of the change process, rather it represents a new beginning as adults and young people collaboratively review the implementation of the intervention, evaluate its effectiveness and the elements of the intervention that relate to its success, in order to refine and improve it (Cowie et al. 2004).

Systematic and impartial implementation of a whole-school community needs analysis

School bullying comes in many forms as defined in Chapter 1. No two schools will experience the same combination of school bullying issues. Furthermore, risk factors such as individual characteristics, interpersonal relationships, community contexts and wider societal factors as outlined in Chapter 1 will each impact differently on the ways in which individual pupils respond to incidents of school bullying (see Chapter 3). To develop an appropriate intervention or set of inventions, therefore, requires a whole-school needs analysis that involves the systematic collection and analysis of data regarding the full scale and nature of the phenomenon. The methods established to identify, measure and monitor school bullying therefore represent the foundation of any intervention (Leather et al. 1999). In order to develop an appropriate and effective set of interventions, the aim of such data gathering is not just to ascertain the incidence and nature of school bullying, but to identify why and where it occurs, its causes and the risk factors for involvement in bullying incidents. Data collection of this kind includes documentary evidence relevant to the reduction and prevention of school bullying (e.g. the School Development Plan, school policies, curriculum); school-based monitoring data (e.g. bullying incident records, absence and exclusion records); questionnaires (see Resources and References sections for examples of standardized measures), interviews and focus groups with representatives from all sections of the school community; and observations in different parts of the school at different times during the school day (Galvin 2006). Case Study 2.1 provides an example of the systematic and impartial implementation of a whole-school community needs analysis.

Case Study 2.1 Systematic and impartial implementation of a whole-school community needs analysis

In the light of the recently published *Safe to Learn* guidance from the Department of Children, Schools and Families (DCSF 2007b), Kerry Comprehensive decided they wanted to review and revise their anti-bullying policy. In 2007–8 a working group was established, which included the head teacher, one of the deputy head teachers, the Educational Psychologist, the school counsellor and two representatives each from the teaching staff, the non-teaching staff, the lunchtime supervisors, the School Council, parents/carers and governors. Following the establishment of the working group, a questionnaire survey was carried out in the autumn term with all pupils using *The Revised Olweus Bully/Victim Questionnaire* (Olweus 1996), the aim of which was to identify the scale and nature of the bullying that was being experienced in their school. In the spring term, members of the working group conducted focus groups composed of either staff, pupils or parents/carers to establish the views of these groups with regard to reporting, recording and follow-up of bullying incidents. The aim of conducting the focus groups was to use participants' views to inform the future monitoring and management of bullying incidents. Data analysis, undertaken with the help of a psychology under-graduate from the local university, highlighted high levels of cyber bullying and suggested an absence of systems to address it.

Following an invitation to join the working group, the information and communication technology (ICT) coordinator helped the group to redraft the anti-bullying policy to include reference to cyber bullying, which was distributed to staff, pupils, and parents and carers for their comments. The policy was revised in the light of the feedback, and existing incident report forms were adapted to log cyber bullying incidents. It was also apparent from the data that adults both inside and outside of the school were unaware of the potential for the misuse of mobile phones and the Internet. The school, therefore, organized two two-day training events on cyber bullying and e-safety, one for pupils and one for staff; invited pupils to design class presentations and assemblies on the topic of cyber bullying; and organized a conference on the topic for parents and carers, which involved substantial input from pupils.

Relational approach to the planning and implementation of the intervention or set of interventions

Given our understanding that the social context plays an important role in whether or not school bullying takes place (see Chapter 1), it is vital that the phenomenon is addressed using a relational approach if it is to be effective. Such an approach adopts an ecological framework for the prevention and reduction of school bullying, as described by Malley et al. (2001), which focuses on:

- emphasizing the primacy of human relationships as the medium for learning;
- cultivating contexts that bring out the best of human qualities;
- creating communities that emphasize the development of the whole person;
- emphasizing cooperation over competition;
- valuing individual differences.

From this perspective, 'the process of arriving at order is more significant than the process of imposing control' (Malley et al. 2001: 25). Thus, pupils will play an active role in policy making that promotes pro-social behaviour within the educational system. All school community members will listen to pupils. In addition, all school staff will emphasize the relationship as the crux of student learning, with respect and responsibility forming the foundations of the whole-school community. To prevent and reduce school bullying, requires the creation of a social context within which children, young people and adults feel a sense of belonging, of connectedness, of community.

This can be achieved by promoting a whole-school community response to school bullying based on a relational approach to building safe and emotionally supportive school communities. A relational approach puts community, interdependence, cooperation and belonging, which foster empathy and connectedness, over and above bureaucracy, control, independence and competition, which foster alienation, isolation and rejection (Malley et al. 2001). The approach focuses on the quality of relationships among staff and pupils; the quality of communication within schools, including staff–student communication regarding bullying incidents; the range of policies and practices available for addressing bullying, and other relationship difficulties, and its potential emergence; and the relationship between the school and its local environment (Watkins et al. 2007). The approach emphasizes the development of emotional and social skills, and concern for healthy interpersonal relationships, alongside the academic considerations of the school curriculum. Such an approach involves not only developing a range of appropriate interventions that address bullying at targeted and intensive levels, but also involves the development of proactive strategies that support the promotion of healthy interpersonal relationships, cooperation above competition and the education of emotional literacy and shared values.

Interventions range from whole-school strategies aimed at the whole-school community to targeted and intensive strategies for specific groups and individuals (see Figure 2.1). The whole-school support level is directed at all members of a school community in order to develop a strong normative climate and ethos of caring and respect, a sense of belonging and connectedness, and the development of strong social and emotional skills. At this level, emphasis is placed upon developing and maintaining pro-social relationships among all members of the whole-school community. This is achieved through the development of whole-school activities that promote and create positive relationship practices as exemplified in the development and maintenance of school policies, and through whole-school activities, including awareness-raising in the school as a whole, assemblies, classroom activities, for example use of circle time, and curriculum opportunities, such as Personal, Social, Health and Citizenship Education (PSHCE) and Social and Emotional Aspects of Learning (SEAL), school councils, emotional and social skills programmes, proactive home–school communication, and adult modelling of pro-social and respectful behaviour.

The group support level involves some members of the whole-school community, for example, a class or a circle of friends, with the aim of managing those

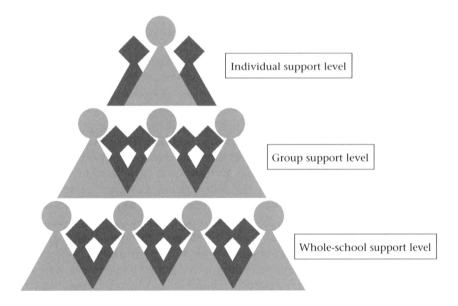

Figure 2.1   A relational model for addressing school bullying

individuals at risk of developing relationship problems, or who may be at risk for engaging in bullying and violent behaviour. At this level, school staff, parents or carers and pupils are encouraged to develop the capacity for cooperation in order that bullying and other relationship difficulties can be addressed through the everyday practices of the school. The aim is to create a culture in which collaboration is modelled and relationship difficulties are treated as an opportunity to learn, and where empathy, responsibility, and interdependence are fostered. This is achieved through strategies such as active listening, problem-solving circles, and cooperative group work, peer support and peer mediation.

The individual support level is intended for those pupils already experiencing distress as a result of bullying and violent behaviour. This level involves the participation of a wider cross-section of the school community, including parents or carers, social workers, and other individuals who have been affected when serious incidents occur within the school. At this level, the emphasis is on building a sense of belonging and a sense of connectedness in order to foster children and young people's capacity for empathizing with the school community. This is achieved through individual support using, for example, restorative conferences and mediation, individual interventions and classroom conferences.

Case Study 2.2 outlines the example of one Lewisham school, which embraced all three levels of support using a restorative approach to address negative student behaviour as an alternative to sanctions.

Case Study 2.2 Forest Hill School

This boys' secondary school has a long history of good relationships and strong pastoral support. Despite this, in 2002 staff were concerned about the high rates of detention and exclusion. Following initial use of restorative conferencing in early 2003, the school carried out a pilot with Year 7, the aim of which was to demonstrate and evaluate the impact of using a restorative approach prior to taking the decision to implement it across the whole school. During the pilot all Year 7 students were offered a restorative process as an alternative to exclusion wherever possible and, if a fixed term exclusion was considered unavoidable, a restorative conference as part of the reintegration process. The pilot was a success, which led the senior management team to give full support to the idea of making restorative practices 'the starting point for dealing with issues where harm has been caused to relationships' (head teacher). The school has subsequently undertaken a root and branch review of all its behaviour management systems to bring them in line with restorative principles. Over 25 staff have been trained as conference facilitators and all staff have received training about restorative approaches, in particular the use of restorative language and mini-conferences. 'Four years on, restorative language has become the norm by which we operate. We have found that systematically using these techniques has helped us to create a better environment, a less punitive culture. We haven't abandoned sanctions but we are always able to offer a restorative alternative, so students have the choice' (deputy head teacher).

The results of the shift in culture have been very encouraging: compared with 2003–4 figures school detentions (the most serious level of detention) have fallen by about 80 per cent; incidents of students being sent for referral has dropped by 45 per cent and fixed term exclusions have fallen by 75 per cent.

A number of activities were key to the introduction of restorative approaches into the whole-school community. At the whole-school community level, these included developing a vision and a team; developing a formal strategy that included a thorough plan for staffing, training and communicating with staff, students and parents and carers; building awareness among staff and parents and carers; reviewing the school detention system; and investment in staff training and a redefinition of key roles. At the group support level, these included training groups of Years 8 and 9 pupils as peer mediators; introducing classroom conferences to address problem behaviour in class; introducing a programme of life skill capacity-building for older pupils; and providing a reflective programme for staff. At the individual support level, this included introducing a conferencing initiative for more serious incidents.

(adapted from Warren and Williams 2007)

It should be noted that a relational approach runs counter to the notion of zero tolerance, which typically focuses on punishment of major and minor offences through discriminatory practices such as suspensions and exclusions and which avoids addressing social and emotional issues (Morrison 2007). Nevertheless, there is no evidence to suggest that zero tolerance works. For example, in their evaluation of zero tolerance policies, Skiba et al. (2006: 113) concluded that:

> zero tolerance policies as implemented have failed to achieve the goals of an effective system of school discipline ...[they have] not been shown to improve school climate or school safety ...[and]... its application in suspension and expulsion [sic] has not proven an effective means of improving student behaviour.

Morrison (2007) suggests that not only does zero tolerance fail to work, it also promotes intolerance and discrimination, since such a policy works to discriminate against a minority of the most vulnerable pupils. Indeed, adherence to such an approach will neither satisfy children's rights as set out in the UNCRC (1989), nor will schools be able to meet the five outcomes identified in *Every Child Matters* (DfES 2004), that is, be healthy, stay safe, enjoy and achieve, make a positive contribution, and achieve economic well-being.

In contrast, there is a growing body of evidence, which emphasizes the need to ensure a healthy, sustainable human community, which pays specific attention to the contextual aspects of the school environment to ensure that the emotional needs of all its pupils are being met (Malley et al. 2001). Malley et al. (2001) argue that post-modern school systems must focus on creating a sense of community and belonging to promote emotionally and psychologically healthy individuals. Children who feel a sense of belonging to a community will have an increased capacity for empathizing with other members; in turn, the presence of empathy is likely to reduce bullying and violent behaviour. For example, Grossman et al. (1997) demonstrated that the Second Step programme, a violence prevention curriculum that covers the teaching of empathy, impulse control, problem-solving and anger management skills, led to a decrease in observed physically aggressive behaviour and an increase in neutral/pro-social behaviour among primary school children.

Training in policy and practice

It is essential when planning your needs analysis that resources are allocated to training, since training ensures successful implementation of the intervention and the policy that supports it. In addition, school staff need general information regarding the incidence and nature of school bullying, and training and ongoing support in understanding and monitoring less observable bullying behaviours such as relational bullying (e.g. rumour-spreading, social exclusion) (see Chapter 1). School staff also need equality and diversity training in order to address sensitive aspects of bullying, related to issues such as race, ethnicity, disability, sexuality and gender (see Chapter 1). Our work with schools suggests that ongoing support for new policies and practices in the form of a rolling training programme for all staff and induction training for new staff, governors, pupils and parents or carers is critical. Case Study 2.3 highlights the importance of initial and ongoing training of the whole-school community.

Case Study 2.3. Woodside School

This large inner city secondary school situated in an area characterized by racial tension and high levels of poverty and unemployment, and a student intake that reflected the diverse local population, was experiencing high levels of bullying and violence. Following the implementation of a conflict resolution programme, which involved a one-day training for all Year 9 pupils and their tutors, a handful of Year 9 students were offered further intensive training as peer trainers over a residential weekend, to deliver training to Year 7 pupils, the idea being that as pupils moved up the school, over time all pupils would be trained. The residential training weekend was also attended by staff volunteers. Evaluation of the intervention revealed a number of benefits including a positive change in school culture and ethos, staff confidence to deal with conflict, greater self-confidence among pupils who had received the training, a significant reduction in high-level conflicts, an increase in annual attendance figures, a fall in the number of permanent exclusions, and a general improvement in academic achievement.

In addition, the evaluation identified a number of key considerations. In order to ensure that all staff have knowledge and understanding of the intervention, or set of interventions, training of non-teaching staff, for example, lunchtime supervisors, school counsellors and special educational needs coordinators as well as teaching staff is essential. To ensure a whole-school approach, new staff and pupils who have missed the initial training require an induction programme regarding the school's anti-bullying policies and practices. Since the long-term nature of anti-bullying work requires the need to keep the initial momentum of the launch of an intervention or policy going in terms of publicity, awareness-raising and ongoing support and induction of new staff, pupils and parents/carers could provide an opportunity for ongoing training for all members of the school community.

(adapted from Cowie et al. (2004)

Ongoing review and evaluation

An essential part of culture change is the provision of information about the implementation of the intervention and its effectiveness. As we have stated elsewhere, effective review and evaluation is not something that happens at the end of a project, rather it is an evolving process that enables the working group to understand the intervention and its anticipated effects better, thus aiding its refinement and improvement (Cowie et al. 2004). According to Riley and Segal (2002), evaluation has three major purposes. First, to review the extent to which each part of the school has implemented the key components of the intervention, which aspects work well and which are problematic, and what obstacles may be preventing individuals from fully implementing it. The second aim is to determine the impact of the intervention on key indicators of school bullying, such as reduced incidence of bullying, increased attendance, increased academic achievement and reduced discipline visits to the school office. The final purpose of evaluation is to describe which aspects of the intervention work well within which contexts. For example, evaluation should seek to identify which characteristics of classrooms, schools and neighbourhoods affect intervention outcomes and which elements key stakeholders value (e.g. training, materials, use of outside agency, sense of community, and levels of involvement and ownership).

A school's recording and monitoring systems, established to monitor bullying incidents, will provide some of this feedback. However, there is no substitute for a rigorously designed evaluation exercise. This need not be as daunting as it sounds, since the methods used for data collection in the needs analysis (documentary evidence, monitoring data, surveys, interviews, focus groups, observations) can be used, not only to collect baseline data, but can be administered one year on, for example, to ascertain whether the intervention has had any impact.

Learning points

- The understanding and management of school bullying must be informed by a sound knowledge base that can be used to design effective policy, procedures and systems and behaviour management practices, and develop a positive culture and ethos.
- A sound knowledge base can be achieved by conducting a needs analysis.
- Central to conducting a successful needs analysis are the acceptance of the existence of school bullying, visible support and participation from senior staff, a working group, systematic and impartial implementation, an integrated approach, training in policy and practice, and ongoing review and evaluation.
- The management of a needs analysis and subsequent implementation of an intervention or set of interventions requires culture change that may be challenging.
- A relational approach that draws upon a range of practices and processes to support the development of all members of the school community's emotional and social skills offers a comprehensive means of preventing and reducing school bullying.
- Zero tolerance not only fails to work, it fosters intolerance and discrimination against a minority of vulnerable pupils.

Resources

Arora, C. M. J. and Thompson, D. A. (1999) 'My life in school checklist', in N. Frederickson and R. J. Cameron (series eds.) and S. Sharp (vol. ed.), *Bullying Behaviour in Schools: Psychology in Education Portfolio*. Windsor: NFER NELSON.

Event Mapper: Mapping Attitudes. Curriculum, Evaluation and Management Centre, Durham University (www.cemcentre.org/RenderPage.asp?LinkID=31820000).

Gittins, C. (ed.) (2006) *Violence Reduction in Schools: How to Make a Difference*. Strasbourg: Council of Europe Publishing.

Olweus, D. (1996) *The Revised Olweus Bully/Victim Questionnaire*. Bergen, Norway: Research Centre for Health Promotion (HEMIL Centre), University of Bergen.

O'Moore, M. and Minton, S. J. (2004) *Dealing with Bullying in Schools: A Training Manual for Teachers, Parents and Other Professionals*. London: Sage Publications.

Rivers, I., Duncan, N. and Besag, V. (2007) *Bullying: A Handbook for Educators and Practitioners*. Westport, CT: Praeger Publishers.

Web sites

Anti-Bullying Alliance Bullying Audit Toolkit (www.anti-bullyingalliance.org.uk).

Rights Respecting School Award (www.unicef.org.uk/rrsa).

School Councils UK (www.schoolcouncils.org).

School Self-evaluation (www.sheu.org.uk/survey/sse.htm).

Training in restorative skills and interventions (www.transformingconflict.org).

Social and Emotional Aspects of Learning (SEAL) primary and secondary versions (www.standards.dfes.gov.uk/primary and www.standards.dfes.gov.uk/secondary).

3   WORKING WITH THE RELATION-SHIP TO HELP THE BULLIED PUPIL

Chapter overview

In this chapter, we consider some of the ways in which adults can work with young people's relationships in order to understand more deeply why bullying takes place and how they can counteract it. We draw on up-to-date research findings on children's relationships with key figures in their lives and how these can play a critical part in the ways in which they relate to their peers. We also show how educators can use this knowledge to help young people themselves understand more about the nature of their relationships with others. We provide up-to-date research findings, case studies of educators working with the relationship to alleviate the negative effects of bullying, examples of young people's perspectives and key learning points.

Understanding relationship difficulties in children and young people

The happiness of children and young people depends greatly on the quality of their relationships. Friends mutually validate one another so heightening self-esteem; friendships lead to other networks of peers so widening that experience as well as providing fun and support along the way. As Dunn (2004: 3) puts it:

> We are missing a major piece of what excites, pleases and upsets children, what is central to their lives even in the years before school, if we don't attend to what happens between children and their friends. The pleasures but also the betrayals, the jealousies and tangled intrigues, make friendships key to the quality of children's lives.

Not only does the experience of friendship, with all its ups and downs, provide an essential feature of the child's development, but also friends are there as a source of emotional support when things go wrong. The quality of children's friendship is an important factor in whether a child is protected from bullying or not. Children whose friends are low in protective qualities (possibly because they are weak and vulnerable as well) have an increased chance of being bullied and also of developing internalizing problems such as depression.

There are different ways of classifying bullied children. Olweus (1978) distinguished early between *passive* and *provocative* victims. Passive victims often show characteristics of insecurity and helplessness, sensitivity, nervousness and submissiveness. By contrast, provocative victims are anxious and defensive, often hyperactive and apt to irritate and annoy other children to such an extent that they appear to provoke aggressive behaviour. Later researchers (e.g. Ma 2004; Perry et al. 1988) distinguished a third category, the *bully–victim*, who is typically trapped in a cycle of rejection through being aggressive towards peers and is also the target of peer aggression; these children appear to be the most emotionally disturbed and are most likely to be chronically involved in bullying for long periods of time.

The impact on bullied children's relationships

Recent research evidence confirms that the experience of being bullied is potentially damaging to the young person's sense of self, their sense of others, their capacity to trust and their ability to enjoy relationships with the peer group (Boulton and Underwood 1992; Hartup 1996; La Greca and Harrison 2005; Marini et al. 2006). Being bullied also has an adverse effect on friendship and attachment and can lead to social isolation of the victim (Nangle et al. 2003).

As we learn from a number of large-scale longitudinal and cross-sectional studies, there are damaging outcomes for children who are bullied by their peers, especially when the bullying is longterm. Arsenault et al. (2006), as part of a longitudinal study of 2232 twins, identified those who had experienced bullying between the ages of 5 and 7, either as 'pure' victims or as bully–victims. Both 'pure' victims and bully–victims showed more adjustment difficulties and unhappiness at school than controls. The 'pure' victims showed a higher incidence of internalizing problems and unhappiness at school. Girls (but not boys) who were 'pure' victims also showed more externalizing problems than controls. However, the bully–victims had the highest levels of difficulty since they showed more internalizing problems than either pure victims or controls. A significant number of the children identified in this study as victims of bullying had come to school with pre-existing problems and were less happy than non-bullied peers during their first year at school. The authors suggest the possibility that bullied children may exhibit some behaviours or characteristics that elicit aggression from peers; for those reasons, the bullies may identify them as vulnerable and so target them from the start.

As we saw in Box 1.1, Hawker and Boulton (2000), in a meta-analysis of cross-sectional studies of bullying carried out between 1978 and 1997, found that the experience of being bullied was positively associated with depression; victims of bullying were consistently more depressed than non-victims. Similarly, they found that loneliness was also positively associated with the experience of being bullied. Both social and generalized anxiety were significantly related to bullying, though the effects were not as strong as those for depression. Bullied children were also found to have significantly lower self-esteem than non-victims. Hawker and Boulton (2000) strongly recommended that future research should focus on risk factors in bullying and matters concerned with causation.

Bosacki et al. (2007) took account of earlier research in their large-scale survey of the multiple dimensions of adolescent peer relationships, including quality of friendships, perceived loneliness and peer victimization. In their sample of 7290 adolescents aged between 13 and 18, they investigated the ways in which these dimensions were linked to depression and social anxiety. They were especially interested to find out how self-esteem acted as a mediator between social isolation on the one hand and the 'internalizing problems' of both depression and social anxiety. They found the following statistically significant results:

- Self-esteem did appear to mediate between peer relationship difficulties and depression and social anxiety.
- Social isolation, friendship alienation and friendship trust were significantly related both to self-esteem and to depression and social anxiety.
- Self-esteem, in turn, was significantly related to depression and social anxiety independent of peer relationship difficulties.
- The direct association between peer relational difficulties and depression and social anxiety was significantly reduced once self-esteem was entered into the equation.

These findings indicate a complex multi-directional process. The young person's self-esteem is likely to be adversely affected by relationship difficulties – a situation which, in turn, increases the emergence of depression or social anxiety. However, self-esteem partially mediates between some peer relationship difficulties and internalizing problems, such as depression and social anxiety, though this effect is more pronounced for depression than for social anxiety. In the Bosacki et al. (2007) study, the degree of emotional distress about peer relationship difficulties was more likely to be expressed by those who also scored high on depression and social anxiety than by those who simply described their perception of relationships factually, even if these were problematic. This suggested that some young people react more emotionally than others when they are having friendship difficulties or are being bullied, possibly because of their temperament or as a consequence of experiences of rejection or loss earlier in their lives. In other words, the individual experience of an apparently similar event depends on the young person's emotional makeup, their history of friendship and intimate attachments or some inner strength that emerges despite the suffering that they are experiencing. (See the case study of Sophie in this chapter and refer to Chapter 1 for the discussion of risk factors for bullying.)

The results of a longitudinal study provide further evidence of the mediating role of resilience in overcoming bullying. Smith Talamelli et al. (2004) found that 'escaped victims' (those who were no longer being bullied after a period of two years) did not differ substantially in terms of their profiles from non-victims. However, the pupils who had escaped from being bullied reported a number of useful strategies, such as telling someone, actively trying to make new friends and even befriending the bully – strategies which the 'continuing victims' (those who had been bullied for more than two years) were less likely to possess. The continuing victims were also more likely to blame themselves. These results suggested that low self-esteem and poor social skills may pre-date victimization and may well affect how successful the individual is in taking steps to escape.

It is not easy to test whether low self-esteem causes victimization, although a number of non-experimental studies provide some clear evidence for this relationship. For example, Egan and Perry (1998) measured the self-reported victimization and global self-worth of 189 schoolchildren (mean age 10.8 years) at the beginning of the school year and again five and a half months later. They found that self-worth decreased over time as a function of victimization, suggesting that low self-worth was a result of victimization. Despite this finding, Egan and Perry cautioned that the self-esteem/ victimization relationship might be a reciprocal one, with victimization and self-esteem mutually influencing each other. Not only are those low in self-esteem possibly lacking the resiliency afforded by higher levels of self-esteem, but also being victimized may further reduce their self-esteem, thereby perpetuating a vicious cycle and making these individuals even more susceptible to the effects of victimization. This corresponds with research showing that those low in self-esteem are more likely to perceive an incident as peer victimization and to interpret events more negatively than children whose self-esteem is high (Verkuyten and Thijs 2001). Therefore, not only do victims report low self-esteem, possibly as a direct result of being victimized, but also their low self-esteem primes them to view events negatively, making it more likely that they will consider a particular incident to be victimization. In addition, Verkuyten and Thijs (2001) conclude that victims' low self-esteem also reduces their resiliency to deal with being victimized.

Escobar (2008) carried out a study of 392 children aged 9 to 12 in four Spanish elementary schools. Her aim was to discover the impact of such factors as daily hassles/stresses and coping styles on the strength of the association between peer acceptance and the following variables: emotional symptoms, unhappiness at school and personal adjustment. She found predictably that daily hassles were a strong moderator between peer rejection and both emotional difficulties and unhappiness at school. Personal adjustment also seemed to depend on positive peer acceptance, low level of daily stresses and a positive problem-focused coping style. Paradoxically, however, for children rejected by their peers, there was an adverse effect from adopting the coping strategies of seeking social support from the peer group and making use of professional help, such as counselling. In other words, coping strategies that were effective for emotionally adjusted children became dysfunctional for those in greatest need of support. These findings confirm earlier research indicating that children's peer relationships are strengthened if they tackle difficulties immediately, seek relaxing diversions, engage in physical recreation, work hard to achieve and think about the positive things in life. But, the study also indicates the complexity of the dynamics of peer relationships. A vulnerable child who is rejected by the peer group may be perceived as too 'needy' and demanding when they seek out social support. There may also be a stigma attached to those who receive professional help for emotional difficulties.

The evidence from the different research studies offers useful insights into a possible chain of events that may arise from the experience of being bullied, and indicates the crucial part that close intimate relationships play in the emotional health and well-being of young people. Low self-esteem and interpersonal difficulties like being bullied may interact with one another over time. Children with low self-esteem may be more vulnerable to attack in the first place; the bullying undermines their self-esteem even further; in turn, this leads to further victimization and so the cycle continues if nothing is done to intervene. Teachers, parents, carers, health professionals and all those who work with young people should be knowledge-able about interventions that help children develop social skills necessary for building and maintaining friendships. We also recommend interventions that bolster self-esteem, such as assertiveness training and practice in positive self-statements, for young people who are being bullied. In the next section, we see an example illustrating how one young girl overcame the social anxiety that was the direct outcome of the bullying she had experienced at school.

Overcoming social anxiety: case study of a bullied girl

Ferrazzuolo (2004: 185–202) describes the case of Sophie, whose experience of being bullied about her bushy hair led to acute social anxiety. In Sophie's words:

> 'It used to be really thick and they called me 'Afro' and I used to be really miserable about it for a really long time ...I used to cry a lot ... I never put it down. Never! And even when I went out with my friends, if somebody from school passed by, I put it up again, just to avoid it (the bullying). It affected everything, my whole life, really. I didn't want to go out. I didn't put my hair down. I didn't speak to my friends. It was like that ... So it (the bullying) changed me.'

The turning point came when Sophie told her Mum who then informed the school about what was happening. However, of even more significance was the change that took place within Sophie so that she began to feel strong enough to deal with the bullying herself. She was then able to speak directly to the girls who were making nasty comments about her appearance and say calmly and clearly to them that she did not like it. That gave her strength so that even when people did make adverse comments she was able to ignore them. Sophie's resilience enabled her to challenge the bullying behaviour when it occurred. In fact, not only did Sophie gain enough self-esteem to address her own social anxiety issue, she became strong enough to challenge bullying against other pupils and so became in her own way a defender. Ferrazzuolo (2004: 191) concludes that 'Sophie revealed the process that produced her personality growth, the reinforcement of her self-esteem and the acquisition of valid problem-solving strategies'.

Working intensively with bullied pupils

Studies like these indicate the importance of building up the inner strengths of bullied children so that they can discriminate among strategies that are effective for them and those that are counter-productive, for example, when they bottle up their feelings, over-react emotionally or try too hard to elicit social approval from their peers. The most successful solutions to the problem appear to be those that acknowledge the moderating power of high self-esteem reinforced by the support of key adults and members of the peer group. For example, assertiveness training can provide bullied children with a set of skills to protect themselves against the hurtful behaviour of bullies, including 'I' statements, such as 'I don't like it when you call me that name' or 'I want you to stop doing that'.

As Sullivan (2000) argues, being assertive can enable bullied children to reclaim their personal power and so begin the process of building up their self-esteem. In some cases, it may be necessary to enable children to be aware of the behaviours and characteristics that provoke bullying behaviour (Arsenault et al. 2006; Pikas 2002). Without condoning the bullying behaviour, it may be helpful for supportive adults (e.g. a teacher, parent, carer or counsellor) to encourage the victim to think about ways in which his or her behaviour may have been a contributory factor. If this is the case, then the adult can help the young person to acknowledge this possibility in an assertive way and to consider alternative ways to improve the situation through their own actions. This self-awareness, of course, may be extremely painful to come to terms with. But in the longer term such knowledge can strengthen the bullied child's capacity to defend their own sense of self and find appropriate responses when bullying occurs.

Staying calm in the face of bullying is a difficult task and the strengths required should not be underestimated. While teaching the bullied pupil skills of assertiveness, as described above, will not in itself stop the bullying, it can help the young person to deal more effectively with being bullied and, even more importantly, help to prevent bullying from being established in the first place. As Sharp and Cowie (1998: 111) recommend, assertive behaviour involves being clear, calm and direct. Assertiveness is based on mutual respect for self and others and helps to defuse potentially aggressive situations before they get out of control. Assertive behaviour combines verbal statements with calm and confident body language. Bullied pupils will need time and practice to become skilled in assertive responses. They may also need to learn stress management techniques like physical relaxation, breath control, massage or creative visualization to help them to stay calm.

Repairing the damage

An increasingly popular method for resolving episodes of bullying is derived from restorative practice (Cameron and Thorsborne 2000; Cowie and Jennifer 2007; Morrison 2003; Wachtel and McCold 2001). Restorative practice originally grew out of peace-keeping methods developed by Maori communities and, more recently, has been successfully used in the criminal justice system to repair the emotional damage done to victims of crime by the perpetrators by bringing the two parties together to engage in a process of repair, restoration and reintegration. In May 2000, the Youth Justice Board (YJB) for England and Wales launched a pilot initiative in two schools in London, using restorative justice conferences to tackle exclusions, truancy, bullying, violence and other forms of antisocial behaviour. This pilot was successful, and was extended to include schools across the UK involving nine Youth Offending Teams (YOTs) and 26 schools, all taking different approaches to the introduction of restorative practices. This was evaluated by the YJB in 2004 (YJB 2004). Initial reports demonstrated that the introduction of restorative practices within the school environment was both beneficial and successful.

Since then, more schools have adapted restorative practices to apply to their own particular culture and, when properly used, they can be a very effective tool to tackle bullying (Hopkins 2004; Warren and Williams 2007) since the focus is on healing the harm, addressing the emotions and engaging the active participation of all involved. Most importantly, restorative practice is viewed as a learning process which provides an opportunity for those involved in a bullying episode to reflect on what happened, to become more emotionally aware and, if possible, to experience increased compassion and understanding of different perspectives.

Warren and Williams (2007) make the point that restorative approaches are not a soft option. In fact, the restorative process can be more difficult for perpetrators than sanctions. The reason for this is that, in order to repair the damage, perpetrators have to face up to the full emotional impact of what they did to another person. However, restorative practices are not a substitute for sanctions and schools need to retain sanctions for the most serious incidents. But schools that have adopted restorative policies find that formal sanctions are needed less frequently. (See the earlier discussion of zero tolerance policies in Chapter 2.)

The methods of restorative range from formal processes, mainly designed for very serious incidents, to informal responses to everyday happenings. Formal methods include conferences and adult mediation; less formal methods include peer mediation, buddying, circle time, restorative discussions in class and restorative thinking plans. Central to restorative practice is the concept of community. The bullying episode is harmful to the individuals directly involved but it also harms the whole school community. When bullying happens, as it does in all schools, restorative practices engage the perpetrators, their victims and significant others in the school community in a collective process of problem-solving whose aim is reparation of damage, restoration of the quality of relationships and facilitation of the reintegration of participants in the conflict back into the school community. The method is a form of collective problem-solving whose aims are as follows:

- *Reparation of damage:* Restorative practices aim to heal the emotional damage caused by the bullying behaviour. The aim is that all parties are winners in this process.
- *Restoration of the relationship:* Restorative practices are not about punishment or blame. Instead, they address issues of fairness and justice. The aim is that the bully takes responsibility for the wrong and makes amends in some way. Through the process of open, direct communication between victim and bully, the method potentially transforms the ways in which people relate to one another.
- *Reintegration:* At the broadest level, it provides an arena in which pupils, staff and parents/carers can be part of a just process through which they learn about the consequences of bullying and come to understand the impact of their behaviour on others.

As Cremin (2007) indicates, restorative practice needs to be integral to the school's culture. The approach is most successful when it is embedded in a whole-school commitment to working with the relationship in every aspect of the school's work through, for example, circle time, cooperative group learning, democratic practices, commitment to equality, tolerance, fairness and justice, as well as peer mediation, adult mediation and conferencing for specific use once the bullying episode has occurred. However, if the school is to make real changes, it also needs to attend to the prevention of bullying in the first place. This involves a whole-school commitment to create a culture grounded in fairness and justice, and in an ethos of positive, caring relationships. Warren and Williams (2007), who have documented the successful implementation of restorative practices in Lewisham schools in London, noted that the greatest impact takes place in schools where restorative practice is not only confined to the most serious issues but happens in everyday situations, however minor they may appear. If restorative thinking becomes part of the behaviour management policy of the school, it then becomes part of everyone's repertoire of response to difficulty. In this way, restorative approaches complement other initiatives such as Social and Emotional Aspects of Learning (SEAL) and Personal, Social, Health and Citizenship Education (PSHCE).

In Chapter 6, we provide examples of young people trained as peer mediators to apply relational practice to bullying incidents. Here we describe the process of adult mediation. The facilitator, a trained adult mediator, hears an account of what happened from each party, tries to enable agreement about what went wrong and what harm has been done, and moves towards a way of repairing the damage. The parties (as in peer mediation) agree to make amends in some way acceptable to each one and then to move on. Adult mediation can be used either to avoid exclusion of the bully or as part of reintegration following exclusion. Typically, the adult mediator will go through the following stages, as shown in Box 3.1.

Box 3.1 The stages of the mediation process

Stage 1 Identify the problem

Make the two disputants feel comfortable. Explain what the process of mediation entails. Invite each participant to describe their view of the problem situation without interruption, stating feelings as well as facts. The mediator clarifies the needs and interest of each party, using statements like, 'My understanding of what you said is this ...' Each party is asked to summarize what the other said. The mediator summarizes what each has said.

Stage 2 Explore options

The mediator gives each person an opportunity to explain what has happened from their perspective, and what led up to it; to share thoughts and feelings they had during the time of the conflict and at the moment and talk about who

---

else may have been affected. The mediator encourages both sides to listen to and recognize the other's point of view, then re-frames the stories checking that each party accepts that this is a fair account of what happened. Each party states what ideally they would like to happen and is invited to suggest possible solutions.

Stage 3   Take account of risks and benefits

The mediator notes possible risks and benefits and invites each party to think about the outcomes of the suggested solutions. Each is invited to explore possible risks and possible benefits of the proposed solutions.

Stage 4   Make a plan of action

Each party considers which solutions are likely to meet the needs of both. They are asked to select one or two possible solutions. The mediator clarifies what each party agrees to do and by when. The mediator then draws up a written agreement of future actions which is signed by all present. Both parties shake hands.

Stage 5   Review and evaluate

The parties agree to meet to review outcomes and to evaluate what happened. They agree to renegotiate as appropriate. The mediator praises each party for successes and summarizes in context the values of cooperation and trust. The mediator closes the meeting by acknowledging that progress has been made (even if complete resolution has not been reached). The mediator invites each person to reflect on how they might each behave differently in the future.

(adapted from Cowie and Jennifer 2007: 108)

A more advanced version of adult mediation is the restorative conference in which the process involves all involved in the bullying episodes with their respective parents/carers/supporters, as well as key school personnel and behaviour support staff (where applicable). The conference takes place in a room where everyone can sit in a circle. The facilitator talks personally with those involved prior to the conference to prepare them for the process and answer any queries and concerns. It is essential that everyone present has volunteered to be there and that everyone feels safe. The purposes of the conference are: to establish the context of the bullying incident and why it happened; to hear accounts of the damage to the victim; to discuss ways in which the damage might be repaired; and to discuss and plan ways of avoiding such incidents in the future. An important feature of the conference is the involvement of everyone in planning the way forward, as we see in Case Study 3.1.

Case Study 3.1 Power struggles in the peer group

The dispute

Staff at a primary school had become worried about a group of Year 6 girls because of the constant arguments, including excluding girls from the 'in-group', name-calling, talking behind backs and spreading nasty rumours. The girls' behaviour was having an impact on others in their year group and negatively affecting the school ethos. Teachers and lunchtime supervisors were constantly trying to resolve these girls' disputes but as soon as one problem was sorted another would spring up. Most recently, there had been a series of confrontations between some of the parents at the school gate with a number of angry accusations and threats being exchanged. The issue was spreading out into the community and showing signs of getting out of hand. The head teacher decided to organize a conference involving three of the girls who seemed to be at the centre of most of the disputes: Becky, Amina and Kumika. She invited PC Emma Young, the school liaison police officer who had been trained in restorative practice, to facilitate the conference, as well as the girls' parents/carers; the class teacher, a lunchtime supervisor and the special needs coordinator.

The conference

PC Young made sure that everyone knew each person's name and set out the purpose of the meeting. In turn, she asked the three girls and the staff to describe what had happened, how they felt then and what they were feeling right now. She then asked the parents and the head teacher what they felt when they heard about the series of episodes and what they were feeling now. Then, in turn, she asked who had been affected and what needed to be done to put the damage right. The girls described a web of intrigue in which girls would share secrets, betray these secrets, gossip about one another, regularly exclude a targeted girl from the group and spread nasty rumours about other girls. The teacher and the lunchtime supervisor described the constant unrewarding task of sorting out disputes only to find that they re-emerged in different ways and with different members of the friendship group. They described their feelings of helplessness and frustration as well as their concern about the emotional upset that these intrigues were causing. The parents/carers were very upset that their daughters could be involved in such feuds and betrayals. Becky's Dad reported how angry he had been when he heard about the nasty things that Kumika had been saying about Becky. Kumika's mother reported that her daughter had been distraught when she was excluded from the group, especially when she was the only one not to be invited to Becky's birthday party. Recently she had been so unhappy that she became ill and was refusing to go to school. Kumika said that she had been devastated when Becky told Amina some secrets that she had told her in confidence about her family; she felt betrayed.

PC Young then asked the girls to respond to what they had heard. Initially, Becky and Amina remained silent then Becky spoke up. She said, 'I am really sorry, Kumika, that I did not invite you to my party. I didn't know how upset you were about those things I told Amina but now I do'. Then Kumika said that she too was sorry for saying some very nasty things about Becky. Amina in turn apologized to Kumika and to the school staff for her part in turning other girls against Kumika. The girls then together discussed constructive ways in which they could all get on better with one another and arranged a meeting with teachers and lunchtime supervisors to help them put these ideas into practice. They already had some ideas about setting up a lunchtime club on Tuesdays.

In the group bullying situation described in Case Study 3.1, it was at times difficult to differentiate among bullies and bullied since the roles shifted depending on who was in and who was out of the group. However, the relational process of the conference enabled all to benefit mutually. All three reported that they now felt more confident in themselves and appreciated the opportunity to make good the damage that had been done which, in fact, was making all of them unhappy. Kumika, in particular, felt much more positive about school and was happy to be involved in the planning meeting in which the girls were actively involved in making things better for the whole friendship group. Over time, and following the planning meeting, all three also reported greater insights into why children bully others and why some people are bullied within the friendship group.

Teachers frequently report that the school environment becomes safer and more caring following the introduction of restorative practices, and that peer relationships in general improve (Warren and Williams 2007). The degree to which the school integrates restorative practice into the whole school policy as strategy is central to its success. In Case Study 3.1 we saw how important it was for the head teacher to be actively involved in the conference and in facilitating the planning meetings afterwards. It was also important to involve lunchtime supervisors as well since they were often at the forefront of dealing with disputes at break time as they arose. The parents/carers also needed to know so that they had the broader picture and potentially were now able to see the incidents from different perspectives.

Learning points

- Educators can learn how to remedy bullied children's relationship difficulties by understanding more about their origins and by building up self-esteem.
- Children can be helped to feel better about themselves by placing emphasis on the emotional aspects of their experience.
- Educators can address the emotional needs of bullied children by helping them to rehearse and practise assertive behaviour.
- Restorative practices have an important role to play in fostering a relational approach to helping bullied pupils.

Resources

Cole, T. (2000) *Kids Helping Kids*. Victoria, British Columbia: Peer Resources.

Cowie, H., Boardman, C., Dawkins, J. and Jennifer, D. (2004) *Emotional Health and Well-being: A Practical Guide for Schools*. London, Sage Publications.

Cowie, H. and Jennifer, D. (2007) *Managing Violence in School: A Whole-School Approach to Best Practice*. London: Paul Chapman.

Cowie, H. and Wallace, P. (2000) Peer support in action. London: Sage Publications.

Hazler, R. J. (1996) *Breaking the Cycle of Violence: Interventions for Bullying and Victimization*. Washington, DC: Accelerated Development/Taylor & Francis.

Hopkins, B. (2004) *Just Schools*. London: Jessica Kingsley.

McLauchlin, E., Fergusom, R., Hughes, G. and Westmorland, L. (Eds.) (2003) Restorative Justice: Critical Issues. London: Sage.

Petch, B. and Withers, T. (2006) *Peer mediation: guidance notes for schools*. Solihull: Solihull Metropolitan Borough Council.

Robinson, G. and Maines, B. (2007) *Bullying*. London: Sage Publications.

Salter, K. and Twidle, R. (2005). *The Learning Mentor's Source and Resource Book*. London: Paul Chapman.

Sharp, S. and Cowie, H. (1998) *Counselling and Supporting Children in Distress*. London: Sage Publications.

Warren, C. and Williams, S. (2007) *Restoring the Balance*. London: Lewisham Action on Mediation Project.

Zehr, H. (2002) *The Little Book of Restorative Justice*. Intercourse, PA: Good Books Publications.

Web sites

International Institute for Restorative Practices (www.iirp.org; www.safersanerschools.org; www.realjustice.org).

Massage In Schools (www.misa.org.uk).

Mediation UK (www.mediationuk.org.uk).

Peer Support Networker (www.ukobservatory.com).

Practicing Positive Relationships (www.betterbehaviourscotland.gov.uk).

Restorative Practices Forum (www.iirp.org).

TeacherNet (www.teachernet.gov.uk).

Transforming Conflict (www.transformingconflict.org).

UK Observatory for the Promotion of Non-violence (www.ukobservatory.com).

Youth Justice Board for England and Wales (www.youth-justice-board.gov.uk).

4 WORKING WITH THE RELATIONSHIP TO CHANGE BULLYING BEHAVIOUR

Chapter overview

In Chapter 3 the focus was on helping bullied pupils but, as recent research confirms, the bullies are at risk too. Children who bully have learned to use their power and aggression to control others, a mode that is not conducive to healthy relationships either in the present or in their future lives. Furthermore, there is evidence that children who bully are also likely to have mental health problems that persist into adult life. In this chapter, we show how educators can use this knowledge to help young people who bully develop deeper understanding of themselves and their relationships with others. We provide up-to-date research findings, case studies of educators working directly with young people who bully, examples of young people's perspectives and key learning points.

The impact on bullies' relationships

Kumpulainen and Räsänen (2000) found that children involved in bullying, in particular those who were bully–victims at early elementary school age and those who were victims in their early teens, had more psychiatric symptoms at the age of 15. The probability of being deviant at the age of 15 was higher among children involved in bullying at the age of 8 or 12 than among non-involved children. When concurrent psychiatric deviance was taken into account, involvement in bullying increased the probability of teacher-defined deviance at the age of 15. Similarly, Kaltiala-Heino et al. (2000), in a large-scale survey of 14- to 16-year-old Finnish adolescents taking part in the School Health Promotion Study (8787 in 1995, 7643 in 1997), found that anxiety, depression and psychosomatic symptoms were most frequent among bully–victims and equally common among bullies and victims. Frequent excessive drinking and substance misuse were most common among bullies and thereafter among bully–victims. Among girls, eating disorders were associated with involvement in bullying in any role, among boys with being bully–victims. These authors conclude that bullying should be seen as an indicator of risk of various mental disorders in adolescence.

Bullies can be classified into a number of categories as follows:

- *Aggressive bullies*: These are most likely to be the ringleader bullies. Typically they are low in empathy for others' suffering. They are manipulative, impulsive, assertive, strong and easily provoked; they take the lead in initiating the aggression; they often seek out other bullies to form a coterie of followers who join in with their aggressive behaviour and support it.
- *Anxious bullies/assistants to the bully*: In contrast to the leadership qualities of the aggressive bully, they usually have low self-esteem, lack confidence and are prone to disruptive temper tantrums; they follow the aggressive bully, possibly to compensate for their own feelings of insecurity. They often appear desperate for approval from the aggressive bullies whom they follow.
- *Reinforcers of the bully*: Like the assistants to the bully, the reinforcers are part of the coterie of followers. Their role is to encourage the ringleader bully by, for example, laughing, actively watching the episode, providing an audience for the ringleader's aggressive behaviour.
- *Bully-victims*: As we saw in Chapter 3, the bully–victims are the most emotionally disturbed since they are aggressive towards their peers but are also the target of their peers' aggression.

Although bullies often appear confident, assertive, and, on the surface at least, popular, they also tend to exhibit a lack of empathy for the suffering of their victims (Sutton et al. 1999). The reasons given by a sample of adolescent female bullies for their behaviour included boredom, attention-seeking, revenge, anger and the need for power (Owens et al. 2000). They also admitted that, by socially excluding selected peers, they affirmed their own inclusion in the in-group. Interviews with bullies frequently elicit rationalizations for their aggressive behaviour that minimize the outcomes for victims and provide justification for the actions. For example, bullies will often state that the victim provoked them in some way and so deserved the treatment that they had received. In Case Study 4.1 we present part of an interview with Mark, one of the children who participated in a study of cooperative groupwork in three ethnically mixed primary schools in an inner-city district of Sheffield (Cowie et al. 1994). In each school, the research team worked with two classes, one of which (the control class) carried on with the normal curriculum while the other one (the experimental class) experienced a curriculum that involved intensive cooperative group learning. The effects of this type of curriculum on the children's attitudes and behaviour were determined by a range of quantitative and qualitative measures, including interviews, sociometric tests and parenting style questionnaires.

Case study 4.1   Mark: a bully who became a victim

Nine-year-old Mark, nominated by the majority of his classmates as a bully, was tall, fashionably dressed and physically fit. Mark perceived the world as a dangerous place to be where you needed to be on the alert and prepared to attack others before they attacked you. For that reason, his main hobby was practising karate, justified, in his words, in the following way:

> Karate is defence, so if someone came up to you and hit you, I've got licence even to kill. You know, if you killed someone doing karate, yeah, you can't get done because it (the licence) tells you that you're doing it for self-defence.

Scores on the parenting style questionnaire (PSQ), one of the measures used in this study, indicated that, while he perceived his parents as high on emotional warmth, they also scored high on neglect. He reported that their disciplinary methods were harsh and included such punishments as locking him in his bedroom, making a fool of him in front of other people and calling him nasty names. His dad often threatened to punish him while his mum let him stay out late, did not mind if he did dangerous things and did not monitor where he was. He had bullied other children since first school. His usual pattern of responding to other children was to counter-attack. He showed no remorse for his over-reaction and always appeared to be convinced that his victims deserved all they got, even when no-one else could see any reason for the provocation. Here is one example of his justification for violence:

Mark: When it was my ball, I brought it to school. He goes, 'I'll pop it,' and I said, 'I'll pop *your* brain!' Then he popped it and I gave him one ... [pauses] ... and he had a broken nose. I broke his nose.

HC: You broke his nose?

Mark: He was on the floor before it got broken. I just stamped on it like that.

HC: You stamped on his nose? Were you sorry afterwards?

Mark: No ... He admitted that he started the fight.

HC: That's quite a reaction on your part now, wasn't it? To break his nose you must have stamped on it pretty hard.

Mark (coolly): Not pretty hard 'cos on the side it's soft there.

HC: How do you think he felt?

Mark: Nowt. He just ran out and went home.

Not surprisingly, other children were wary of him and he found it hard to make friends. Even constructive feedback in small groupwork enraged him leading him to shout, 'Shut up!!' or 'You liar!!' During the first year of the study, it appeared that no-one dared to challenge his dominance. However, over the course of the next year Mark, now 10 years old, became increasingly subdued. The main reason for this was that he, in turn, was being bullied by tougher, stronger boys who were threatening him and extorting money from him. Only 38 per cent of his classmates now rated him as a bully while 69 per cent nominated him as a victim. His lack of supportive friends made him all the more vulnerable to attack so confirming his negative view of relationships. Even his faith in the protection of karate was reduced. Although he still practised, he was less confident that physical aggression could solve his problems.

(Cowie et al. 1994: 166–170)

The precarious nature of the bully's power, as shown in the case study of Mark, is confirmed by Besag (2006) in her longitudinal observational study of girls' relationships. She observed that if a girl wished to retain her power within the group she needed to be constantly aware of the needs of individual members as well as the shifting dynamics of the group. Skill at manipulating others (often covertly) may be an effective means of retaining dominance over others in the short term, but it can backfire if the group collectively decides that the behaviour is unacceptable. Kaukiainen et al. (2002) found that 11- and 12-year-old bullies tended to fall into two groups: socially skilled and socially unskilled. This is an important distinction to make. For example, Besag described the unsuccessful bids for leadership on the part of one girl (Rachel) that failed since her repertoire of tactics included a bullying, autocratic manner and the tendency to act in such a way that vulnerable members were disadvantaged. She was large and powerfully built so could be very intimidating but in the end the others usually managed to reject her attempts to dominate, so indicating the potential of the group to challenge the power of the bully, if it chooses.

Low fear reactivity seems to be a strong risk factor for aggressive behaviour since it prevents the development of a sense of conscience about harming others, undermines the quality of empathy for another's suffering and acts against the internalization of pro-social norms of behaviour. Terranova et al. (2008), in a sample of 124 middle-school children, investigated whether the children's fear reactivity and their 'effortful control' (i.e. their ability to inhibit dominant responses) would influence whether they engaged in bullying. They found that children who carry out direct physical bullying (as opposed to psychological or indirect bullying) lack the qualities of self-regulation and also do not fear the consequences of their aggression. They noted that deficits in effortful control disrupt the development of pro-social skills and values so reducing the repertoire of responses available to bullies when they interact with their peers.

These examples of the bully's personal characteristics also appear to confirm what some researchers have identified as a narcissistic preoccupation with the self and oversensitivity to any form of actual or perceived criticism. Those high in narcissism appear to be self-confident with high levels of self-esteem but they are often considered by others to be egotistical and conceited individuals who have a grandiose conception of themselves. Narcissistic individuals also tend to be self-focused, highly competitive, exhibitionistic and aggressive people who lack empathy and who tend to be manipulative and self-seeking in their interpersonal relationships (Raskin and Novacek 1989). Baumeister et al. (1996) further propose that aggression is related to high self-esteem through what they define as *defensive egotism*–a tendency to hold favourable self-appraisals that may not be grounded in reality or may be exaggerated, combined with difficulty in accepting any criticism. Threats to such self-appraisals are met with aggression. This type of self-focused person tends to be highly competitive, manipulative, lacking in empathy and self-seeking in their relationships with others; they also score highly on measures of narcissism. Baumeister et al. (1996) argue that it is at the point where such a person's self-appraisal is perceived to be under threat that they become aggressive.

Research has given us some insight into the bullies' need for dominance within the group and their use of aggression and psychological manipulation to maintain their power, characteristics that clearly reflect the above descriptions of narcissism and defensive egotism. From this perspective, it would appear that bullies take advantage of the social structures in their peer groups and their skill at manipulating others to use bullying strategies, often indirectly, to deflect perceived threats to their own self-esteem. Salmivalli et al. (1999) investigated the relationship between bullying, self-esteem and defensive egotism in a sample of 148 female and 168 male adolescents. They found no relationship between global measures of self-esteem and bullying behaviour. However, they found a correlation between defensive egotism and bullying among boys, such that boys who were classed as bullies had higher levels of defensive egotism. Building upon the earlier research, Daly (2006) investigated the links between narcissism (as a component of defensive egotism), self-esteem and bullying in a large sample of Australian adolescents (Box 4.1).

Box 4.1   Bullying and narcissism

Daly, in his study of 1628 adolescents in six Australian schools, tested the hypothesis that high self-esteem in conjunction with high levels of narcissism would predict greater levels of bullying. His findings challenged the commonly held view that bullies use aggression to bolster their low self-esteem. The adolescents in this survey who scored highly on measures of self-esteem and narcissism also scored highly on aggression. He concluded that programmes of intervention that aim to increase the self-esteem of bullies may be counterproductive since this may simply reinforce unacceptable social behaviour. Like Terranova et al. (2008), he recommended that interventions that focus on building the capacity for empathy among young people who bully may actually be more effective in reducing aggression. Examples of such interventions would include training in peer support and in restorative practices, each of which works through the relationship to develop qualities such as respect for the other, a problem-solving approach to conflict and the experience of active, empathic listening. Additionally, interventions such as the support group method (described later in this chapter) work directly to enhance empathy and to foster pro-social attitudes within the group. When these methods are successful, they enhance a group ethos in which it is possible to make reparation for the emotional damage that arises from bullying and increase the repertoire of responses to situations of conflict.

(adapted from Daly 2006)

It is essential to view the research that documents *personality* characteristics of bullies in the wider *social* context in which children and adolescents are growing up, and so to take account of such factors as social class, ethnicity and sexuality. This is graphically illustrated in an innovative study of adolescent boys by Frosh et al. (2002). These researchers discovered that it was very difficult for boys to experiment with alternative ways of being masculine outside of the narrow stereotypes provided by their culture. In the researchers' words, 'the dominant form of masculinity is associated with heterosexuality, toughness, power and authority, competitiveness and the subordination of gay men' (Frosh et al. 2002: 75–76). As mentioned in Chapter 1 in the section on homophobic bullying, many boys do not attain this masculine 'ideal' and have to find strategies for dealing with the sanctions of bullying, ostracism and name-calling meted out mercilessly to those who do not fit. The most common terms of abuse concerned being 'gay' but boys who were studious, sensitive or in some way emotionally vulnerable did not fare any better at the hands of the peer group. Even boys who were willing to defend bullied peers had to be careful in case the group turned on them. Here one boy, Thomas, describes how he attempts to defend James whom others label as a 'boff' or a 'geek':

> There's a boy in our year called James and he's really clever, and he's basically got no friends and that's really sad because he's such a clever boy and he gets top marks in every test and everyone hates him. I mean I like him, when I see someone bullying him I just tell them to go and get lost. I just find that really annoying.

> (Frosh et al. 2002: 199)

In general, within that peer group, it was necessary to 'get by with cussing and comradeship at best, alienation at worst' (Frosh et al. 2002: 260–61). Being 'hard' conferred high status and being studious or sensitive meant ostracism. Yet most of the boys in the study had a clear awareness of moral codes, understood the need for close supportive relationships and were able to talk about these aspects of relationships in one-to-one interviews with the researchers.

Working intensively with bullies

In Chapter 3 we saw how supportive interventions can raise the self-esteem of bullied children and give them a repertoire of skills with which to relate to their peers more positively. However, we also need to work with the bullies in order to change their domineering and manipulative ways of relating to others. As Daly (2006) suggests, it may be counterproductive to use interventions that boost self-esteem. Interventions with bullies, if they are to succeed, must aim to achieve not only prevention but also rehabilitation. As we argue throughout this book, this can only achieved through a consistent whole-school approach that addresses the issue at different levels: working therapeutically with the individual, strengthening positive relationships within the classroom and the school community, creating and implementing fair policies and practices to ensure agreement on behaviour that is acceptable and forging links with the wider community to share values and reinforce strategies. Here we focus on direct therapeutic work with bullies but need to state clearly that, on its own, such intervention is less likely to succeed in its goal of changing the individual bully's behaviour and attitudes unless it is embedded in a wider whole-school approach.

As discussed in Chapter 2, Skiba et al. (2006), in their report to the American Psychological Association Zero Tolerance Task Force, concluded that zero tolerance policies were ineffective in changing the behaviour of bullies. In fact, they found that, contrary to popular belief, the removal of disruptive pupils from school actually had the opposite effect to that intended since pupils in schools with the highest rates of suspension rated the ethos of their schools as less satisfactory than did those in comparable schools without such policies. Not only that, the researchers found a negative correlation between the use of suspension and academic achievement in general in these schools. The overzealous use of zero tolerance policies also shows a serious infraction of fundamental rights by threatening the opportunity to learn for large numbers of young people. The authors recommended that zero tolerance strategies should only be used in the most extreme and severe cases of bullying and even then used with great thought for the needs and rights of all the individuals involved, including those of the bullies. Some practitioners (e.g. Hazler 1996a) argue the case for reinforcing bullies' good behaviour when it occurs–'catching them being good'–by using a traditional behaviour modification approach, indicating that the rewarding of low-level pro-social behaviour is likely to promote its recurrence, provided that the reward is offered in a consistent manner. But at a deeper level it is also necessary to work therapeutically to change the cognitions that many bullies hold and which, too often, are reinforced by the supporters in their immediate peer group.

As the research indicates, children engage in bullying for a range of different reasons, so the interventions need to be adapted to the particular needs of the individual and take account of that young person's peer group, their family values and behaviour patterns, as well as the characteristics of their community. In Box 4.2, Hazler (1996a) describes the promoting issues in common (PIC) method, which works to change the bully–victim relationship by enabling bullies to understand the fears and anxieties that they have in common with those they bully. The rationale behind PIC is that everyone benefits when people seek to understand, work with and care for others.

Box 4.2 Helping the bullies to change

The adult facilitator (who may be a counsellor or a trained member of the pastoral care team) has to demonstrate willingness to listen to all involved in the bullying episode and commitment to working fairly and transparently in order to repair the damage that has been done. The method works best when the school efficiently and fairly develops and implements clear and consistent procedures that clarify the negative consequences that arise from being a bully. The task facing the adult facilitator is to educate the bully to recognize what the consequences of bullying are but also to help the bully to see the perspective of others. To help in the process, the facilitator offers the bully opportunities to improve their problem-solving skills and to teach them strategies for managing their anger. Questions that the facilitator may need to consider include:

- What underlies the bullying behaviour?
- Is the child being bullied in other contexts, such as the community?
- Is there fear underlying this child's anger?
- What disciplinary methods are being used within the child's family?
- Why has the child not developed empathy for more vulnerable peers?

Hazler recommends that the facilitator takes on the very challenging task of helping bullies to recognize that there are personal gains for them if they follow the rules and values of their school. It will be necessary to use sanctions on occasion when all else has failed, but it is equally important to educate the bullies to behave differently on a longer-term basis. Suggested goals include getting the bully:

- to recognize that there are legal, social and personal consequences if they continue to act in a bullying way;
- to identify and seek support from others who care about them;
- to work on their skills of empathy;
- to be more realistic about their own self-perceptions;
- to work on their own anger management skills.

(adapted from Hazler 1996a: 167–80)

There are close parallels with well-documented interventions such as the Support Group Method (Maines and Robinson 1997; Robinson and Maines 2007) which aims to change the behaviour of children who bully others by actively working to increase their empathy for the bullied pupil's feelings and by making constructive use of group processes to offer care and support. The support group method creates a forum consisting of bullies, bystanders and defenders that focuses on the feelings of all participants, including those of the bully. The support group is a reflective, cooperative space within which these young people can develop problem-solving skills and the capacity to help others. The method does not apportion blame. Instead, the process of working cooperatively in the group changes the power structure within the group by discouraging negative behaviours and empowering group members to devise strategies for helping the bullied peer. There are particular outcomes in the process. The first is that the method creates a context in which the bully is given the opportunity to reflect on the victim's feelings by imagining what it must have been like to be a victim. The bully is encouraged to express concern for the victim within the safety of the group and, if possible, to come to some form of realization that the bullying actions were wrong. The second key outcome is that, since the facilitator places the emphasis on the expression of feelings, the process of change is a collective one involving not only the perpetrators but also the bystanders, onlookers and potential defenders. With the help of the facilitator, the group explores the empowering effect of working through the relationship to help another person in distress. The issue is one of shared concern and again the power base is shifted away from the bullies. A consistent finding, as evaluations have shown, is that participants feel better about themselves through the experience of helping others. Young (1998), for example, found that the support group method altered the dynamics of the group so that the benefits for helping the victim of bullying outweighed the costs. Details on how to implement this method can be found in Cowie and Jennifer (2007) and Robinson and Maines (2007).

There are close parallels between the support group method and the method of shared concern, developed by Pikas (2002). The aim of this method is to create a set of ground rules that will enable children who engage in bullying behaviour and those whom they bully to coexist within the same school community. They do not necessarily have to be friends and no punishment is involved but their behaviour has to change. There are three stages to the Pikas method process:

1   individual chats of around 7–10 minutes with each of the pupils involved in the bullying episode;
2   follow-up individual interviews of around three minutes with each pupil
3   a group meeting with all involved of around 30 minutes.

The time that elapses between the initial chats and the follow-up interviews is usually one week. The chats and interviews are scripted. The basis of the method of shared concern is for those involved to agree that there is a problem; that is, that the bullied pupil is unhappy. Individual discussions with each pupil involved in the bullying episode establish that this problem exists. All that is needed is for each young person to agree that the pupil who is being bullied is having a difficult time. Once they have agreed this, the adult facilitator asks each individual pupil to suggest what can be done to make the bullied child's life better. At no point does the adult apportion blame. The emphasis is on finding a solution. Solutions can be quite small ones, for example, 'Leave the bullied child alone'. When each child produces a solution the agreement is made to implement it and to meet again in a week to review progress as a group. In this final group meeting, the facilitator praises all participants for their efforts to reduce the bullying behaviour and generates a wider discussion aimed at promoting values of helpfulness and cooperation. The adult who facilitates the Pikas method is trained to adhere to the exact wording of the script. This person must also remain very calm, non-judgemental and clear about their goals. Specific details on how to run the method can be found in Sharp et al. (1996: 80–88) and in Sullivan (2000: 184–192).

Besag (2006), on the basis of her in-depth observations of girls' friendship groups and her extensive knowledge of therapeutic interventions, confirms the value of this non-punitive approach that takes account not only of the individual needs of the young person but also places the intervention firmly in the context of the peer group. As she points out, it is rarely enough to rely only on punishment if we wish to change the behaviour and attitudes of those who bully. Her solution is to start with low-key strategies and move towards heavier sanctions only when all else has failed. Much of this involves the participation of the victims and their defenders, the supporters of the bully, the bystanders, the families and, at times, the wider community. In the next section we take this one step further by exploring ways in which the whole school can counteract bullying by working consistently to create positive, harmonious relationships.

Working relationally with smaller groups: the example of nurture groups

In the next section we turn to nurture groups (NGs) which have been designed to address the needs of children identified as having social, emotional and behavioural difficulties (SEBDs). Our particular emphasis here is to examine how effective this nurturing approach is in changing aggressive and antisocial behaviour. For over 30 years, NGs have demonstrated that, with the right type of emotional support, children who are having emotional and behavioural difficulties at home and school can be successfully included in mainstream school. More recently, the NG movement has been extended into secondary schools where it has been shown to be very effective in enabling children to make the transition from primary school. NGs create a school-based environment specifically designed for pupils whose behaviour indicates unmet early emotional needs (Bennathan and Boxall 2000). Nurture-based practice (Bennathan and Boxall 1998: 2000) is an increasingly influential approach to the inclusion of pupils with SEBDs and as such is highly relevant to the issue of bullying.

The theory underlying NGs is that many children who exhibit emotional and behavioural difficulties experience emotions and demonstrate behaviours that are developmentally inappropriate. As Cooper (2004: 59) points out, normal infant behaviour is characterized by egocentrism and a disregard for the needs and feelings of others (see Case Study 4.2). In order to progress from this state to the level of social competence that is required in mainstream infant classrooms, it is helpful for such individuals to go through a nurturing process which enables them to meet their own needs through social interaction with others and in a manner that is compatible to the needs of others. Cooper argues that this process is essential for healthy emotional development since without such progress these children will be unable to regulate their behaviour and emotions, form relationships and communicate effectively with others. The NG is part of integrated provision; all staff involved work towards the reintegration of the child back into mainstream education. Its emphasis is on supporting positive emotional and social growth as well as on cooperation and play with others.

Many of the children who are placed in NGs have experienced disruptive or dysfunctional parenting in their early years and their social and language skills tend to be poorly developed. These children behave inappropriately, show limited capacity to regulate their emotions and consequently experience acute difficulties in their relationships with peers. Within the NG they discover an environment that is predictable, secure and structured. Cooper and Whitebread (2007) make the point that there is no intention to pathologize certain parents, but rather to acknowledge the fact that some children reach school age with every sign that their early attachment needs have not been sufficiently met. While NGs have many of the features of family life, such as soft furnishings, kitchen and dining facilities, the NG staff do not aim to usurp or challenge the parent–child relationship but to support it by creating an educational environment in which the children can learn how to engage in group activities in a constructive way and to learn group participation skills. The ultimate aim is to equip the child with the skills appropriate for reintegration back into mainstream education. At the heart of the NG concept is:

- an understanding of the development needs of children;
- a recognition of the interdependence of social, emotional and cognitive factors in the child's development;
- a commitment to the fostering of positive, healthy development.

(Cooper et al. 2001).

Each one of these aspects is consistent with the whole-school approach that we promote throughout this book. NGs usually consist of between six and eight pupils, supported by the staff and by their parents. There are always two members of staff present in a NG. The children typically spend a large part of the week in the NG, gradually joining in with mainstream activities as they become ready. The rationale that underpins NGs is that the children have, for a number of reasons, missed out on the early experiences in the home that promote positive, trusting relationships with peers and adults. Because they cannot relate well to others, such children find it very difficult to settle in school. The NG teachers' role is to understand the gaps in these children's development and to try to meet their particular needs. The children are given work that is adapted to their own level and which also takes account of their emotional needs. There is a great emphasis on language. The relationship with the NG teachers is supportive and these teachers provide a role model that the children observe and, over time, begin to incorporate into their own relationships. Two adults are always present in the NG in order to model positive social interaction and cooperation. The NG routine is structured and predictable. Mainstream curriculum is interspersed with programmed activities, such as free play and physical activity. A crucial feature of the NG is 'breakfast' which usually occurs mid-morning. Pupils and teachers share in a simple cooked meal (usually toast and jam) and interact socially as they eat it.

The social and developmental targets for each child are based on the psychometric assessment of their needs and functioning (derived from the Boxall profile) (Bennathan and Boxall 1998). The work of NGs can apply to children who are bullied as well as to children who bully.

Case study 4.2 Nurturing Shafida: an aggressive girl

Shafida at five years of age was out of control. She was unable to share anything with her classmates and her play mainly consisted of fighting. She bullied the others, especially smaller, younger children, by biting them and scratching them. Understandably, her classmates were wary of her and she had no friends. In class she had frequent tantrums and her teacher had observed that, when thwarted, she would lash out, throwing toys and books around and running out of the class. She could never accept praise when her teacher offered it and was destructive of her own and others' work. The school knew that there were family risk factors that contributed to her behaviour. She frequently saw and experienced violence at home. Her parents drank to excess and on those occasions would engage in physical and verbal violence towards one another. If she got in the way, they would hit her and her two younger brothers as well. Her father often threatened to leave the family. When the children annoyed him, he would lock them in their bedroom. When they were not actually being disciplined, Shafida and her brothers were often out in the street until late. Mealtimes were erratic and it was rare for the family to sit down all together. When they did, usually a row erupted.

In the light of her disruptive behaviour and as a matter of urgency, Shafida was given a place in the school's NG. Initially, she behaved as usual, with temper tantrums and erratic, violent activity. During the course of the first term in the NG, however, she gradually began to respond to the consistent, supportive care that her teachers offered her. Slowly she started to enjoy playing and even began to accept a little praise without destroying her work. She learned to enjoy the experience of eating in the group and began to form positive relationships with the others. Over a period of three terms, her behaviour improved, she demonstrated trust in her teachers and appeared happier. During this time, she showed, for example by her willingness to accept and give praise to others in the group, that she was beginning to trust other people. Her aggressive, bullying behaviour became much less frequent after she began attending the NG. A year later, her class teacher commented on her cooperative, helpful behaviour in class and her genuine interest in her school-work. Importantly, Shafida had made friends in the NG and had learned to play constructively with the others. Her new friendships endured over time so that she now had a supportive peer group at school.

Evaluations of the impact of NGs (e.g. Bennathan and Boxall 1998;. 1998; Cooper and Whitebread 2007) reveal statistically significant improvements in terms of children's social and emotional development, social engagement and behaviours showing secure attachment. Pupils with global ESBD difficulties, antisocial and disruptive behaviours tend to generalize improvements that they gain in the NGs into main-stream education. Reynolds and Kearney (2007), studying 179 pupils with SEBDs aged between 5 and 7 of whom half were in schools with NGs and half in mainstream provision, found that the NG pupils made significant gains in self-esteem, self-image, emotional maturity and attainment in literacy when compared with those without NGs.

Cooper and Whitebread (2007) found that the presence of the NG in a school adds substantially to the work that the school as a whole is carrying out with SEBD pupils. Having the NG on site appears to improve the effectiveness of the school's work with all children with SEBDs, even those who do not actually participate in the NG itself, suggesting that the mainstream staff as a whole develop a more nurturing approach to all of their pupils through their interactions with the NG staff. The experience of NGs has an impact on the other children and their teachers in the school at large. Significantly, the experience of the NG also appears to have a positive influence on the ways in which parents interact with their children.

Cooper and Whitebread (2007) argue that their findings have implications for practice in the wider school environment. They discuss the fact that the social-emotional developments are on the whole maintained by SEBD children after they leave the NG but there is some deterioration in some areas. It may be difficult to maintain the intimacy of the small group interactions in a class of 30. Cooper and Whitebread (2007) argue that there are implications for reviewing current practice with regard to the structure and organization of the classroom if teachers are to facilitate positive relationships among their pupils.

There are important implications for intervention work with young people to change the quality of their peer relationships and to give them contexts in which to explore their own emotions and identities. A large body of research now confirms and gives added insight into what many educators know from their practice; that is, that good quality relationships are as integral to the child's healthy development as academic attainment (Cowie et al. 2004; Cowie and Jennifer 2007; Goleman 1995; Hartup 1996; Marini et al. 2006; Weare 2004).

Working with the relationship enhances positive mental health, helps young people deal with key social and emotional issues in their lives, creates a positive learning environment and increases academic performance (Weare 2004). There is great scope within these initiatives to embark on a variety of more thorough studies on the effectiveness of this kind of involvement and participation on the part of young people and to evaluate successes and failures in their implementation.

Learning points

- The behaviour of children who bully can be changed by placing emphasis on the emotional aspects of their experience.
- There are some evaluated strategies such as the *support group method* and the *method of shared concern* that have been shown to change the behaviour of bullies.
- Educators can address the emotional needs of all children by creating nurturing communities in the classroom where relationships are valued and people are encouraged to care for one another.
- Educators can learn how to remedy children's relationship difficulties by understanding more about their origins in the family and the community.

Resources

Hazler, R. J. (1996) *Breaking the Cycle of Violence: Interventions for Bullying and Victimization*. Washington, DC: Accelerated Development/Taylor & Francis.

Robinson, G. and Maines, B. (2007) *Bullying*. London: Sage Publications.

Sharp, S., Cowie, H. and Smith, P. K. (1996) How to respond to bullying behaviour, in S. Sharp and P. K. Smith (eds.) *Tackling Bullying in Your School* (pp. 79–101) London: Routledge.

Sullivan, K. (2000) *The Anti-bullying Handbook*. pp. 184–192 Oxford: Oxford University Press.

Web sites

Antidote (UK) (www.antidote.org.uk).

Collaborative for Academic, Social, and Emotional Learning (CASEL) (www.casel.org/home/index.php).

Committee for Children (www.cfchildren.org).

Department for Children, Schools and Families (DCSF) (www.dcsf.gov.uk).

Materials including the Social and Emotional Aspects of Learning (SEAL), and Social, Emotional and Behaviour Skills (SEBS) materials (UK) (www.teachernet.gov.uk/teachingandlearning/socialandpastoral/sebs1/seal/themes/).

UK Observatory for the Promotion of Non-Violence (www.ukobservatory.com/).

5 WORKING WITH THE RELATIONSHIP TO HELP THE WHOLE CLASS

Chapter overview

Cooperative learning in groups teaches the values of respect for others, empathy for the feelings of others, sharing of ideas and the promotion of cooperative, democratic values (Sharp and Cowie 1998). In addition, research demonstrates that cooperative group learning can be effectively used to enhance positive relationships and reduce school bullying.

Given our understanding that bullying is a relational issue that permeates many areas of school life, approaches and strategies for addressing the phenomenon must be integrated into the classroom. In this chapter, we focus on the opportunities presented by the use of cooperative group learning in the classroom for developing tolerance of individual difference, improving friendship networks and reducing interpersonal conflict.

Essential aspects of cooperative group learning in the classroom

It is now widely acknowledged that social interaction plays a key role in children's learning. Cooperative group learning as an educational strategy builds on social learning processes and also the pupil's own role in the learning process (Johnson et al. 1994a). The use of the cooperative group as a basis for learning in the classroom has been a methodological strategy used, researched and validated for many years. According to Johnson et al. (1994b), learning in a cooperative group appears in all learning situations where the participants' objectives are tightly linked in such a way that everyone can only achieve their own objectives if others achieve theirs. Groupwork is about a group of individuals 'working together to achieve common objectives' (Johnson et al. 1994b: 14). The group works jointly towards a shared outcome, which can be a product (e.g. a presentation on friendship for an assembly) or something less tangible, such as a summary of a discussion (Steiner 1993). Cooperative group learning compares favourably with individualist and competitive approaches to learning in that it has been shown to promote more complex reasoning processes as well as enhancing the capacity to express opinions and critique those of others (Bossert 1988; Steiner 1993). When schools promote individualist and competitive learning styles, pupils learn that they are alone in the learning process and view others as their rivals. Such competitiveness promotes relationships based on hostility, lack of confidence and aggressiveness.

By contrast, studies of cooperative group learning reveal that when pupils work in groups they discuss and negotiate their ideas and learn to help one another (Bossert 1988; Steiner 1993). Johnson et al. (1994a) noted greater transference of knowledge in cooperative groups in comparison with those students working competitively or individually as well as a greater ability in solving problems and assimilating new concepts. Candela (2005) found that students' knowledge and understanding improved when they played an active part in contributing to the cultural practices of their schools. Group learning, if properly structured, encourages questioning, evaluating and constructive criticism, so leading to a restructuring of knowledge in a friendly, supportive environment (Cowie et al. 1994).

In addition, research demonstrates strong evidence that intensive, regular contact of a cooperative nature among children has the potential not only to improve academic skills (Wegerif and Mercer 1997), but also to enhance friendships and social networks (Slavin 1987; Warden and Christie 1997), and to improve pro-social behaviours (Aronson 1978; Johnson and Johnson 1987; Kagan 1986; Sharan 1985; Slavin 1987). Since cooperative group learning is more engaging to students than individualist approaches, it offers opportunities for pupils to practise their personal and social skills (Dusenbury et al. 1997). Furthermore, there is a great deal of evidence to show that cooperative group learning promotes self-esteem and a sense of positive identity (Candela 2005; Slavin 1995; Steiner 1993). Steiner's (1993: 49) research with a group of 40 teachers and their classes of 8- to 13-year-olds from schools around England which looked at the effectiveness of cooperative group learning over a period of two and a half terms demonstrates that cooperative active working 'in small groups contributes significantly to children developing communication, cooperative and critical thinking skills'.

Recently cooperative group learning has been recognized as a method that can play a key role in addressing the issue of school bullying. A number of large-scale European projects to counteract school bullying have involved the use of cooperative group learning as a central focus, for example, the Sheffield Anti-bullying Project in the UK (Cowie and Sharp 1994); the Seville Anti-violence in Schools (SAVE) Project in Spain (Ortega, et al. 2004; Ortega and Lera 2000) (see Box 5.1); the Donegal project in Ireland (O'Moore and Minton 2001, 2004); and the Rogaland project in Norway (Galloway and Roland 2004; Roland 2000; Roland and Munthe 1997). In these projects, cooperative group learning has been used to promote pupils' interpersonal skills in order to prevent school bullying. From this perspective, school policies to prevent school bullying should include teaching methods that promote cooperative values and that train pupils in effective communication, to include skills of dialogue, debate, critique and negotiation. If children learn to work cooperatively with one another in the same classroom, they are building the foundations for their future roles as citizens.

Box 5.1 Cooperative group learning in an English Language Class in Seville

This cooperative group learning intervention was carried out for six months in three classes of the foreign languages department of a secondary school in a deprived area of Seville, Spain, as part of the Seville Anti-violence in Schools (SAVE) project designed to reduce bullying. The research team, in partnership with the language teachers, developed a cooperative group learning approach using narratives, videos and role plays. Prior to the start of the intervention, researchers administered the Participant Role Questionnaire (Salmivalli et al. 1996), a scale which uses peer nomination to identify bullies, victims and bystanders (see Chapter 1). During the first two weeks, cooperative group learning activities were introduced gradually into the English language curriculum in order to teach the pupils interpersonal skills, to promote positive interdependence, to develop a sense of personal responsibility and to facilitate group processing. After these two introductory weeks, the cooperative group learning approach played a central role in the language teaching, including the use of narrative, video and roleplay as a working methodology to support the learning of English as a foreign language. Examples of narrative tasks included: within a group, to create a common story (in a foreign language) about a boy with interpersonal problems in school, or a story about conflict in the local neighbourhood. In these stories, teachers asked students to follow the grammar content explained in the lesson (e.g. using present simple, present perfect ...). Also, students altered or completed a story or scene to practise putting new information into a familiar context, or familiar information into a new context. The stories and scenes were taken from written sources, photos, pictures, cartoons, videos, verbal sources, and so on. Role play was introduced in different ways. For example, groups created stories and dialogues about interpersonal peer relations, with different protagonists that were then dramatized in the classroom.

At the end of the intervention, students completed the Participant Role Questionnaire again, as well as a test of their opinions on such factors as the class climate before and after the intervention; the academic content of the lessons; the effectiveness of narrative and role-play methods; the development of communication and language skills; and the incidence of bullying during lessons. Sixty-four per cent of the pupils reported that learning in a cooperative group had helped to improve the social climate of the class. They also reported that they enjoyed the lessons and felt that they learned the material more effectively and with greater enjoyment. The cooperative group learning approach was especially valued by those pupils who had been nominated as victims of bullying by their peers and by those who were neither bullies nor victims. Only 13 per cent said that it had directly reduced the incidence of bullying, however, suggesting that cooperative group learning had a more positive impact on improving interpersonal relationships than on actually reducing bullying. The fact that children nominated by their classmates as bullies were less enthusiastic about the method could suggest that they found the method challenging to their power base and that they were resistant to the democratic values inherent in cooperative group learning.

(adapted from Ortega et al. 2003)

However, Cowie and colleagues (Cowie et al. 1994; Cowie and Berdondini 2001) have observed that a minority of pupils are not receptive to cooperative group learning. For example, boys rejected by their peers and those who bully others are particularly uncooperative; these children dislike cooperative group learning on the grounds that they prefer to work with their friends. If they are boys, they are likely to express displeasure at being placed in multi-ethnic groups and do not like working with girls. Smith et al. (1994) concluded that such pupils view cooperative group learning as a threat to their power base. The values of cooperative group learning, that is, sharing with peers, supporting others, learning from one another, and reflecting on interactions within the group, are not attractive to these children and their non-cooperative attitude regularly causes difficulties within their groups. In addition, Cowie and Berdondini (2001) found that victims had difficulties expressing themselves within the group, remaining silent or denying their genuine feelings. Nevertheless, this study showed that cooperative group learning is a useful strategy for enhancing peer relationships among bullies, victims and bystanders.

The aim of the study was to explore the impact of cooperative groupwork on children's attitudes towards other group members and to analyse their ability to express their own emotions in the context of working cooperatively in groups (Cowie and Berdondini 2001). A sample of 117 pupils, aged 8 to 11 from Florence, participated in the study. Peer nominations for bully, victim and bystander were nominated for each participant according to the methodology described by Bowers et al. (1994). Teachers were trained in the following cooperative groupwork activities: role play, literature as a stimulus, group discussions and debriefing. The role-play activity was based on scenarios regarding the phenomenon of bullying from different perspectives, including those of the bully, the victim and the bystander. Scenarios also included parents' reactions to different episodes of bullying. Literature as a stimulus involved children reading stories such as 'The Daydreamer' (McEwan 1994) or 'The Diddakoi' (Godden 1991). To stimulate group discussions about the issue of bullying, relevant sections of the books were used to question and analyse personal narratives and solutions. Sometimes the situations depicted were used as a basis for role-playing. Group discussions took the form of focus groups, based on a specific topic, identified by all participants as an interpersonal issue of importance to them.

At the end of every cooperative groupwork session a debriefing was conducted, which consisted of a series of open questions to explore group members' emotions and the quality of the group process as experienced by the participants. The main ground rule was that the class teacher had to involve all the participants and offer all the children the opportunity to speak. Teachers were involved in the composition of the working groups, comprising five or six children, and including at least one bully and one victim in each. Group activities were carried out for approximately two hours, once a week, for a period of eight months. The final 20 minutes of each session was dedicated to the debriefing process. Each working group was video-taped in the classroom for about five minutes, once at the beginning of the study (Time 1) and once at the end (Time 2). Either the same day, or the day after the video-recording session, each group was interviewed by the researcher for 20 minutes using the method of Interpersonal Process Recall (IPR) (see Box 5.2).

Box 5.2. Interpersonal Process Recall

IPR involves the presence of two roles, the *inquirer* (or researcher) and the *recaller*. The inquirer facilitates recall of the event through a series of open questions (see below). A key point of IPR is that the recallers have the responsibility for stopping and starting the video at points which are important to them by physically pressing the pause button at the point they choose. The questioning stance of the inquirer (after the child stops the video) helps recallers to explore in more detail aspects of the group experience that might otherwise not be expressed in more common debriefing sessions. Inquirer prompt questions include:

1   How were you feeling then?
2   Did you have any feeling towards the other person?
3   How do you think the other person saw you at that point?
4   What do you wish you had said to him/her?
5   What do you think he/she would have said or done if you had said that?
6   What would have been the risk in saying what you wanted to say?
7   If you had the chance now, how might you tell him/her what you are thinking and feeling?
8   Were there any other thoughts going through your mind?
9   How did you want the other person to see you?
10 Were those feelings located physically in some part of your body?
11 If that feeling had a voice, what would it say?
12 What did you want him/her to tell you?
13 What do you think he/she wanted from you?
14 Did he/she remind you of anyone in your life?

At the end of the intervention period, some children spoke more, responded more specifically to the interactions recorded on the video-tapes, and discussed issues arising from the interactions at greater length. This was particularly pertinent for the victims, whose expressions of feelings of enjoyment were more in line with other children, both bullies and bystanders, at Time 2 than they had been at Time 1. Similarly, by Time 2, victims expressed less fear than other children did and were more similar to other children with regard to this emotion. However, at each of the two time points, victims tended to deny their feelings or to report emotions that were clearly inappropriate for the unpleasant treatment that they had experienced. In addition, victims appeared to find it difficult to share genuine feelings within the group. While at Time 2, bullies and victims demonstrated increased awareness of others' feelings compared with Time 1, the authors observe that this awareness does not necessarily result in increased empathy. Interview data suggested that bullies and some bystanders appeared unconcerned about the feelings of group members even though they were aware of them.

In addition, the authors calculated the frequency of times that each child fell into the category of 'interrupting others' or 'being interrupted'. At Time 1, there was a significant result with bullies interrupting others more than bystanders and victims did – victims never interrupted. At Time 2, there was a significant result with bullies still interrupting others more than bystanders and victims did. At Time 1, victims were interrupted significantly more than bullies and bystanders were, while at Time 2 there were no significant differences among the three participant roles.

While this study demonstrates that cooperative groupworking had an impact on the expression of emotions, it also highlighted the tendency of victims to deny their feelings in comparison with bullies and bystanders. However, it does draw attention to some of the issues for consideration for teachers working with challenging groups in terms of individuals who feel unable to express authentic emotions in a cooperative groupwork context.

This study highlights the use of literature as a stimulus to generate discussions about issues related to bullying. Reading lists of children and young people's literature that address the topic of bullying are available to download from the Anti-Bullying Alliance (see Resources section at the end of this chapter). Film and DVD, for example *Bully Dance* (Perlman 2000) or *Silent Witnesses* (O'Moore 2006) can also be used as a basis for understanding and exploring the phenomenon. For a more detailed discussion of the role of narrative approaches in addressing school bullying, see Chapter 7.

Cowie and Berdondini (2001) suggest that an understanding of bullying as a social phenomenon, that is the recognition of the participant roles that children take in the bullying process (see Chapter 1), can offer insights into the processes that emerge when children are asked by their teachers to work cooperatively in groups. Since peers within school classes form spontaneous peer networks, with children and young people with similar behavioural tendencies with respect to bullying tending to associate with each other, Salmivalli (1999) suggests that restructuring of social networks for cooperative group learning purposes may prove useful in preventing and diminishing bullying. In this way, bullies receive different feedback than they would otherwise receive in their own aggressive friendship group. A good example of an intervention that enables pupils to work confidently with children outside their usual social networks is R time (**R**elationships **t**o **im**prove **e**ducation; see Case Study 5.1).

Case Study 5.1 R time (Relationships to improve education)

R time provides a structured programme for schools that aims to develop positive relationships among children. It achieves this by creating a supportive environment that enhances good manners, attainment and citizenship through a process called 'random pairing' in conjunction with interesting, non-threatening and easily achievable activities for children from Nursery to Year 7. R time consists of 30 weekly sessions each lasting 10–15 minutes. Each session comprises five component parts, that is, random pairing, introductions, an activity, a plenary session and a conclusion.

Random pairing: Each session the children work with a different partner enabling them to work with all members of their group.

Introductions: Once the children are in their random pairs they greet one another with a positive statement, for example, 'Hello, my name's Simon. I'm glad that you're my partner today Faiza'.

The activity: There are 30 short, easily achievable, age-appropriate activities for each year group for the children to do with their partner.

The plenary: The children feed back their experience to the whole group and the teacher helps them to reflect on their learning.

Conclusion: At the end of the session, each child thanks their partner and says something positive with which to complete the activity.

While R time was not specifically designed as an anti-bullying programme, it teaches skills that contribute to the reduction of bullying, including acceptance, respect, valuing diversity, creating ways to support one another, enabling children to succeed in one-to-one friendships and to handle peer conflict. A survey of 1140 pupils from eight primary schools, before R time was introduced and then again at three and six months, post-intervention, by the Leicestershire anti-bullying team suggests that R time has had a positive impact on social inclusion, contentment in school, relationships and promoting a positive ethos (Osborn 2007). Indeed, the evaluation showed that pupils perceived that their school was against bullying, and were increasingly willing to talk about it. Furthermore, results of Leicestershire's annual Pupil Attitude Survey suggest a significant decline among primary pupils reporting that they have been bullied, since the introduction of R time.

Numerous teachers, as well as children, find group work problematic (Blatchford et al. 2006). Cowie et al. (1994) document the difficulties experienced by many teachers when they try to create a cooperative learning environment in certain groups, particularly where group members engage in bullying behaviours or sabotage activities designed to promote a climate of co-operation. Nevertheless, recent research suggests that successful implementation of groupwork into everyday school class-rooms improves pupil interactions, providing teachers take the time to train pupils in the skills of group working (Blatchford et al. 2006). Box 5.4 summarizes this research.

Box 5.3 The effect of a new approach to group work

The SPRinG (social pedagogic research into grouping) programme was designed to create connectedness among group members in terms of sustaining a positive and inclusive group ethos and with regard to increasing the degree of participation of all group members. It had three key principles. First, the SPRinG programme adopted a relational approach to groupwork, which assumed that in order to engage in collaborative work, children need effective social and communication skills, such as listening, explaining and sharing ideas, they need to be helped to trust and respect each other, and they need skills in how to plan, organize and evaluate their work. Second, it assumed that teachers could adapt grouping practices for different learning objectives, in order to support children in taking responsibility for their own learning. Third, the approach rested on the view that to be successful, groupwork must be integrated into overall classroom organization and management, by adapting classroom seating arrangements, and characteristics of groups, such as size, composition and stability over time, to make the groups work more constructively. Full details of the approach, including strategies for teachers and activities for children, can be found in the handbook for teachers and practitioners (Baines et al. 2008).

The main research question was whether the SPRinG groupwork programme would lead to classroom interaction patterns supportive of learning. Effects of the groupwork programme were addressed in comparison with a control group and in terms of changes over the whole school year. The experimental sample, receiving the SPRinG programme, consisted of 21 classes and 135 pupils, and the control sample, receiving a parallel project, consisted of 32 classes and 179 pupils. Data were collected using on-the-spot systematic classroom observations and video-taped observations.

On-the-spot and video-based systematic observations showed more active, sustained engagement in group activities; more connectedness within the group; and, more higher-order inferential forms of reasoning with SPRinG groups than in control group comparisons. Despite teachers' concerns that introducing groupwork might be detrimental to pupil conduct and bring about more off-task behaviour, the researchers actually found that behaviour improved.

(adapted from Blatchford et al. 2006)

As we mentioned earlier, challenging behaviour sometimes arises as a result of the social dynamics within the group. According to Tuckman (1965), group relationships progress through a developmental process, which includes five stages: forming;

storming; norming; performing; and dorming (see Table 5.1). A failure at any point in the developmental process will result in a reduction in the group's effectiveness and in the quality of the relationships among members of the group (Sharp and Cowie 1998). Ineffective groups tend not to move beyond the first two stages.

Table 5.1. Developing effective groups (Sharp and Cowie, 1998)

Forming (awareness)	Individuals coming together; establishing a common set of ground rules
Storming (conflict)	Competing for status and power; expressions of criticism, manipulation, direct or subtle aggression; alliances formed and reformed; possible scapegoating of a member of the group
Norming (co-operation)	Involvement with the task; support for one another; effective communication; offering and receiving constructive feedback
Performing (productivity)	Achievement of goals; pride in collaboration; problem-solving; completion of the task
Dorming (separation)	Celebration or positive affirmation of a task well done; satisfaction in the group process; evaluation of accomplishments; review of relationships within the group; closure.

The central point of cooperative group learning is that it provides the opportunity for individuals to express and explore a range of ideas and experiences in the company of others. Groups that are working well will display the following characteristics:

- Group members are putting forward more than one point of view in relation to the task they face.
- Group members are encouraged to explore these different points of view.
- The interaction process facilitates learning and knowledge about the topic under consideration.
- The interaction process also facilitates tolerance of different points of view and openness to new ideas.

In effective cooperative group learning, members are given the opportunity to draw up, and agree to abide by, a set of social ground rules whose values reflect equality, respect for others, freedom to explore ideas and openness to new perspectives. Cooperative group learning takes a variety of forms, which we outline below.

Buzz groups

These provide an opportunity for greater participation by pupils in a large class event. The teacher may invite pupils to turn to their immediate neighbours and, in threes or fours, to spend a few minutes exchanging views about, for example, things they do not understand about a topic, things they disagree with, things that have not been mentioned, and so on. Buzz groups enable participants to express difficulties that they would have been reluctant to reveal to the whole class without the initial push of being obliged to say something to an immediate neighbour.

Circle time

Here pupils come together in a safe supportive environment where they can learn about one another, build a team, develop communications skills, share issues of shared concern (such as friendships, being lonely, being bullied) and celebrate achievements. Circle time provides a space in which to develop active citizenship skills.

Discussion groups

Here a larger group of pupils and their teacher, or a smaller group of pupils without their teacher's constant presence, work to share understanding and ideas. The focus might be, for example, a poem written from the perspective of a young person who has been bullied or a newspaper report on an extreme case of violence in school. Discussions may lead to enhanced understanding on the part of each individual or they may require negotiation in order to arrive at a group consensus.

Problem-solving circles

These usually depend on the discussion of a range of possibilities as a medium for constructive interaction. Often the same task is set simultaneously to a number of small groups of three or four pupils, for example, designing a logo for the school anti-bullying policy or planning strategies to create a friendlier environment in the school. Box 5.5 presents the quality circle method, a participative approach to problem-solving originating in industry, which can be used with pupils to actively engage them in school decision-making (Cowie and Sharp 1994).

Box 5.4 Quality Circles

Cowie and Sharp (1994) have used quality circles (QC) with children and young people, a technique that offers a participative problem-solving approach for addressing the issue of school bullying. Originating in industry, the aim of the QC, which consists of a group of between five and twelve young people who meet together on a regular basis, usually weekly, is to devise practical solutions with which to address school bullying. The process involves five steps: (1)

identifying the issue; (2) analysing the issue; (3) developing solutions; (4) presenting solutions to the working group and; (5) reviewing the solutions.

Step 1 Identifying the issue

Using brainstorming, the QC lists all the issues related to bullying that they wish to address. When all issues have been identified, the group prioritizes one issue on which to focus first by way of a vote.

Step 2 Analysing the issue

At this stage of the process, group members consider the possible causes of their chosen bullying issue, deciding which causes are the most important, using the Why? Why? technique (see Figure 5.1). The group asks themselves the question

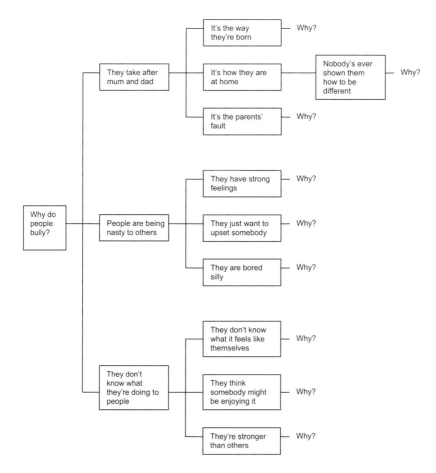

Figure 5.1 Why? Why? diagram: a 10-year-old's responses
Source: Cowie and Sharp (1992).

'Why?', at which point several causes may be identified. These are annotated on the first branch of the Why? Why? diagram. The group then ask 'Why?' of each first-level reason and continue to do so until an original causal factor has been identified.

Having considered the possible causes, the group then explores the issue, trying to find out as much factual information as possible about it, by collecting data about the nature and extent of the problem. Useful activities at this stage of the process include conducting a survey (e.g. regarding types of bullying behaviours experienced by pupils), interviewing a sample of young people about their experiences of being bullied, carrying out observations at a particular location (e.g. in the dining hall) at a specific time (e.g. between 12.00 and 1.00 p.m. on a Friday). Once the information has been collected, the QCs then need to analyse the data and ask themselves 'What does this information tell us about the problem?'

Step 3 Developing solutions

Once a cause has been identified and analysed the QC members begin to explore alternative solutions using the How? How? technique. The group asks themselves the question 'How?' to every solution that is suggested until it culminates in some practical action that can be taken. These are annotated on the first branch of the How? How? diagram (see Figure 5.2). The group then asks 'How?' of each first-level solution and continues to do so until the list of alternative solutions has been narrowed down. After this process has been carried out a number of times, the QC lists the advantages and disadvantages, chances of success and relative costs of each alternative solution in order to facilitate a more objective selection process. The How? How? diagram enables QC members to explore solutions creatively and consider numerous alternatives instead of jumping to an immediate solution. At the same time, the structure of the How? How? diagram highlights the steps which QC members have to take in order to implement their solution. This enables them to form a specific action plan. Once a solution has been agreed upon, it is often useful to check that it works in practice by running a small pilot.

Step 4 Presenting a solution

The QC members prepare a presentation of their solution for the working group. Time needs to be allowed for preparation of the presentation, including paying attention to the content of the talk and ensuring that the message is conveyed clearly and succinctly. Groups will need to rehearse their presentations, and consider what visual aids they may need to support them. Finally, they need to prepare to handle questions from the working group.

Step 5 Reviewing the solution

If the working group decides to implement the proposed solution, they must evaluate how effective it has been and feed this back to the QC. If the solution

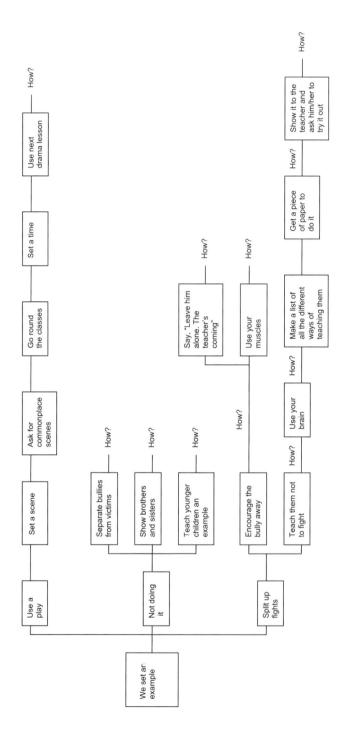

Figure 5.2 How? How? diagram: a 10-year-old's response to the issue of bullying suggested by the quality circle
Source: Cowie and Sharp (1992)

is not implemented, there must be discussion between the working group and the QC about the reasons for this decision. The members of the QC can then review and modify their solutions or can move on to another issue of concern.

Full guidance on how to carry out QCs over one term can be found in Cowie and Sharp (1994).

(adapted from Cowie and Sharp 1994)

Production activities

Here pupils may be working in teams to produce a magazine or film, with one team responsible for the research, another for the technical support, one for the sequencing, and so on. This is sometimes called 'the jigsaw method' and, as in problem-solving, there are regular reviews of the progress of different parts of the jigsaw and a constructively critical review of the finished product. Box 5.6 highlights an example of the use of such activities to promote social and emotional skills in science lessons, which resulted in the reduction of peer conflict.

Box 5.5 How pupils can be helped to develop socially and emotionally in science lessons

Morrison and Matthews (2006) argue that the development of emotional literacy can be integrated into academic subject lessons, such as science, through the use of collaborative groupwork. They suggest that, as with most subjects, there are many opportunities for pupils to work collaboratively in science lessons, for example, while completing a worksheet or a practical activity. To this end, they carried out a study with three Year 7 (aged 11 to 12) classes in two coeducational schools. The authors provided pupils with a framework for use in groupwork, which enabled them to monitor themselves and their interactions, and feed back the results to the group for discussion.

  Within each class, the teacher organized the pupils into groups comprising two boys and two girls. Initially, another pupil observed each group. The composition of the groups was changed regularly in order that every pupil in a class had the opportunity to work with and get to know every other pupil. As each group was working, the pupil-observer monitored how each group member contributed to the task, and how each group member talked, interrupted, listened and/or was supportive, on a pre-prepared form. At the end of the task, the group members themselves estimated these aspects of their contributions. Following completion of the task, a discussion took place whereby each member of the group contributed their individual viewpoint, which was compared with each other's experience and with the observer's notes. This formed the basis for the pupil-observer to lead a discussion on how the group worked together and how the group members felt. As the pupils became familiar with the process, the researchers dispensed with the pupil-observer. Instead, each group member completed an opinion sheet, and then discussed their completed sheets among the group. The discussion that followed formed a key part of the process as group members could begin to understand how others had perceived their interactions in the group differently. Sometimes the focus of the group discussions was on reflexive questions posed by the teacher, such as, 'When I was working with my group I felt …', 'How well did you get on with the rest of your group?' and 'Were there any differences with sex or race?'.

Interviews with the science teachers some time after the research period revealed a number of benefits:

- pupils getting to know those peers that they would not normally interact with;
- pupils learning to support each other in their learning, and having the confidence to engage with and make known their emotions without fear of being laughed at or made fun of by others;
- improved communication and social interactions among pupils (e.g. pupils learning the skills to listen to get their point of view of across, rather than shouting at each other).

Outside of the classroom context, pupils were observed to develop their own systems to support one another, which was picked up by new pupils moving into the research groups after the study had ended.

This research suggests that not only can pupils collaborate in the classroom on their academic tasks but at the same time they can also engage with the social and emotional aspects of working together, as a means of promoting an understanding of diversity and learning skills to deal with a range of social situations, including interpersonal conflict.

(adapted from Morrison and Matthews 2006).

Simulations

Here participants take on the situation of a supposed real life group. They might, for instance, become a staff team carrying out a needs analysis on the problem of bullying in the playground at break time. Within simulations, participants are free to contribute from their own strengths or perspectives, although sometimes they may be assigned specific roles and the simulation then merges into our next category – role play.

Role play

Here each pupil is given a character or perspective within the framework of an event or situation. The role becomes like a mask and the characters interact according to their interpretation of the role. Roles are usually assigned to reflect different perspectives on an issue or event. For example, pupils might enact an argument at a bus stop and take on such roles as aggressor, reinforcer of the aggressor, victim, bystanders and defenders.

A review of the literature suggests a number of key considerations for successful cooperative group learning, for example, Johnson et al. (1994a) refer to the following three points:

1 Positive interdependence

To achieve positive interdependence, it is important for group members to feel that their efforts are necessary for the group's success, and therefore that each member is responsible for the common effort. Teachers can facilitate such positive interdependence in a variety of ways by: encouraging open communication among all members of the group; by distributing distinctive tasks to each group member; and identifying clear roles within the group, such as *scribe, chairperson, observer and mediator*. Commonly a diversity of opinions appears in groups over how things must be done. Such conflicts are constructive and, if properly managed, lead to effective group bonding and facilitate the development of social skills. The cooperative group learning approach offers teachers the opportunity to train children to solve conflicts when they inevitably arise within the group.

2 Interpersonal skills

In order to be sure that the group is working well, it is essential that there is a focus on such interpersonal skills and processes as *effective communication, dialogue, listening, respect for others* and *tolerance of difference*. A key long-term outcome of cooperative group learning in the context of this book is to encourage children to work collaboratively with one another to enhance pro-social peer relationships and reduce peer conflict.

3 Group evaluation

An important component of cooperative group learning is the opportunity for reflective evaluation of the process that the group has experienced as they completed the task. Most types of cooperative group learning include some form of debriefing or group processing activity. While structured evaluation and reflection enables children to focus their debriefing on the problem, project or discussion they were working on, it also enables them to concentrate their attention on the group process itself (Steiner 1993). Their feelings about the experience of cooperative group learning, and their analysis of its effectiveness, will facilitate self-awareness of how they and others learn in such a context, which will enhance their group working skills and effectiveness (Steiner 1993). Furthermore, Sharp and Cowie (1998) highlight the importance of 'closure' in which celebration or affirmation of the group's achievements takes place. They suggest that it is important for the group to acknowledge that their work together is done in order that they can move on to a new task, and possibly a new group. In addition, it is important to keep the following issues in mind.

Group membership

It is important to take into consideration the individual characteristics of group members, their cognitive and social skills, their participant roles in bullying (bullies and victims should not be in the same group), their interests and attitudes, as well as their gender, social and cultural background, ethnicity, sexual orientation and ability. Students should feel comfortable in their groups and have the opportunity to change roles and responsibilities. Such individual characteristics can help children to learn to tolerate difference and appreciate diversity (Steiner 1993).

Task

The nature of the task is important for cooperative group learning. We recommend easy tasks when groups are inexpert. Once groups have experience in cooperative group learning, students can be given more complex tasks.

The duration of the group

This variable depends on the type of cooperative group selected. In this sense, for curricular subjects, some authors underline the importance of stable groups for developing basic intra-group dynamics, which facilitate the work. In other cases, as in role play, the group is formed to represent a story or a situation.

Learning points

- Cooperative learning in the classroom has the potential not only to improve academic skills, but it also enhances friendships and can play a critical role in reducing bullying.
- The values of cooperative group learning can prove challenging for some groups of pupils.
- Many teachers, as well as children and young people, find facilitating cooperative group learning problematic.
- Research suggests that providing teachers take the time to train pupils in the skills of groupworking, successful implementation is possible.
- Cooperative group learning takes a number of forms, including buzz groups, circle time, discussion groups, problem-solving circles, production activities, simulations and role play.

- Successful cooperative group learning requires consideration of a number of issues, including positive interdependence, interpersonal skills, group evaluation, group membership, the nature of the task and the duration of the group.

Resources

Bliss, T. and Tetley, J. (2006) *Circle Time*. Bristol: Lucky Duck Publishing.

Hopkins, B. (2004) *Just Schools*: A Whole School Approach to Restorative Justice. London: Jessica Kingsley.

O'Moore, M. (2006) *Silent Witnesses*. Ireland: Trinity College Dublin Anti-Bullying Research and Resource Centre (www.abc.tcd.ie).

Perlman, J. (2000) *Bully Dance* (*La Danse des Brutes*). Canada: National Film Board of Canada (www.bullfrogfilms.com/catalog/bully.html).

Sharan, S. (1999) *Handbook of Cooperative Learning Methods*. Westport: Praeger.

The SPRinG Group Work Project (www.SPRinG-Project.org.uk).

Web sites

Anti-Bullying Alliance Reading Lists (www.anti-bullyingalliance.org.uk/downloads/pdf/draftbullyingbooksforchildrenandyoungpeople210601.pdf).

R time (**R**elationships **t**o **im**prove **e**ducation) (www.rtime.info).

6 PEERS HELPING PEERS

Chapter overview

Peer support programmes are becoming internationally popular in schools as anti-bullying interventions that enhance pupil safety and empower young people to take action against injustices in their school community (Cowie et al. 2004). Peer support systems can be adjusted to suit children and young people of all ages. For example, circle time (for younger pupils) and active listening services (for older pupils) can provide arenas in which young people can offer support to one another and address issues of shared concern, such as conflicts and bullying.

In this chapter, we outline the essential aspects of peer support, provide up-to-date research findings on how effective peer support is as an anti-bullying intervention and discuss main implications for practice. We provide case studies of peer support in action, give examples of young people's perspectives on peer support, and end with key learning points.

The essential aspects of peer support

Essentially peer support systems provide a flexible framework within which children and young people are trained to offer emotional and social support to fellow pupils in distress. Peer support takes a number of forms (Figure 6.1) including:

- methods that focus on the emotional and social support of bullied pupils;
- methods that facilitate the resolution of conflicts between pupils in dispute before they escalate into bullying and other forms of oppression;
- methods that involve social action on the part of young people to create systems that challenge bullying in their school community.

Systems of peer support vary quite widely across schools and according to the age groups of the peer supporters themselves. Primary school schemes generally adopt a buddying/befriending approach or a conflict resolution approach; secondary school schemes build on the methods adapted for younger age groups, for example, by running a lunchtime club, being available in a 'drop in' room, facilitating workshops in tutor groups, or mentoring younger pupils in need and make use of a more sophisticated range of active listening and problem-solving skills (Cowie and Wallace

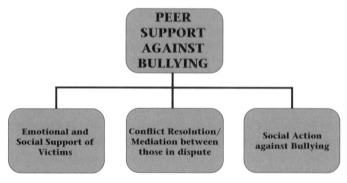

Figure 6.1 Forms of peer support

2000; Smith and Watson 2004). The schemes evolve over time and change in line with local needs and pupil perceptions of the effectiveness and acceptability of this type of intervention. With advances in technology, methods also take account of distance-learning types of support, including use of the Internet and email support (Cartwright 2005; Cowie and Hutson 2005; Hutson and Cowie 2007).

Peer support is not about giving advice. Rather it involves training pupils to listen to their peers, responding genuinely and authentically to the needs and feelings of those seeking help and liaising with appropriate adults when necessary. This is where good communication skills, emotional literacy and a problem-solving stance are essential. There should also be some form of supervision and debriefing by adults (usually the coordinator of the peer support system) to allow time for peer supporters to process what they do and collectively to address the issues that they encounter. There are a number of strands in the development of peer support. These we have broadly categorized as: *counselling-based approaches*; *befriending/buddying*; *conflict resolution/mediation*; *cyber peer support*; and *social action*. To some extent there is an overlap among the strands but they offer a useful typology for training and evaluation. We describe each strand in turn.

Counselling-based approaches

The earliest types of peer support were grounded in a counselling model. Pupil helpers were trained (usually by a qualified counsellor or psychologist) to use active listening skills to support peers in distress, often the victims of bullying; and (less frequently) to challenge pupils who bully. Regular supervision (whether by a qualified counsellor or by the teacher who managed the peer support scheme) was an essential feature. Peer counsellors were likely to see users of the service in a specially designated room just as counsellors see their clients in a private consultation.

Although the method of peer counselling had been quite widely used in Canada and Australia since the 1980s, it was unknown in the UK until it was pioneered in 1990 by Netta Cartwright, the school counsellor at a Midlands secondary school, who trained students in basic listening and co-counselling skills as a critical part of the school's anti-bullying policy (Cartwright 1996; Glover et al. 2000).

The theory behind Cartwright's training was re-evaluation counselling, a person-centred approach proposing that everyone has a natural ability to recover from the effects of the hurts that they have experienced through a process of healing that takes place when we discharge our distress. The approach involves re-evaluation of self through reflection and exercises in self-awareness. The intensive training aims to give participants fresh insights into self and others, increased awareness of how oppressive systems operate to the detriment of the school community, and the opportunity to act on this heightened awareness by offering emotional support to fellow pupils in need. Over the years, as Cartwright trained cohorts of students, she demonstrated that young people can be trained to use a counselling approach very effectively to help bullied peers. Evaluation indicates that students report feeling safer, whether or not they actually used the service, and the whole culture and climate of the school becomes more positive (Cartwright 2005).

Influenced by Cartwright's work, the team at the Department for Education and Skills (DES) funded an anti-bullying project (Smith and Sharp 1994) which implemented peer counselling methods in two Sheffield secondary schools as one of the interventions to be evaluated as a method to counteract bullying. A counselling approach was adapted for use with young people and cohorts of students were trained to use active listening skills, to facilitate supportive relationships and to reflect on the helping process (Sharp et al. 1994). The method spread from Sheffield to Acland Burghley School, where students were trained to offer peer counselling and mediation as part of their anti-bullying campaign (Paterson et al. 1996). The unique contribution at Acland Burghley School was to involve both bullies and victims in encounters where each was invited to reflect on their behaviour and where the peer supporters played a facilitative role in resolving the conflict between the two parties. The filming of this pilot work by Windfall Films and the subsequent showing on UK television in April 1994 led to considerable national and international interest in peer support schemes, their principles and practices.

Befriending/buddying

Over time, peer counselling services evolved into befriending/buddying schemes that still involve active listening skills and a person-centred approach during training, but which, in their implementation, adopted a much more informal approach. Usually befrienders are same-age peers or older pupils, who are selected by teachers on the basis of their friendly personal qualities. In some systems existing befrienders or classmates are also involved in the democratic selection and interviewing of volunteers. In addition, these schemes often incorporate other activities for peer supporters such as leading games activities, supporting learning at a homework club, or one-to-one work with very young pupils who need support in learning how to be friends with others. Secondary school peer support schemes usually involve *peer mentors*, who may offer support to pupils with difficulties in a 'drop in' room, help primary school pupils make the transition to secondary school, do groupwork with a tutor group, offer one-to-one contact with a pupil in need over a period of time, or run a lunchtime club for younger pupils (Andrés 2007; Cowie and Wallace 2000; Smith and Watson 2004).

A pioneering example came from the work of Athy Demetriates, founder of *Children of the Storm*, a charity designed to help young refugees (Demetriades 1996). Her approach was more characterized by befriending than by counselling and contained a strong educational component. The peer partners played a central role in the planning and organization of the support work and had an equal role alongside the adult trustees of the *Children of the Storm* project. This demonstrated the potential of young people for playing an active role in responsible decision-making on important issues in their everyday lives. Many of the peer partners were young people who had, as refugees, been themselves greatly helped by their peers in the initial difficult months of their stay in the UK. The peer partners' task was to assist refugee peers with practice in English language, to help them with homework and to facilitate their integration into the school community. As the project evolved, it became clear to both pupils and teachers involved that there was a need for the peer partners to be trained in listening skills so that they could help war-traumatized peers to deal with difficult feelings and to affirm their attempts to grow and survive despite the unbearable memories that they all carried.

Since then there have been a number of very influential peer support initiatives, particularly funded and produced by charities including ChildLine in Partnership with Schools (CHIPS), the National Children's Bureau (NCB), the Mental Health Foundation (MHF) and the National Society for the Prevention of Cruelty to Children (NSPCC). Excellent training of peer supporters also takes place through local consultants and trainers, such as ABC Training and Support (www.abcservices.org.uk). The following scenario, as shown in Box 6.1, illustrates a typical ABC training session involving peer supporters know as PALS from Northgate High School, Ipswich.

BOX 6.1   Out and about: using role play to train peer supporters to befriend bullied pupils

The role-play incident

A group of pupils have snatched Tom's bag and emptied the contents onto the ground. They have grabbed his keys and are throwing them from one to the other while he frantically tries to retrieve them. The more upset he gets, the more hilarious the group becomes. Tom is smaller and younger than the others so it is easy to throw the keys over his head.

Freeze

At this point Jill, the trainer, asks the audience of peer supporters to suggest some options for action on the part of a peer supporter who happens to be passing by. The scenario is re-enacted with each of the options and the audience and the role players are invited to discuss their feelings and perceptions.

Option 1: Confront the bullies

Sarah, a peer supporter, confronts the group publicly. She joins in and tries to retrieve the keys. The group responds by throwing the keys over her head so she, in turn, becomes a target.

The audience and the role players discuss the outcome. Tom feels even more humiliated than he did before. Sarah feels that she has failed in her role and so feels disempowered. The audience comments that the incident has become even more public since a larger crowd would gravitate towards the group. Furthermore, Tom may well be targeted by the group in the future. As he reflects, the intervention may have made things worse for him.

Option 2: Offer immediate help to the pupil who is being bullied

This time, Julie, a peer supporter who is taller and older than the group members, goes straight into the group, easily retrieves the keys and then publicly tries to comfort Tom. As before, a group of bystanders gather round to watch. Julie kneels down on the ground and starts to gather all Tom's possessions back into his bag. The group members and bystanders jeer as she does this.

The audience and role players discuss this outcome. The advantage to Tom is that he now has his keys and his possessions have been returned to his bag. However, as he reports, Julie's public intervention makes him look weak and ineffective. The group's fun has been disrupted so they may pick on Tom again. The intention was good but the outcome may not have been successful.

Option 3: Offer help in private to the bullied pupil

This time, Anne joins the group and says loudly and firmly 'Game over!' and leads Tom away to a quiet place where they may talk about what has happened. Since the target is no longer there, the group drops the keys and disperses leaving Tom's possessions on the ground. Anne quietly checks that he is OK, shows empathy for what has just happened and finds out from Tom what it is that he would find most helpful now. She offers to keep an eye on him during breaks and suggests a number of clubs and activities that Tom might like to join so that he can make some new friends. At a later stage, Anne returns with Tom and helps him repack his bag. The audience and role players discuss and conclude that this is the best of the three options for all involved.

Studies of befriending indicate a number of advantages, not least the recruitment of bystanders to tackle the problem of bullying. Over the years, the shift from a counselling-based approach to a more informal befriending approach has often been initiated by peer supporters themselves who report that both they and the users of the schemes have difficulties with a formal counselling approach and prefer the anonymity of an informal befriending scheme. For vulnerable pupils, the experience of being befriended can be a critical part of the process of feeling more positive about themselves. Through the process of experiencing the empathic response of a peer supporter to their distress, these pupils are given an opportunity to express their feelings about upsetting aspects of their lives. Befrienders report that they too benefit from the helping process, that they feel more confident in themselves, and that they learn to value other people more. Teachers frequently report that the school environment becomes safer and more caring following the introduction of a befriend-ing scheme, and that peer relationships in general improve (Andrés 2007; Cowie et al. 2002; Menesini, Codecasa et al. 2003).

Cyber peer support

With advances in technology, peer support methods now take account of distance-learning types of support, including use of the Internet and email support (Cartwright 2005; Cowie and Hutson 2005; Hutson and Cowie, 2007). Peer supporters in the UK have begun to develop systems that ensure confidentiality by working anonymously through their school's intranet (Cartwright 2005; Cowie and Hutson, 2005; Hutson and Cowie 2007). Typically, small groups of peer supporters work together on a rota system to respond to emails during certain time slots so that everyone who uses the system will receive a reasonably quick response. Peer supporters also have a useful role to play in evaluating existing web-based resources to help bullied children and are often more pragmatic than adults in designing useful ways of dealing with the experience of being bullied. For example, they are often realistic about the pointless-ness of reacting punitively to the bully and are trained to discourage bullied pupils to harbour wishes for revenge. They recognize the necessity of coexisting with the bullies in the school community.

BOX 6.2   How peer supporters responded by email to a typical issue

One boy wrote just before the Easter holidays to the email peer support team:

'My friend is sometimes nice to me ...but at other times he plays jokes on me and embarrasses me in front of the class ...Should we still be friends or should I tell my Mum to call his Mum so she tells him off about it?'

The peer supporters responded:

'How long have you been friends? Is this a recent development? You don't say whether you have told him yourself what effect this has had on you. It may be your opinion has changed since the end of last term so we look forward to hearing what you think'.

The boy wrote:

'Thanks a lot. We met over Easter and I told him that I don't want to have to be in touch with him anymore, and he said fine and now he ignores me which I suppose is a good thing. But he is one of the cool boys in the class, and I want to be popular like him, because I don't have any other friends'.

The peer supporters responded:

It's good that you took the initiative and spoke to him in the holidays. Having this space may be hard at first, but will give you a chance to look for friends who share your interests outside class as well as inside. Let us know how it goes. Write back whenever you like'.

(adapted from Hutson and Cowie 2007)

The Internet has great potential for helping young people to find resources to help them and to offer strategies for overcoming the threats posed by cyber bullying. Cyber peer support systems make use of the new technology by providing anonymity and by providing an open space where young people can meet more freely than they may feel is possible when face to face. Some researchers have welcomed the use of the Internet as a key medium for breaking down barriers and for connecting people who would otherwise be marginalized (McKenna and Bargh 2000) or whose culture shames and embarrasses the bullied child (Toda 2005). The Internet is especially attractive to young people who might otherwise fear that their issues will not be treated in confidence. By preventing the need for pupils to be physically present when talking to a peer supporter, this barrier is removed. Box 6.2 gives an example in which the peer supporters enable a boy with a friendship issue to work out his own solutions while still offering to support him through the process and acknowledging that it may be emotionally painful for a while. The issue is common in this age group yet many young people feel deeply ashamed about their friendship difficulties. Specifically, email peer support has the potential to reach vulnerable young people who might otherwise stay silent about their distress.

Conflict resolution/mediation between those in dispute

Another strand in the peer support process involves training young people to act as mediators in a dispute (Andrés 2007; Cremin 2007; Cunningham et al. 1998; Fernandez et al. 2002; Stacey and Robinson 2003). The mediators can be the same age as those in dispute where, for example, pupils are elected within their year group to offer a service to fellow pupils when a dispute arises. Training is intensive and allows time for team-building, time for developing good communication skills, practice in the necessary skills of mediation through role-playing typical scenarios, and time for reflection on the process of conflict resolution and on the nature of the strong emotions that are usually involved in disputes. There must be a follow-up meeting at which participants review the success or otherwise of the solution and acknowledge their willingness to make adjustments if necessary. At the heart of the process of mediation we find the quality of *active listening* and the ability to respond authentically to the needs and feelings of the participants. Mediators are trained to use empathy as well as a rational problem-solving stance so that the disputants can move through their conflict into a resolution.

Cremin (2007) reports on research that she carried out by interviewing teachers and peer mediators from 15 Birmingham schools with mediation schemes in order to identify what the critical elements for success were. She found that it was necessary for the whole school to be committed to the mediation service by embedding it in the school's policies on behaviour management and linking it with other pupil-led bodies such as the school council. The regular use of circle time in the whole school prepared all pupils for mediation through practice in essential social and personal skills such as cooperative groupwork, active listening, turn-taking, respect for others' point of view. Circle time provided an arena for preventing conflicts in the first instance and for giving all pupils the awareness that conflicts can be resolved peacefully. Additionally, successful schools provided designated time for staff and peer supporters as well as financial resources to the schemes. She also found that peer mediation services worked best when the pupils themselves were involved in the selection of mediators through such experiences as democratic elections and active involvement in the interviewing processes. Mediators felt most satisfied where there were clear boundaries and where the limits of their expertise were identified and made explicit. They appreciated regular supervision and opportunities for training and documented the value of regular debriefing meetings to keep up the momentum. In essence, then, Cremin's research emphasized the need for schools to demonstrate their commitment to the empowerment of young people and their belief that young people have the potential to resolve many of their everyday disputes and so come to a greater understanding of the concepts of responsibility and justice.

Evaluation of this approach indicates that there is a substantial decrease in the incidence of aggressive behaviour. Typically, over 80 per cent of disputes mediated by peers result in lasting agreements (Cunningham et al. 1998)

Community action against bullying

The most recent form of peer support is expressed through the democratic participation of young people in identifying issues in their own school community, such as bullying, and working collectively to address them. Student Councils can be used to deal with problems that arise in the school, and initiate methods to improve the school climate. They are usually initiated by a group of elected peers who start by generating a series of 'ground rules' for their peers to follow. These ground rules are then presented to the whole school during assembly. Students on the Council are generally elected by the student body, though some may be appointed by staff. The Council then convenes once a week to deal with social problems at school which they then provide solutions to. Other students evaluate how well the Council fulfils their role throughout this process. The idea of Student Councils is that decisions about issues within the school are made via a democratic group decision-making process.

An example of the perceptiveness of young people in addressing the problem of school violence appears in the European Charter for Democratic Schools without Violence (Council of Europe 2004). Young people from across Europe prepared the Charter which they based on the fundamental values set forth in the Council of Europe's Convention for the Protection of Human Rights and Fundamental Freedoms.

The group of young people recommended that schools throughout Europe seriously consider using this Charter as a model with which to further the cause of democratic schooling without violence. The seven points of the Charter are:

1.   All members of the school community have the right to a safe and peaceful school. Everyone has the responsibility to contribute to creating a positive and inspiring environment for learning and personal development.

2.   Everyone has the right to equal treatment and respect regardless of any personal difference. Everyone enjoys freedom of speech without risking discrimination or repression.

3.   The school community ensures that everybody is aware of their rights and responsibilities.

4.   Every democratic school has a democratically elected decision-making body composed of representatives of students, teachers, parents, and other members of the school community where appropriate. All members of this body have the right to vote.

5.   In a democratic school, conflicts are resolved in a non-violent and constructive way in partnership with all members of the school community. Every school has staff and students trained to prevent and solve conflicts through counselling and mediation.

6.   Every case of violence is investigated and dealt with promptly, and followed through irrespective whether students or any other members of the school community are involved.

7.   School is a part of the local community. Co-operation and exchange of information with local partners are essential for preventing and solving problems.

Other schemes such as *Checkpoints for Young People* (Varnava 2002) involve a peer support process by encompassing principles of democratic participation on the part of children and young people. *Checkpoints for Young People* is a resource aimed at primary and secondary school students. It is particularly applicable at the transfer stage — when children move from primary to secondary school. The resource was developed after consulting with young people, and aims to improve the school environment to achieve a safer and happier school life for all by providing the peer group with a tool to identify the social and interpersonal issues, such as being bullied, that they face at school. It also helps to identify the gaps in the school's pastoral care system. *Checkpoints for Young People* was published to encourage students' active involvement, establish their ownership of the intervention process and reinforce its messages through the channel of communication to the home.

   Discussions with 10 to 11-year-olds, for example, reveal their inner fears about transferring to secondary school: 'bigger children', 'getting lost', 'too many people' and 'queuing for food'. In one school, *Checkpoints for Young People* was used as the agenda for a Student Council conference, putting issues and their solutions firmly in the hands of young people themselves. In another, *Checkpoints for Young People* served as the basis of a whole-school development plan.

Using a test-retest design, the efficacy of *Checkpoints for Young People* and its companion resource *Checkpoints for Schools* (Varnava 2000) was evaluated by Jennifer and Shaughnessy (2005) as a strategy to support young people and schools in promoting non-violence. They found that in three of the four (two primary and two secondary) UK schools where it was implemented, there was a reduction in overt bullying behaviours, such as hitting, tripping and shouting, in comparison with control schools, as measured by the *My Life in School Checklist* (Arora and Thompson 1999).

Children's views and experiences

Traditionally, adults as experts in child development gathered evidence about children 'objectively'. More recently, researchers have seen the need to record children's own perspectives on the grounds that children themselves are the most important source of evidence on how they experience their lives. In other words there is a movement to engage in research *with* rather than *on* children (e.g. Greene and Hogan 2005; James and Prout 1997; Veale 2005) where children are active participants in the project. In our culture, we do not have a strong track record of listening to children or of understanding children's lives in their own terms and as a primary source of evidence. The field of peer support seems to be an ideal arena in which to put more innovative child-centred methods to the test, for example with the peer supporters in the role of active researchers into their own experience. More use could be made of anonymous feedback on the part of users while still respecting the confidentiality of their interactions with peer supporters. Recent developments in the use of the Internet as a vehicle for peer support could be mobilized in this domain.

Qualitative responses by peer supporters have indicated their awareness of the moral dilemmas faced by bystanders when they observe pupils being mistreated and abused by peers. The practice of peer support appears to give direction to young people's altruistic wishes to address injustices such as bullying and deliberate social exclusion in their school community. This is the moral stance taken by those bystanders who – unlike the silent majority – are prepared to demonstrate publicly their stance against injustice (Cowie and Hutson 2005; Hutson and Cowie 2007). The skills of peer support are potentially present in anyone provided that they have the willingness to offer help to peers in distress. They can be drawn from the ranks of bullied, bullies and bystanders. Some young people are naturally friendly and spontaneously reach out to help a fellow pupil in distress. Salmivalli et al. (1996) found that around 17 per cent adopted this participant role of defenders of victims who would challenge bullies and support victims either during or after the episode. Hutson and Cowie (2007) interviewed pupils who had volunteered to become peer supporters and found that they represented a range of participant roles, not only those of defender, indicating the enormous value of peer support training in harnessing, or even unlocking, the potential to reach out to another person in distress. The following extracts from these interviews (Box 6.3) reveal the different reasons that underpin the wish to volunteer to offer help in addressing the issue of school bullying.

BOX 6.3 Why young people become peer supporters

The first statement come from a pupil who had never been bullied himself but nevertheless had empathy for other bullied peers:

'I have always liked school and have never been bullied myself but I do get really fed up with the cliqueyness of the school. If you're good at sport then you're in with the right crowd, but people can be really narrow-minded. I've seen a few boys in my year have a really tough time. There are a couple of boys who are constantly picked on and most of the time they don't deserve it at all. They're just unlucky. I'd like to feel that I'm doing something about it, and this is why I'd like to be a peer supporter'.

A proportion of peer supporters are former victims of bullying who often are so appreciative of the help that they received from peer supporters that they would like to offer something back in return, as the following quotation indicates:

'When I was in Year 8, my best friend turned against me. We had a stupid fall out in the autumn term and for some reason my whole group of friends then turned against me too. I spent most of break time alone, and nobody wanted to sit next to me in class. I was really unhappy ... I didn't know how awful it can be until it happened to me, so I think I'd be good at being a peer supporter as I know what boys are going through ...'

At the same time, even bullies may feel guilty about their cruel behaviour towards peers and may welcome the opportunity to change their ways and so make atonement, as the following quotation reveals:

'Last year when we moved up from primary to secondary school I know I bullied quite a few of the kids in my class – nothing physical, just picking on them and trying to make them feel bad. I guess I look back on that now and feel quite bad, so I'd like to do something positive to make up for it ...'

(adapted from Hutson and Cowie 2007)

It is also worth including the perspective of parents here since research indicates that they notice changes in their children once they have participated in the peer support training. Cremin (2007: 118) gives an extract from an interview with the parent of a primary school peer mediator:

> When my son was chosen to be a mediator, I felt very proud of him. Being a shy child, I felt that it helped him to become more confident to approach his peers, and to help them with their disputes if they had any. He would tell me when he was on duty and be pleased to wear his jumper and cap. I believe that the experience was rewarding for Michael. I hope that many more children will have the same experience as he had ...

Does peer support work? Key research findings

Cowie and Smith (2008 forthcoming) carried out an international review of the effectiveness of peer support schemes and identified a number of key outcomes for peer supporters, users of peer support systems and for school climate in general.

Outcomes for peer supporters

Evaluations of peer support schemes have consistently indicated certain advantages of peer support for those who are trained to implement the schemes. Benefits reported by peer supporters include: being more confident; developing a sense of responsibility; valuing people more; feeling gratification at doing something to help improve the quality of life in their school community; and satisfaction at learning skills such as conflict resolution (Cowie 1998; Cowie et al. 2002; Naylor and Cowie 1999) At the same time, some peer supporters report difficulties that include: hostility on the part of peers, with boys especially vulnerable to taunts about their masculinity; and jealousy because of their role or because of the attention they received from the school, the community or even the media; undervaluing of their skills by some staff (Andrés 2007; Naylor and Cowie 1999; Smith and Watson 2004). In some very violent contexts, peer supporters report feeling overwhelmed by the magnitude of the task that they were expected to do (Cowie and Olafsson 2001).

Overall, despite the difficulties reported by some peer supporters, on the basis of this evidence about the impact of peer support systems on peer helpers, Cowie and Smith (forthcoming) conclude that the practice of peer support appears to give direction to some young people's altruistic wishes to address injustices such as bullying and deliberate social exclusion in their school community, and that the training enhances their communication and problem-solving skills and their capacity to feel empathy for peers in distress. There is also informal evidence that peer supporters' career goals are clarified through experiences of helping others and that interview panels regularly express interest in this aspect of a young person's *curriculum vitae*.

Outcomes for users of peer support systems

A number of studies have interviewed or surveyed pupils who have used peer support systems and have asked them how satisfied they were with the quality of the service they received. On the whole, reports are positive for those pupils who actually use the systems. For example, Naylor and Cowie (1999) found that 82 per cent of users reported that they found peer support 'useful' or 'very useful'; 82 per cent said that they found these helpful in giving them the strength to cope with bullying; and 80 per cent said that they would recommend the system to a friend. In the follow-up study two years later, Cowie et al. (2002) confirmed these findings; overall, 87 per cent of bullied pupils said that the system had been useful or very useful to them, the most frequent reason given being that it helps to talk to a peer. Even in the adverse circumstances of the underprivileged school investigated by Cowie and Olafsson (2001), the majority of users reported that they valued having a peer to listen to their problems and found it helpful to have the protection of a peer supporter's presence. Similar levels of satisfaction were reported by Smith and Watson (2004) who found that 44 per cent of primary school users said it helped a lot, 50 per cent said it helped a bit, and only 6 per cent said that it did not help. Cowie and Smith (forthcoming) conclude that the majority of users report finding the schemes helpful.

Outcomes for school ethos

Teachers frequently report that the school environment becomes safer and more caring following the introduction of a peer support scheme, and that peer relationships in general improve (Cowie et al. 2002; Cowie and Sharp 1996; Cremin 2007; Hurst 2001; Mental Health Foundation 2002; Naylor and Cowie 1999; Smith and Watson 2004). Lane-Garon and Richardson (2003) studied the impact of a peer mediation scheme on school climate in a sample of 300 elementary school pupils in the USA. Both mediators and non-mediators perceived the school climate to be safer than had been reported in the year prior to the introduction of the peer mediation scheme. This represented an increase from 56 per cent (in 1999) to 66 per cent (in 2001) of pupils who either agreed or strongly agreed that they felt safe on campus. Responses to the items *Other students treat me with respect at school*, and *I feel like I belong here*, both increased from 47 per cent to 58 per cent over this period. However, other studies have been less positive in this domain. Naylor and Cowie (1999) found that peer support systems did not appear to reduce bullying, since its incidence as measured by an anonymous questionnaire was similar to that reported in other surveys at that time (e.g. Whitney and Smith 1993). Nevertheless, on the basis of users' responses to their questionnaire, they argued that the presence of a peer support system reduced the negative impact of bullying on victims and made it more acceptable for them to report it, especially as it was perceived by both users and potential users that peers are able to detect bullying at a much earlier stage than adults can.

Salmivalli (2001b) reported mixed effects of a small-scale peer-led intervention in a Finnish secondary school of a general awareness-raising nature. Seventh- and eight-graders (13–15 years) were assessed. For seventh-grade girls there were positive outcomes (reduction in self- and peer-reports of victimization), but these were not found in eighth-grade girls, or either year group of boys. Girls showed an increase in willingness to influence bullying problems, but boys actually increased in pro-bullying attitudes. However, this intervention was very short and there was no control group comparison. Cowie and Olafsson (2001), in their study of one secondary school with high levels of violence, administered the Olweus bullying questionnaire before the introduction of the peer support service and seven and a half months after. The high incidence of bullying in the school showed little change over the period when the peer support service was in operation. When asked how often teachers, peer supporters and other young people tried to put a stop to someone being bullied, pupils tended to perceive all three parties as intervening less in June than in the previous November. However, results from a recent study in inner-city schools in Madrid have produced very encouraging results, as reported in Box 6.4. Think back to Chapter 1 where we discuss Salmivalli et al.'s (1999) research into the impact of group dynamics and participant roles on bullying.

Box 6.4 A longitudinal study of peer support and its impact on *convivencia*

Andrés (2007) carried out a longitudinal study in two secondary schools in Spain: an experimental school which had developed a system of peer support to enhance the school's ethos (or, to use the Spanish term, its *convivencia*) and a second school in the same catchment area which acted as a control. There were 778 pupils, 65 teachers and 242 families in the experimental school and 462 pupils and 53 teachers in the control school. (Note that the families were only asked questions that related to the impact of the peer support system so these were only drawn from the experimental school.) The study took place in a social-cultural context of major difficulty with a large influx of families from other cultures and an ongoing concern about rising levels of violence, both in the community and in school itself. In each class of the experimental school, the pupils democratically elected classmates to act in the role of peer helpers. The elected pupils were then given training that enabled them to intervene directly to resolve peer group conflicts, with a particular brief to intervene in cases of bullying and the abuse of power.

Andrés (2007), Andrés and Barrios (2006) and Andrés et al. (2005), using quantitative measures of psychological qualities, including empathy, problem-solving ability, pro-social behaviour, self-efficacy and emotional efficacy and qualitative interviews and focus groups, found that the programme had a very positive effect on the social development of those who participated as peer helpers, with boys demonstrating greater gains than girls. All the peer support-ers improved in their communication skills. The study indicated the value of the training for enhancing these qualities and for providing an opportunity for young people to develop in pro-social behaviour and attitudes, self-efficacy and empathy.

Regarding the influence of this learning on her social world, Nina, a 12-year-old peer supporter, said of the training that it was: '... useful. It gives you the basis to intervene. You learn, for example, to listen, which is very important. Moreover, you make friends with other peer supporters and learn to make new friends in other places and get along better with the ones you already have'. The perceptions of teachers and pupils in the experimental school were that *convivencia* improved during the period of the intervention. At the same time, they observed that despite the emergence of a number of conflicts in the local community, the implementation of the programme played a vital part in protecting *convivencia*. As a senior teacher put it: 'Yes, we are having interpersonal conflicts but the peer supporters intervene positively ...These problems come up. That is, the number of disputes obviously have increased because of the circumstances, but they have been reduced by the programme'.

The head teacher reported that preventive actions against bullying had taken place in all the classes and grades, pointing out the challenging nature of some of the work that the peer supporters did. She quoted one example of how a group of 15-year-old girl peer supporters resolved the very cruel, insidious homophobic bullying of one boy in their own year group: '... They were friends of the perpetrators and of the bullied pupil, Javier. ... Two boys started calling him names, like 'flaming faggot'. ... they wrote very offensive Christmas cards during a class activity designed to enhance *convivencia*. When the peer supporters became aware of it, they informed their class teacher and she told the peer support team ...The peer supporters also spoke with the aggressors, who had mobilized the other boys in the class against Javier, doing all sorts of harmful things to him ...Javier had been feeling very, very frightened for three or four months. ... The girls intercepted one of these terrible Christmas cards sent (anonymously) to Javier which said, 'We are going to kill you'. The peer supporters then spoke to the aggressors [...] but the damage had already spread to the rest of the class ...In the end, we [the teachers] were very strict with the whole class and managed to solve the problem ...all thanks to the girl supporters. Though they were friends of the perpetrators, morally they couldn't stand it ... They were really worried ...'

This is one extreme example of how bullies can sabotage cooperative group learning in the classroom. Yet at the same time, the action of the peer supporters facilitated the reparation of the damaged relationships in that class and affirmed the value of taking a moral stance. This incident also provides an example of the limits of the expertise of peer supporters. On their own, they could not resolve the issue but by working with the school staff they were able to bring the cruel behaviour out into the open and so resolve it.

The greatest impact of the programme in general appeared to be on psychological or indirect bullying. For example, social exclusion decreased significantly in the experimental school during this study. In-depth interviews revealed that during the third year of the programme *convivencia* improved substantially, indicating that the work of the peer supporters was becoming more effective. The programme has now been running for eight years and has become an integral part of the school culture.

(adapted from Andrés 2007)

Investigations into pupil reports on experiences and perceptions of safety at school reveal mixed results when similar schools, those with and those without a peer support system in place, are compared (Cowie and Oztug 2008). Cowie et al. (2008) surveyed around 900 secondary school pupils in total, and found that the pupils in the non-peer support control schools reported feeling no safer in the toilets, the playground, corridors and in lessons than their counterparts in schools with peer support. However, a different picture emerged when they separated out those pupils who knew of their school's peer support system from those who did not. Those who were aware of the peer support system in place in their school felt significantly safer than those who were not (see Box 6.5).

BOX 6.5 Pupils' perceptions of safety among those who were aware (APS) and those who were not aware (NAPS) of their schools' peer support system

The research was carried out in four secondary schools in a small rural town, each with a well-organized pastoral care system and an active anti-bullying policy. The study involved a total of 931 pupils (49.5 per cent boys, 50.5 per cent girls) aged between 11 and 15. Two schools (A and B) that already had established peer support schemes (PS) were matched with two schools (C and D) which had yet to commence their peer support training (NPS). Pupils responded to the School Climate Checklist (Secondary Version) that was developed by Carrie Myers and Nicky Hutson, and published in Cowie and Jennifer (2007: 133–36). Questions covered issues such as perceptions of safety within school, anxieties about being bullied; engaging in bullying behaviour; and telling someone about experiences of school violence and bullying. Specific questions about awareness, use and evaluation of peer support were also added for peer support schools only. There were also some open-ended questions, such as: 'How much do you agree most people in school trust one another?'; 'Do you worry about being bullied?'; 'Where do you feel least safe and why?'; 'Where do you feel most safe and why?'; and 'What are your suggestions for making the school a better place?'.

Within each of the peer support schools there was a substantial proportion who did not know about the existence of the peer support system. In School A, 25 per cent of pupils were not aware that their school had a peer support system in place; in School B the percentage was even higher at 33 per cent. The pupils who were not aware (NAPS) were matched randomly by age and gender with pupils within their school who were aware (APS) and their responses to the questionnaire compared. There were no differences between APS and NAPS pupils in terms of their perceptions of safety in the toilets, playground and corridors; however, significantly more of the APS pupils reported that they felt safer in lessons. Significantly more of the APS pupils perceived their school as 'a friendly place to be', compared to NAPS. In answer to the question, 'Do you worry about being bullied at school?' significantly more of the NAPS pupils reported that they worried 'a lot' about being bullied at school.

In answer to the question, 'When bad things happen do you tell anyone?' there were no significant differences between PS and NPS pupils though older PS pupils were significantly more likely to tell a friend, boy/girlfriend than NPS pupils. In other words, only older pupils in peer support schools were different from pupils in non-peer support schools in terms of telling someone about negative experiences. However, within the peer support schools, APS pupils were more likely to answer 'Yes' than NAPS pupils. In other words, NAPS pupils were significantly more likely to keep silent about a negative experience than peers who knew about the existence of their school's peer support system. Additionally, APS pupils were significantly more likely to report to a member of their families when bad things happen than NAPS pupils.

In answer to the question, 'If you do bad things at school whom do you tell?', there were no significant differences between PS and NPS pupils. However, within the peer support schools, NAPS pupils were significantly more likely to tell no-one than APS pupils. Additionally, APS pupils were significantly more likely to report to a member of their families if they did bad things at school than NAPS pupils.

The most immediate conclusion to be drawn from these results is that schools need to be much more proactive in advertising their peer support schemes to the school population if they are to reach out to as many people as possible. It is not enough to have a launch and then to consider that everyone knows about the system. Schools need to disseminate and publicize the service in as many ways as possible, through posters, announcements, assemblies, parents' evenings, the local media and direct contact through tutor groups and year groups, and maintain the advertising momentum over time.

At a deeper level, the results indicate that it is not so much that the existence of a peer support service reduces bullying and violence by its presence and the actions of the peer supporters. Rather, it is the awareness that peer supporters are there to help that enables pupils to create a social construction that school is a safer place to be. These findings suggest that for those pupils who know about their school's peer support system one important outcome is that they feel empowered to talk about negative things that happen to them, or that they do to others, with someone else, not necessarily a peer supporter. In other words, the observation (and in some cases the experience) of the helpfulness of sharing worries and anxieties with another has become an accepted method for coping with issues of concern. At the same time, the pupils who are unaware may well be young people who are particularly hard to reach and who are most at risk of being adversely affected by school violence, whether as bullies or as victims. Peer supporters and the teachers in charge of schemes need to make greater efforts to communicate with these pupils and to convince them of the value of the service that they have to offer.

(adapted from Cowie et al. 2008)

The evidence gathered from the survey reported in Box 6.5 indicates too that unless a peer support system is widely disseminated as part of the whole-school strategy to counteract bullying and violence, it will fail to reach a proportion of pupils who may well be those in particular need of help. Further research could identify who these pupils are and discover better ways to meet their needs.

Given the extensive evidence from earlier studies of the impact of peer support training on the young people who take part, there is a case for arguing that peer supporters should be given additional training on how to challenge bullies and bystander apathy as well as the more traditional forms of training in active listening and empathy. Such training, of course, should not push peer supporters beyond the limits of their expertise. Additionally, peer supporters would benefit from consulting more extensively with the school population to discover what their common fears and anxieties are and how their needs might be met. A range of different strategies is essential if schools and their pupils are to be successful in the ongoing effort to create and sustain social and learning environments that are friendly and safe. (For further discussion of the school ethos, see Chapter 8.)

LEARNING POINTS

- The most well-established findings concern the benefits of peer support systems for the peer supporters, which have been nearly universally reported in the studies reviewed.
- These benefits probably stem from the quality of training and supervision received, and the practice of skills in a context generally valued by other pupils and the school.
- Users also report benefits, with only a minority saying that peer support is unhelpful. It is also worth noting that a proportion of former victims of bullying are consistently present among the ranks of peer supporters, demonstrating the value of peer support training and practice in restoring the self-esteem and confidence of vulnerable pupils in the context of a supportive, well-motivated group.
- The extent of the impact of peer support systems on the general climate of school is less clearly documented. There are subjective impressions that school ethos improves and that rates of bullying decrease, but objective, unbiased evidence of such improvements is less frequent.
- Research into peer support illustrates the ongoing difficulty involved in measuring the processes that take place when people intervene to reduce bullying. There is a need to develop a wider range of studies that explore the complex social and personal processes of change both in those who participate (whether users or helpers) and in the wider school population as a whole.
- There is also a need to involve young people themselves, perhaps as peer researchers, in order to gain richer insights into the ways that peer supporters might influence relationships in the peer group and the techniques that have the greatest impact. Such research could include observations of peer support in action and peer-led reflections on the experience of peer support.

Resources

ChildLine in Partnership with Schools (CHIPS) (2006) *Peer Support Toolkit*. London: NSPCC/ChildLine.

Cole, T. (2000) *Kids Helping Kids*. Victoria, British Columbia: Peer Resources.

Cowie, H. and Wallace, P. (2000) *Peer Support in Action*. London: Sage Publications.

Department for Children Schools and Families (DCSF) (2000) *Bullying: Don't Suffer in Silence: An Anti-bullying Pack for Schools* (2nd ed.) London: Her Majesty's Stationery Office.

Petch, B. and Withers, T. (2006) *Peer Mediation: Guidance Notes for Schools*. Solihull: Solihull Metropolitan Borough Council.

Salter, K. and Twidle, R. (2005) *The Learning Mentor's Source and Resource Book*. London: Paul Chapman.

Scherer-Thompson, J. (2002). *Peer Support Manual*. London: Mental Health Foundation (www.mentalhealth.org.uk/peer http://www.mentalhealth.org.uk/peer/).

Web sites

ABC Training and Support (www.abcservices.org.uk).

Bullying – A Charter for Action (www.teachernet.gov.uk/publications).

ChildLine (www.childline.org.uk).

Cowie, H. and Jennifer, D. et al. (2006) *School Bullying and Violence; Taking Action* (www.vista-europe.org).

National Children's Bureau (www.ncb.uk).

National Society for the Prevention of Cruelty to Children (NSPCC) National Society for Prevention of Cruelty to Children (www.nspcc.org.uk).

Peer Support Networker (www.peersupport.ukobservatory.com/).
UK Observatory for the Promotion of Non-violence (www.ukobservatory.com).

7 THE ROLE OF NARRATIVE IN COUNTERACTING BULLYING

Chapter overview

In this chapter, we consider some of the ways in which researchers can use narrative methods with children to gain insights into the phenomenon of bullying. We also show how educators can use narrative to help young people understand more about themselves and the nature of their relationships with others. We provide up-to-date research findings, case studies of educators using narrative in the creative arts to alleviate the negative effects of bullying, examples of young people's perspectives and key learning points. Narrative approaches, in particular those that encourage interaction with characters, participation in the plot development and reflection on outcomes, have direct application to the issue of bullying. First, we provide an overview of different forms of narrative that have direct relevance to the study of bullying: symbolic play, narratives of everyday life, children's fiction, role play and drama, and virtual reality narratives. Then we explore three key aspects:

1   using narrative to gain insights into children's construction of bullying episodes and their perspectives on those who bully, those who are bullied and those who stand by and watch;
2   using narrative approaches to raise awareness about bullying and change attitudes towards it;
3   using narrative therapeutically to help children who have been emotionally damaged by experiences of bullying.

The essential aspects of narrative in counteracting bullying

Through the medium of story, the child can move into an imaginary world where all things are possible, whether by listening to a story-teller, by reading a book or comic, by watching a DVD or television, or by going to the cinema, and where important learning takes place about life, relationships and the self. The characteristics of stories have particular relevance for those who would like to address the issue of bullying. In the classroom they enable children to discuss and explore different aspects of bullying through direct interaction and through the child's emerging sense of audience. Since stories operate in the world of the imagination, they can bypass everyday resistances, such as shame, guilt and embarrassment, which may inhibit those who bully and those who are bullied from examining the problem. Stories have the potential for developing children's problem-solving skills since within the narrative there is scope for trying out a range of outcome possibilities. Stories also invite children to be reflective by providing opportunities to see the world from different perspectives, including those of the victim, the bully and the witnesses. The characters in stories can facilitate bonds between teller and audience and so can challenge accepted ideas and provide role models for future behaviour.

Symbolic play

Children's fascination with story begins early. From around 12 months of age, they begin to engage in fantasy play, initially with the parents but this mode of representation develops increasingly with peers throughout the pre-school years. During this time, children derive a great deal of fun and enjoyment out of socio-dramatic play episodes in which children act out scripts and stories around themes drawn from real life, such as mum and dad putting children to bed, doctors treating patients, firemen rescuing people from buildings, and from fantasy worlds, such as monsters from outer space or dragons and witches. From quite an early age children seem to be able to make a distinction between what is real life and what is make-believe (Scarlett and Wolf 1979). The child will often signal that the story is make-believe by saying 'Once upon a time' or 'Let's pretend'. By the age of 3 or 4, children are expert at moving swiftly between reality and fantasy through complex systems of tone of voice, gaze, gesture, position and posture, often with the help of toy figures and dolls. The stories that children enact in their play tend to be based on real life experiences or on stories that they have heard from books or the media. Telling and retelling stories through their play can enable children to understand their own experiences and to communicate to others what these experiences mean.

Narratives in everyday life

Part of the child's reality inevitably involves relationships with others, including difficulties with members of the family and the peer group. Narratives of everyday life offer opportunities for the child to learn to take the perspective of others by recounting shared memories and important family events, such as birthdays or holidays (Engel 1995).

Working within the attachment theory perspective, Bretherton (1990) argues that emotional openness between parent and child facilitates children's ability to form coherent internal working models of relationships. These coherent representations are in turn reflected in coherent child narratives about parent–child relationships. Dunn et al. (1991) have also found relationships between the quality of children's conversations about emotions and later differences in the child's capacity to discuss their emotional states. Dunn et al. 1991 studied children's close relationships. They found that from their second year children are increasingly articulate in discussing their own relationships and can from this age talk about feelings, including those of other people. The researchers found that pretend play in particular provides children with a chance not only to explore social roles and rules of their world, but also to play with feeling states. For example, in pretend play, children will talk about pain, distress, being sleepy, feeling hungry or feeling sad. This demonstrates their capacity to 'take on' a feeling stance that is not their own, to assign a feeling state to a character, and to share this feeling state with another person. This process involves co-construction of a shared experience or memory.

Experimental and observational studies indicate that there is a consistent relationship between cooperative co-constructors and a rich, embellished, frequent style of 'memory talk'. That is what Oppenheim et al. (1997) found when they examined the nature of early mother-and-child co-constructions of narratives about separation and reunion, focusing in particular on the child's capacity to view interpersonal situations from multiple perspectives and see the self as having multiple sides or 'narrative voices'.

In their experimental study, they found that there were clear associations between children's co-constructed narratives with their mothers and two aspects of their development: (1) their ability to construct emotionally well-organized and regulated narratives independently; and (2) their behavioural and emotional regulation in everyday life. Children who were rated higher on emotional coherence during co-constructed narrative-making had higher ratings on their independently created stories in terms of emotional coherence, the presence of pro-social themes and the absence of aggressive themes. In addition, they were rated by their mothers as having fewer behavioural and emotional problems at the time of the study, and also one year later than control group children. There are clear implications here for the role of parenting in preventing bullying characteristics and behaviour from evolving, and in enabling their children to develop the quality of empathy which, as we saw in Chapter 4, is so often lacking in children who bully.

Children's fiction

Parents and teachers can continue this process by reading fiction with children so creating a space within which it is possible to explore everyday anxieties, worries and insecurities about self and others. Protherough (1983) found that young readers reported that they often imagined that they were one of the characters or that they were in the places where the events of the story took place. Some reported that they were trying to make links between the world of the book and their own life experiences. It appeared that the young readers' values and experiences interacted with those portrayed in the story. The themes of most literature are those of life – relationships, conflict, love, betrayal, death, danger – and can be applied directly to the issue of bullying. Literature helps us to learn about the impact of similar life events on the characters within the text, their emotions, their thoughts and their actions.

Of course, there are wide individual differences in children's capacity to respond to fiction, and research studies of adult–child interaction indicate that these processes may be nurtured or inhibited by the responses of other people, especially those who are significant to the child. Bruner (1986, 1990) has suggested that the concept of 'scaffolding' is a useful way for explaining the processes that parents and their children go through as they jointly create or co-construct stories about their shared experiences. Recently, researchers have acknowledged the status of talk about the past – or the 'there and then'. This is one kind of memory and it can pave the way for different types of story-telling. Bruner argues that narrative is an important means through which individuals build systematic representations of experiences to interpret the past and to anticipate the future. Bruner (1990) suggests that stories achieve their meanings by representing deviations from the ordinary in a comprehensible form. The viability of a culture, he argues, lies in its capacity to resolve conflicts, explore differences and renegotiate communal meanings. In other words, any culture needs to have a set of norms but it must also have procedures for making departure from these norms meaningful. Through story this kind of meaning is often achieved. He argues that the telling of stories within a community or a family constitutes a form of social memory. The idea of 'the other' is therefore central to understanding the processes that the child engages in.

Other researchers, influenced by the psychodynamic tradition, argue that the symbolic images of fantasy can help children to distance themselves from the fears and anxieties that formed an inevitable part of their lives. Bettelheim (1976) argued that pre-school children could understand the underlying themes of fairy stories, such as *Little Red Riding Hood*. This understanding has an important therapeutic function in helping the child to explore moving experiences from the inner world, and to achieve some form of resolution of emotional conflicts. Guggenbhul (1991) encouraged children to supplement everyday anxieties about common problems with their own fantasies by making up new episodes or enacting new scenes in role play. Through the ensuing discussion, the children were able to move from the imaginary to the real, and could apply the lessons learned from fiction to their own lives.

But literature also has an important function in documenting, in symbolic ways, the large-scale aggression endemic in modern society. Rustin and Rustin (1987: 250) refer to this key aspect of story in their discussion of Tolkien's *The Lord of the Rings* which, in their view, evokes 'the climate of world struggle against the forces of totalitarian darkness which belongs to the Second World War and Cold War periods'. The continuing popularity of Tolkien in the form of epic films and the more recent widespread fascination on the part of children with the saga of Harry Potter illustrate the great potential of story, in whatever form, to offer young people an arena within which to experience not only a particular world in the imagination but also to reflect on broad issues such as violence, and war. Stories also give the child the opportunity to think about moral issues that arise when one person deliberately inflicts harm on another or when characters are involved in a conflict. (See Box 5.1 for further discussion of the use of literature in groupwork.)

Drama and role play

Drama and role play in school carry on this narrative process. The learning that children experience in drama has the advantage that it happens within the safety of a playful situation. It is possible in this medium to address disturbing aspects of life through the voices of imaginary characters and in the company of other participants and members of an audience. Many children and young people might find it difficult to talk directly about their own fears and anxieties but find that in role play the self is protected so freeing the character in the role play to try out a range of behaviours, experiment with outcomes and reflect on possible solutions. Again, as we saw in our discussion of play, children are thereby enabled to explore a range of perspectives on any issue, however troubling.

When using role play and drama to work therapeutically with children and young people, teachers are not concerned with public performance but rather with creating a space within which to explore ideas about, for example, relationships that are unequal, relationships that turn sour, and conflicts and emotions, such as jealousy and anger. An integral part of the role play will be the opportunity to stand back from the drama in order to reflect on key matters that arise from it. Conn (1997) describes the successful use of dramatherapy as a tool for working with children whose behaviour in school is challenging. One example that Conn uses concerns her work with aggressive children where she gives them the chance through therapeutic role play the chance to shift from the image of being 'bad' or 'criminal' to the more noble image of 'warrior' or 'guardian'.

Virtual reality (VR) narratives

Traditionally, stories were told by a narrator or author directly or shown to an audience through dramatic characterization. Most recently, with developments in the world of VR, narrative approaches have evolved into a medium that involves interactivity since the audience can actively engage with the characters, the plots and the environment (Aylett et al. 2005; Hall et al. 2006; Louchart et al. 2005). The resulting participative narrative approach has much in common with Boal's Forum Theatre and street theatre (Boal 1999) where participants enact unscripted dramatic episodes and in which, at critical points, the director can pause the role play to question both participants and audience. This creates a context for reflection on what is happening now in the role play and what may happen in the future. (See Box 6.1 where this method is used to train peer supporters.)

Using narrative to gain insights into children's construction of bullying

Recently, researchers have used narrative methods to enhance understanding of how children actually describe experiences and perceptions of bullying and victimization in their own words rather than through the lens of existing adult constructions. As described in Box 1.2, Bosacki et al. (2006) invited 82 children aged between 8 and 12 to draw a bullying episode and then questioned them about the emotions and motives of the characters in their drawings. The researchers were interested to find out from children themselves what their moral views were on how bullies justify their actions as well as how they portrayed the emotions experienced by bullies, victims and (if they included them) bystanders. Although the majority of the drawings depicted a dyad, the number of characters in the bullying scenarios increased amongst the older children, confirming Salmivalli's (2001a) view that, as they get older, children develop a view of bullying as a more complex, social process involving bystanders in different roles. Most of the drawings showed the bully as bigger than the victim (40 per cent) or the same size (57 per cent). Most of the bullies were portrayed as smiling (78 per cent) whereas victims tended to be crying or upset (48 per cent).

In the older children's drawings, the victims were given voice bubbles much less frequently than in the younger children's drawings, dropping from 53 per cent among the 8-year-olds to 40 per cent for 10-year-olds to 23 per cent for 12-year-olds. The authors note that this 'silencing' of the victims is also expressed in the passive acceptance of the situation which appeared more frequently among the older children. For example, one 8-year-old gave the bully a speech bubble that said, 'You're smaller than me. Ha! Ha!' to which the victim replied, 'Big or small, it does not matter.' By contrast, a typical 12-year-old drawing gave the bully a speech bubble that said, 'You're a loser!' to which the victims made no reply. Older children were also more likely to draw thought bubbles in which, for example, bullies were thinking things like, 'You're too small to do anything' but victims were portrayed as thinking things like, 'Boo hoo!'.

Seventy per cent of children when interviewed about their drawings indicated that bullies had psychological motives for behaving the way they did (e.g. wanting to make someone sad), often in a sadistic manner for the fun of it, confirmed by the fact that so many of the bullies were smiling in the drawings. The children also commented that 'being different' was a feature common to many bullied children rather than the possession of a skills deficit.

The authors conclude that anti-bullying policies should adopt whole-school initiatives that aim to create a positive school climate and that educate children about qualities of caring, responsibility, compassion and respect for others. These ideas are in harmony with the philosophy of this book and with peace-oriented approaches such as those advocated by Fonagy et al. (2005).

Using narrative approaches to raise awareness about bullying

Many children spontaneously engage in aggressive play involving, for example, imaginary guns and weapons of attack. Some researchers, for example, Gunter and McAleer (1997) and Sutton-Smith (1988), argue that children clearly understand the difference between reality and fantasy. These researchers point out that much of the violence features fantasy figures like Batman and Superman or animals (as in cartoons like *Tom and Jerry*) and that children are able to distinguish clearly between these characters and people in real life. These researchers conclude that war-play demonstrates just one aspect of the child's imaginative development. From their perspective, aggressive play has a therapeutic dimension and so it may be counterproductive to forbid it.

Costabile et al. (1992) interviewed parents in Italy and the UK to establish their views on whether to tolerate or actively discourage war-games. Some parents tried to forbid it on the grounds that it made their children behave badly and become more disobedient. Others tolerated war-play but still worried that it might have a negative influence on their children's emotional development and sensitivity. Carlsson-Paige and Levin (1990) argue that war-play has a very bad impact on children's emotional and social development since it impoverishes the child's imagination by narrowing stories down to good versus evil and by dulling the child's sensitivity to the suffering caused by violence. Their recommendation for parents and teachers is to intervene when children play war-games and turn their attention to more constructive forms of play. This advice is, in practice, adopted by nurseries and schools and by most parents. The evidence remains uncertain but it seems likely that a proportion of very disturbed children may be put at a greater risk if their aggressive play is not channelled into other, more productive, types of play.

One result has been to alert adults for the need to take account of the baseline attitudes and perspectives that children already hold when they listen to a story or watch a film. For example, Tulloch (1998) found that a film drama on bullying was perceived differently by two groups of pupils — those who initially disapproved of bullying and those who tolerated bullying or considered it amusing. In Tulloch's study, instead of fostering anti-bullying attitudes in all pupils, the film actually appeared to reinforce pro-bullying attitudes in those who were already predisposed in favour of the bully. Jennifer et al. (2006) evaluated the impact of showing a cartoon film specially designed to heighten children's awareness of bullying and to broaden their perspectives on the different participant roles involved in most bullying episodes at school. As you can see in Box 7.1, the film affected boys differently from girls. The findings indicate how alert teachers and researchers need to be to the fact that some children actually admire bullies and despise victims. The advantage of the cartoon format is that the children can identify with the characters in the story and can explore outcomes in a non-threatening context since the narrative is 'make-believe'.

BOX 7.1 How cartoons can help children understand the social context of bullying

In this study, the researchers organized an activity day centred on *Bully Dance*, a non-verbal cartoon film with a strong message about bullies and how to deal with them. In the film a community of ant-like creatures is disrupted when a bully victimizes a smaller member of the group. Eventually, the whole community becomes involved in dealing with the bully, who is himself a victim in his own home. Issues of peer pressure, accountability and imbalance of power are explored in a story that deals with a sensitive and pervasive problem.

The participants were 34 10 to 11-year-old children from one London primary school. The children viewed the film in the school's performance arts room and then engaged in structured activities such as brainstorming, poster-making, letter-writing and role play around the theme of bullying. The researchers administered the *Children's Attitudes to Bullying Scale* (Eslea and Smith 2000) before and after the activity day. Before the activity day, the majority of the children expressed anti-bullying attitudes. However, over one-third indicated that they could understand how some children might enjoy bullying another person. For example, nearly half of the children thought that a small amount of bullying can be a good thing; nearly half thought that they were pretty tough themselves, and nearly three-quarters thought that children should be able to stand up for themselves. So while most children sympathized with the plight of a bullied pupil, a significant minority despised victims and admired bullies.

After the activity day, the boys' anti-bullying attitudes decreased slightly while those of girls increased slightly.

(adapted from Jennifer et al. 2006)

The results reported in Box 7.1 indicate that while awareness may be raised by an activity day of this kind, it takes a more extended period of intervention to change attitudes which are deeply engrained. The researchers argue that the increase in girls' anti-bullying attitudes may have taken place because the message of the day was already acceptable to them. By contrast, for the boys, the cartoon film may have aroused opposition to the victim and strengthened macho attitudes. The cartoon enabled a forum within which the issue of bullying could be explored and in which antisocial attitudes, such as contempt for bullied children, could be challenged.

One way forward is recommended by researchers who are developing innovative virtual learning environments (VLEs) to educate children in ways of counteracting bullying (Aylett et al. 2005; Hall et al. 2006; Watson et al. 2007) with such programs as FearNot!, an acronym for Fun with Empathic Agents to Reach Novel Outcomes in Teaching (see Box 7.2). These pro-social programs have the potential to challenge educators' and parents' understandable concerns about the violence that is often portrayed on commercial DVDs and computer games.

Newson (1994), for example, produced an influential report on the topic of video violence and its impact on young people. She argued that children in Western society were being damaged by the preponderance of violent images and themes in videos. Most recently, the Byron (2008) report examined the potential risk to children of video and Internet games. While acknowledging that they offer many opportunities for enjoyment and learning, Byron expressed concern that some of the content is extremely violent. Her proposals include the recommendations that there should be a shared culture of responsibility with regard to Internet games, that families, industry, government and others in the public domain should collaborate in order to reduce the availability of violent material to children, and that the current classification system should be reformed in order to raise awareness of content in the games and to enable more effective enforcement.

In the same spirit, there are now new 'emotionally intelligent' games with an educative purpose which build on children's interest in this medium. These games are designed to help players consider the outcomes of certain behaviours (for example, how bullying behaviour makes people sad and lonely, or how peer support builds up their confidence in themselves) and to help players think about the impact of different types of behaviour on characters' emotions in the game.

Box 7.2   FearNot! an anti-bullying intervention: evaluation of an interactive virtual learning environment

The FearNot! method provides 8 to 11 year-old children with the opportunity to explore a virtual school environment complete with bullies, victims, bystanders, assistants to the bully and defenders of the victim. The characters are autonomous agents capable of making their own decisions and acting out their own behaviours. The goal of the game is to educate children on how to deal with bullying behaviour, so the child participant takes the role of peer buddy or friend to the victim character. Participants in the game witness a bullying episode and then 'talk to' the victim characters in order to advise them about what to do next. For example, if a child advises a character to hit the bully back, many different narrative outcomes are possible.

The FearNot! method provides two distinct levels for players:

1   *appraisal*: a fast mechanism for reacting to a given event;
2   *coping strategies*: a mechanism for representing the emotion-focused planning involved in coping, such as acceptance, denial and mental disengagement.

Early evaluations of FearNot! showed that children responded well to this interactive narrative method and enjoyed playing the game. The most liked characters were John, the victim, and Paul, the defender; the least liked was Luke, the bully. Participants reported that they felt sorry for the victim and were angry at the bully. However, the longer-term effects on children's attitudes and behaviour have yet to be established. Zoll et al. (2006) evaluated its impact on 252 school pupils in the UK, Portugal and Germany. Comparing pre- and post-test data did not indicate any rises in empathy for the victim or any decreases in bullying rates in the schools.

However, Hall et al. (2006) had more promising findings. Results from 127 children and 95 adults indicated that children expressed more favourable views towards the characters and the believability of the plots than did the adults. Children were more favourable towards the virtual school environment, the character voices and movements compared to teachers. Similarly, children found the conversation and storylines more believable than did the teachers.

However, there were significant gender differences in which of the characters the children would like to be. Forty per cent of boys and 88 per cent of girls chose to be John, the victim. No girls chose to be Luke, the bully, compared to 44 per cent of boys. Girls expressed most empathy towards the victim and anger towards the bully.

The authors expressed satisfaction that the VLE was so positively accepted by the children since this shows the high potential of this as an educative tool for raising awareness about bullying and how to deal with it. The fact that children liked the VLE more than the teachers did simply indicates that the cartoon metaphor is one that most children engage with naturally.

With regard to longer-term effects, we can only conclude that evaluation needs to take place over time in order to give a realistic picture of impact. It seems likely too that FearNot! could only be effective as part of a wider whole-school policy to counteract bullying.

(adapted from Watson et al. 2007)

We can link this debate back to our discussion of risk and protective factors in Chapter 1. If the number of risks to which a child is exposed is high, then war-play and violent video games may be potentially harmful to that child's social, moral and emotional development. However, if protective factors are present then the risks may be diminished. Actual aggression in the home or in the community is likely to be much more damaging to the child than imaginary episodes on DVD or in play. Responsible parents and teachers need to help the child to keep a check on fantasy that leads to unstable, egocentric patterns of thought with little sensitivity towards the feelings of others. On the other hand, if adults deny the free flow of the imagination, the child may lose the capacity to think and create with an authentic voice, and so to come to a moral stance on aggression and violence that derives from reflective thought and emotional awareness of the needs of self and others. In fact, the more constructive approach than constantly vilifying the media might be for parents and teachers to select plots from television that illustrate contemporary issues and relevant dilemmas for youth in order to discuss the effective and ineffective coping strategies of all participants and the emotional responses of all involved. These approaches work with all children but are especially effective with young people who are experiencing difficulties with peer relationships or aggressive, bullying behaviour.

Using narrative therapeutically

We turn now to therapeutic uses of narrative to help those who are most disturbed by bullying. White and Epston (1990) have developed a narrative approach to therapy which has been used successfully to help children damaged by their experiences of bullying. White and Epston (1990) argue that children, like adults, can redefine their relationships within the context of their life story. What holds people back from doing this is often the range of cultural assumptions, beliefs and practices that exist in our social world.

White became interested in the course of his work as a therapist to discover how certain voices came to dominate a person's description of their reality. So his questions as a therapist became concerned to explore the *absent* voices. He developed a process of deconstruction to create questions that explored the absent voices in order to elicit narratives about why and how they came to be silenced. (Think back to the study by Bosacki et al. (2006) in which the children themselves literally silenced the voices of bullied children in their drawings.) In other words, child and therapist together need to engage in a process of challenging taken-for-granted assumptions about the self through a re-storying process. Through the process of therapy, children and young people are enabled to rediscover subjugated knowledge — the suppressed stories that more fully encompass the experience of the individual. With every telling of the story, the young people are rewriting their lives.

According to White and Epston (1990), some dominant stories are saturated with problems. The role of victim may be deeply internalized in the young person's mind. The first step will be to give the problem a name. Once the problem has a name, the counsellor asks questions that map the influence of the problem, and gauge the relative strength of the person and the problem. This process is followed by identifying the influence of the young person on the problem. The counsellor also takes note of any experience, however small, that stands apart from the problem story. With these fragments, a new story is woven. These 'unique outcomes' illustrate the young person's influence on the life of the problem and will require patient and persistent questioning on the part of the counsellor. Once some unique experiences that are not problem-bound have been explored, the child and therapist begin to 'thicken' the plot of an alternative story. The child is also consulted on whether it is appropriate to continue to live by the problem story or to move on, usually with the help of supportive others, such as friendly members of the peer group.

According to Winslade and Monk (1999:15) 'an appreciative audience to new developments is deliberately sought out. For most of us, it is not possible to make radical changes in our lives without somebody cheering us on'. Burns (2005) has developed a similar therapeutic story-telling method for enabling children and young people to work through damaging experiences such as bullying with the help of healing stories and, through that process, become empowered to deal with the issue. The therapist designs a humorous, playful story that will culminate in a fictitious character finding out his strengths. First, she identifies the *problem* (for example, the character is being bullied), the second, *resources* (the things that the character does to address the *problem*) and the third, *outcome* (finding out what the character is good at and building on it). In one story, for example, a boy discovers by accident that when he takes his socks off, the resulting smell is strong enough to make the cat faint. He decides not to change his socks for some time. His feet become so smelly that he is able to knock himself out when he puts his socks to his nose. He adds to their pungency by spreading Gorgonzola cheese in the socks. Finally, when two bullies corner him in the school toilets, he is able to kick off his shoes and point his feet in their direction. They duly pass out and the boy feels confident now that he has his secret weapon. It is essential for the story-teller to observe the child to see how the story is being received and what needs to be changed and adapted to make it work for that child. The story-teller also needs to ground the story in reality. This helps make listening to the story more engaging for the child and also helps generalize the benefits into the child's day-to-day life. The story-teller is free to incorporate metaphorical events like the powerful socks to symbolize the potential strengths that all children possess within themselves.

Parents and teachers can use the metaphors embedded in all stories to help children deal with experiences of bullying and should not underestimate the power of the imagination to help children think out solutions themselves to their difficulties or collectively to develop a coherent sense of what is right and wrong in acting towards others in the peer group. As Gersie (1997) points out, on the basis of her extensive use of therapeutic story-making, many traditional stories recount the adventures of 'victim heroes' who are invited to wake up and move on in their lives by overcoming many difficulties and obstacles on the way until at last they are strong enough 'to face their reality; their hurts, longings and possibilities – thereby to be transformed' (Gersie 1997: 157). As she puts it (Gersie 1997: 154), 'sooner or later the shed, prison, nest, cottage or cave where a story character abides is turned into a location which must be left'. Parents, caregivers and teachers can use the myriad of stories that children love to explore the meanings embedded in such journeys.

LEARNING POINTS

- Narrative approaches give us insights into how children perceive and experience bullying. It is important for educators to listen to the voice of the child in order to understand bullying more deeply. Many children feel empathy for the plight of victims and anger at the bullying behaviour, but some, especially boys, also express admiration for peers who bully and contempt for those who are bullied.
- Stories teach us about values and acceptable forms of behaviour. For this reason, they are an effective medium for challenging bullying since they can educate children about how to deal with bullying when they encounter it, whether as witnesses or as victims, or when they practise it as bullies.
- Stories have the potential to teach values, but educators need to be aware that children respond differently to awareness-raising interventions.
- Stories give opportunities for children to experiment in the world of the imagination with alternative ways of being, behaving and intervening when they encounter or experience bullying.
- Stories provide understanding of the outcomes of bullying — they create role models on how to behave in different contexts.
- Stories have a therapeutic role in healing the emotional wounds inflicted by the experience of being bullied.
- The use of drama, role play and (more recently) cartoon figures in virtual learning environments has a great deal of potential to prepare children for the future and equip them with strategies for dealing with bullying.

Resources

Brun, B., Pedersen, E. W. and Runberg, M. (1993) *Symbols of the Soul: Therapy and Guidance Through Fairy Tales*. London: Jessica Kingsley.

Burns, G. W. (2005) *101 Healing Stories for Kids and Teens*. Hoboken, NJ: John Wiley & Sons.

Cattanach, A. (1997) *Children's Stories in Play Therapy*. London: Jessica Kingsley.

Freeman, J., Epston, D. and Lobovits, D. (1997). *Playful Approaches to Serious Problems*. New York: W.W.Norton.

Gersie, A. (1997) *Reflections on Therapeutic Storymaking: The Use of Stories in Groups*. London: Jessica Kingsley.

Perlman, J. (2000) *Bully Dance* (*La danse des brutes*). [Film] Available from the National Film Board of Canada: (www.bullfrogfilms.com/catalog/bully.html).

Web sites

ABC Training and Support (www.abcservices.org.uk).

Action Work: Films, Theatre and Education (www.actionwork.com/).

Classroom-based story-telling activities (www.teachit.co.uk/custom_content/newsletters/nationalstorytelling2007.asp).

FearNot! ECircus web site (www.e-circus.org).

The Society for Storytelling (www.sfs.org.uk).

Virtual ICT with Empathic Characters VICTEC (www.ist-world.org/ProjectDetails.aspx?ProjectId=98eb49eb736749cda8037eeb3a35f18f).

White and Epston: Narrative Therapy with Children and their Families (www.narrativeapproaches.com/ntwc.htm).

8 CREATING A SUPPORTIVE ENVIRONMENT

Chapter overview

In previous chapters, we based our arguments on research findings that explored the nature of bullying, the causes of bullying, the characteristics of bullies, victims and bystanders, the contexts where bullying flourishes and a range of interventions that can counteract bullying. Fundamental to our discussion has been the necessity of viewing bullying as a relational issue. In this concluding chapter, we integrate the ideas from the previous chapters into a series of recommendations on how educators can create nurturing and supportive environments that actively prevent bullying before it starts and that empower teachers, parents/caregivers, children and young people to challenge it when they encounter it. We consider both physical and psychological aspects of the environment. We also show how educators can create and sustain environments that foster positive relationships and alleviate the negative effects of bullying. We return to the model that we introduced in Chapter 2 (see Figure 8.1).

What are the essential components of successful interventions?

Too often the school environment is not supportive of bullied children. Many bystanders, even if they feel outraged by the actions of the bully, fail to intervene through fear of retaliation by the bully or derision on the part of the peer group. As children grow older, the percentage of those who believe that in some way the victim deserves to be bullied increases (Slee 1995). Adults and children may fail to intervene because they feel that they lack the skills or understanding to act effectively (Boulton 1997). Many adults — teachers, administrators, parents/carers — ignore bullying or even actively engage in it themselves in their daily interactions with others (O'Moore 2000). Bullies receive a great deal of support from peers and so their deep-seated need for dominance is fuelled (Salmivalli et al. 1999).

As discussed in Chapter 2, Skiba et al. (2006), in their report to the American Psychological Association Zero Tolerance Task Force, concluded that zero tolerance policies fail to make school environments safer. Far more emphasis, they argued, should be placed on the host of existing strategies that already exist to promote school safety and prevent bullying and violence. Pepler, Smith et al. (2004) also identify ongoing controversies in the anti-bullying field, most importantly the debates around whether it is better to apply sanctions to those who bully or to develop educational and therapeutic strategies as preventative measures. As we argued in Chapter 3, relational approaches are not a substitute for sanctions and no schools that we know of have abandoned sanctions from their behaviour management and anti-bullying policies. However, as Warren and Williams (2007) demonstrate, schools that adopt policies and practices based on relational principles of reparation, restoration and reintegration no longer need to use formal sanctions as frequently. When sanctions *are* applied they are more likely to be perceived as meaningful since those involved in the bullying incident have also had a say in agreeing on the consequences.

So how can we actively change the school environment into one that fosters positive relationships and challenges bullying when it occurs? Two useful international evaluation studies (Baldry and Farrington 2007; Smith, Pepler et al. 2004) have systematically reviewed the successes and failures of anti-bullying interventions in order to identify the core elements which have been proved to be effective. Smith et al. (2004) reviewed 13 while Baldry and Farrington (2007) reviewed 16 anti-bullying programmes, together representing work from 12 different countries (Germany, Norway, UK, Canada, Australia, Ireland, Belgium, Finland, USA, Switzerland, Italy and Spain). The programmes were selected because each was a large-scale study involving large numbers of schools and because each had been systematically investigated using experimental methods with controls and a before–after set of measures, or a longitudinal design. The evaluations included self-report questionnaires, peer ratings, teacher ratings or observational data. A main measure of effect size was drawn from the percentage change in rates of bullying in the experimental group (i.e. the group that had experienced the interventions) in comparison with a control group.

In each case, the researchers concluded that the most effective programmes are those that adopt a whole-school approach. For example, the first national programme for the prevention and reduction of bullying carried out by Olweus and his team in Norway (Olweus 1993: 2004) involved families and schools, a national campaign and a comprehensive set of interventions at three different levels: the individual, the classroom and the school. Supervision during break times was improved. The outcome was a substantial reduction in rates of bullying (48 per cent for boys and 58 per cent for girls), especially among the primary school pupils. Similar successes were found in the Sheffield, UK study (Smith and Sharp 1994), the SAVE project in Spain (Ortega and Lera 2000) and the Donegal Primary Schools anti-bullying project in Ireland (O'Moore and Minton 2004). In each case, interventions were carried out at individual, class and whole-school levels. Additionally, the Irish programme included a resource pack for parents and carers. The successful interventions also put in place systems that were sustainable over time and that involved ongoing monitoring of effectiveness. This research confirms the effectiveness of consistent policies and procedures that are negotiated and regularly updated by the whole school community

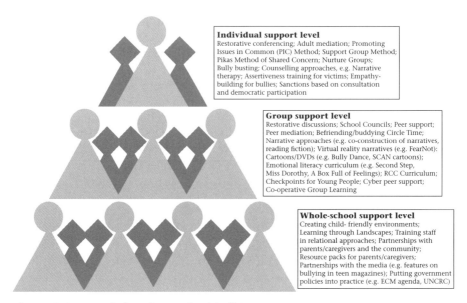

Individual support level
Restorative conferencing; Adult mediation; Promoting Issues in Common (PIC) Method; Support Group Method; Pikas Method of Shared Concern; Nurture Groups; Bully busting; Counselling approaches, e.g. Narrative therapy; Assertiveness training for victims; Empathy-building for bullies; Sanctions based on consultation and democratic participation

Group support level
Restorative discussions; School Councils; Peer support; Peer mediation; Befriending/buddying Circle Time; Narrative approaches (e.g. co-construction of narratives, reading fiction); Virtual reality narratives (e.g. FearNot): Cartoons/DVDs (e.g. Bully Dance, SCAN cartoons); Emotional literacy curriculum (e.g. Second Step, Miss Dorothy, A Box Full of Feelings); RCC Curriculum; Checkpoints for Young People; Cyber peer support; Co-operative Group Learning

Whole-school support level
Creating child- friendly environments; Learning through Landscapes; Training staff in relational approaches; Partnerships with parents/caregivers and the community; Resource packs for parents/caregivers; Partnerships with the media (e.g. features on bullying in teen magazines); Putting government policies into practice (e.g. ECM agenda, UNCRC)

Figure 8.1 Knowledge about school bullying

and the value of direct therapeutic work with individual pupils involved in bullying, whether as bullies, victims, followers or onlookers.

A whole-school approach to the creation of safe environments

The results of these and other studies indicate that the success of any anti-bullying intervention depends on a proactive, consistent whole-school approach that involves ongoing consultation with representatives of all members of the school and its community. The research also suggests that all members of the school community must learn about bullying, its social dynamics, its origins and the impact that it has on everyone's life, as well as the many forms that bullying takes including physical, psychological and cyber bullying, if they are to be knowledgeable about appropriate interventions. As we saw in Chapter 1, without this understanding, it is likely that the more subtle and insidious aspects of bullying will be overlooked. Adults need to be aware of the risk factors that influence bullying behaviour and the extent to which they can minimize them. They also need to be aware that the experience of being traumatized by bullying can lead to reduced concentration and attention on the part of victims, so exposing them to heightened risk of accidental injury in the immediate aftermath (Engström et al. 2005; Laflamme et al. 2002).

Becoming knowledgeable about the range of risk factors is a complex, ongoing process that must continue to be addressed in different arenas, including lessons, assemblies and staff meetings. Adults need to be aware of the array of strategies that exist to prevent bullying. Furthermore, adults need to reflect on their own behaviour

honestly and consider whether they are modelling a positive approach to relationships through their own interactions with children and other adults.

The school needs to be clear about its values. Educators need to be committed
to creating and maintaining an ethos concerned with justice and fairness, empathy
for children in distress, cooperativeness, trust and emotional literacy. As we saw in
Chapter 3, restorative practices in schools have successfully been employed to
challenge aggressive behaviour, to resolve conflicts and to repair the emotional
damage of participating in bullying. In a radical way, the approach challenges the
notion that wrongdoers deserve to be punished and that the threat of punishment is
necessary for the control of perpetrators. Good communication is essential so that
pupils, teachers, parents and all adults involved with the school understand these
values and share in the willingness to promote them. Open, direct patterns of
communication are entirely consistent with policies that counteract bullying and
they flourish in environments characterized by trust and friendliness. These qualities
in turn contribute to high morale among the teaching staff and the pupils. It is
equally important for the school to forge links with key government and local
authority anti-bullying initiatives. For example, at local authority level, it is important to link the school's policies to initiatives based on the *Every Child Matters* (DfES
2004) agenda, such as the Youth Participation Strategy and the Children and Young
People's Plan (CYPP), and Social and Emotional Aspects of Learning (SEAL) in order to
develop a integrated strategic approach to bullying. To this end, the school benefits
from setting up regular meetings with the Local Authority to parallel the procedures
already in place and to forge links with other groups that are developing anti-bullying
initiatives. These links will ensure that the school is up to date on national strategies
and can receive relevant information about training guidance and on funding and
resource opportunities to support innovative work.

The whole school should be concerned to develop policies and procedures to
counteract bullying. This must also be reinforced in the curriculum. The policy must
be regularly disseminated and discussed throughout the school through codes of
conduct that are owned by adults and pupils, through regular assemblies, classroom
discussions, poster displays, drama activities, special days devoted to the topic,
workshops for children, teachers and parents, specialized curriculum materials that
foster an emotionally literate school.

In each school, there must be an ongoing process through which all members of
the school community – or their representatives – are regularly engaged in identifying
the extent, nature and location of bullying. There needs to be a system for reporting
bullying and for responding to bullying episodes. Once reported, there must be an
efficient, child-friendly system in place to address the issue. Students who are
frequently bullied need to be encouraged to feel safe and secure enough to report it.
Parents/carers too need to be informed about the school's anti-bullying approach and
offered opportunities to learn about ways in which they can support what the school
is doing to create a positive school climate and so reinforce at home qualities of
caring, responsibility, compassion and respect for others.

Research findings also indicate the value of working to change the school's
social and emotional environment in order to foster positive relationships, moral

values, rights and responsibilities; in other words, to foster an emotionally literate school. We saw examples, in Chapter 4, of anti-bullying approaches that have very successfully challenged bullying by working with peer relationships through cooperative group learning processes. These include Hazler's *promoting issues in common* (PIC) (Hazler 1996a), the Pikas *method of shared concern* (Pikas 2002) and the *support group method* (Maines and Robinson 1997; Robinson and Maines 2007). Each of these methods, though they differ in some detail of implementation, is grounded in a philosophy based on empathy for others. Each abhors blame and punishment but works through group processes to foster feelings for others and greater awareness of self and the impact of actions on others. We have also outlined the value of such anti-bullying approaches as restorative practice (Chapters 3 and 5) and mediation/conflict resolution and peer support (Chapter 6) which form an integral part of a wider commitment to emotional literacy in schools. We saw in Chapter 7 that schools can be proactive in supporting the development of virtual environments that promote positive, pro-social values through cartoon characters that give children opportunities to rehearse a range of strategies through role play for dealing with bullying when they encounter it. What these approaches also achieve is a positive contribution to the emotional climate of the school which in a broad sense reduces social support for bullies and actively promotes pro-social values among all the children and adults in the whole-school community.

A nurturing school climate creates an environment that reinforces empathy for others in bullies, their assistants and onlookers and, at the same time, provides psychological support for victims, as we saw in Chapter 6 through the work of peer supporters and Chapter 4 in the discussion of nurture groups. In the next section we take this one step further by exploring ways in which the whole school can counteract bullying by working consistently to create positive, harmonious relationships.

Creating an emotionally literate school

The movement towards teaching emotional literacy in schools has been evolving for a number of years since Goleman (1995) popularized the research findings of Salovey and Mayer (1990) in his book *Emotional Intelligence: Why it Can Matter More than IQ*, which has been translated into many languages all over the world. At the heart of this approach is the recognition of the importance of the culture of the whole school and of the active emotional engagement of all pupils and adults in this community. Goleman (1995) argues that in recent years our society has seen a decline in emotional literacy and that this has resulted in an increase in cynicism, social pathology and violence. He maintains that we have overemphasized intelligence and academic achievement at the expense of emotional skills such as empathy, responsibility, persistence, caring for others and the control of anger. He believes that society must help children to recognize and understand their emotions and the emotions of others so that they will be more able to control themselves in positive ways. The emotions play a key role in the ways that adults and children work, interact and learn together. Salovey and Mayer (1990) have identified five key features of EI:

1   *Understanding feelings*: understanding the power of your feelings and the feelings of others. The authors highlight a keystone of emotional intelligence – *self-awareness* – which can be heightened by using materials in schools that help children identify their own feelings, build a feelings vocabulary and recognize links between feelings, thoughts and actions.

2   *Managing feelings:* understanding when and how to use your feelings and help others to understand when and where to use theirs. Managing feelings so that they are appropriate is regarded as an ability that builds on self-awareness. Children can be taught to use strategies such as self-talk, writing down their feelings in a diary, using breathing appropriately, singing, reading or drawing.

3   *Self-motivation:* taking control of your future by making decisions to move towards your goals; developing self-control, like delaying gratification and controlling impulsiveness through self-regulation

4   *Handling relationships:* relating well to other people. This is seen as the skill of managing emotions in others and how this skill will impinge on abilities that underpin popularity, leadership and interpersonal effectiveness.

5   *Empathy:* caring about the feelings of others but remaining detached enough to be able to give them support. Children can be taught listening and communication skills, problem-solving, stress management and negotiation skills. They can learn to be assertive rather than aggressive or passive. Empathy is viewed as another ability that builds on emotional self-awareness.

Essentially the message is that we should never neglect the emotional life of our pupils since emotions and reason are equally important in education. From this perspective, teachers should be prepared to teach their students about self-awareness, life skills, conflict management, self-esteem, empathy and how to work reflectively and cooperatively in groups, since these qualities underpin the strength of each person's emotional competence. Children who are emotionally competent are significantly more likely to lead productive lives and to have satisfying interpersonal relationships. Children with high scores on emotional intelligence receive more nominations for pro-social than antisocial behaviours from their peers and receive more nominations for kindness, leadership and overall peer competence (Harris 2000; Mavroveli et al. 2007; Petrides et al. 2006).

In the UK, the Department for Children, Schools and Families has taken these ideas on board to devise the Social and Emotional Aspects of Learning (SEAL) curriculum in which the emphasis is on teaching children to understand, express and manage their own emotions and respond to the emotions of others in helpful and sensitive ways. From this perspective, the school can play a very significant part in addressing bullying by focusing on relationships among pupils, between pupils and staff, among colleagues and between staff and management, encouraging open, genuine communication, and by devising policies and practices that offer emotional and social support to all members of the school community. Perhaps the most powerful way of counteracting bullying is for the school as a community to offer constructive alternatives to the cruel, manipulative worlds where bullies dominate.

As Cowie and Jennifer (2007) indicate, the implementation of emotional literacy programmes like these over time has a powerful impact on the incidence of bullying. Evaluations of emotional literacy programmes (Aber et al. 2003; Elias and Clabby 1992; Frey et al. 2005; Greenberg et al. 1995; Grossman et al. 1997; Van Schoiack Edstrom et al. 2002) consistently confirm increases in pro-social behaviour, reductions in aggressiveness, effective management of emotions and improvements in children's capacity to develop and sustain interpersonal relationships. The value of such interventions cannot be overestimated.

A key outcome of the emotionally literate school is a concern for those emotionally affected by bullying. Counselling approaches should be available that are suitable and appropriate. Pupils who bully need to have provision for addressing their behaviour. All members of the school community should learn to take responsibility for the part that they play in addressing the issue of bullying. Teachers should create opportunities to celebrate positive achievements and success of pupils, staff and other members of the school community. Emotional literacy should be taught and reinforced across the curriculum and in the staffroom so that a culture of mutual respect and cooperation is fostered between staff, between pupils and between staff and pupils

Designing child-friendly environments for play and discovery

In harmony with emotional literacy programmes has grown a concern to enhance the physical environment of schools. Titman (1994) carried out pioneering consultations with hundreds of children in order to discover what the school landscape meant to them. A significant finding was that very few school grounds actually met children's needs which included the desire for natural colours (not concrete), trees, flowers, places with different levels, places to climb, explore and hide, as well as simple items like informal benches. Her recommendation was that head teachers should look at the whole-school environment rather than the playground in isolation and that they should consult with children at every stage of the process of redesigning their grounds. Out of that earlier research has grown the Learning through Landscapes (LTL) movement which integrates planning of the school environment with a range of other activities in the mainstream curriculum, including drama, design games, questionnaires and surveys, observation, photography and mapping. Children are involved at all stages of the process. The movement has developed and now involves hundreds of schools in the UK.

Blatchford (1998) highlighted the role of break time in providing an opportunity for children to acquire valuable social skills through the process of forming and maintaining friendships. While recognizing the difficulties that some children can experience during break times, notably the danger of being bullied, Blatchford and Sharp (1994) proposed a holistic solution to include training in lunchtime and break time supervision, enhanced opportunities for play, improvements in the environment and greater consultation with children themselves about the environment in which break times take place. Essentially Blatchford and Sharp (1994) proposed that initiatives in the playground should not be peripheral to developments in the curriculum or activities in the classroom. They also argued strongly that children should be involved in decisions about their own school environment.

Research into the impact of a more child-friendly playground environment has indicated a very positive influence on children's behaviour. For example, Spears et al. (2007) introduced teacher-directed unstructured lunchtime physical activities, such as ball games and gym activities, and pupil-led, teacher-supervised structured lunchtime activities, such as music, dance, drama and crafts into one primary school in Australia. The activities were structured to incorporate cross-age tutoring and the teachers consistently provided rewards for positive play. They found significant reductions over a five-year period in aggressive behaviour and bullying with parallel improvements in pro-social behaviour. In this context, it is worth reiterating Dunn's (2004: 105) point that the crowded and public nature of school environments and the constant presence of power and evaluation throughout the school day both combine to make separation of the genders more likely. These characteristics of school life, Dunn (2004) argues, actually increase the appearance of aggressive modes of interaction. This confirms the observations of researchers like Opie and Opie (1969) who noted that, in the community or in local neighbourhoods, boys and girls play much more cooperatively and in more imaginative ways than they do in crowded playgrounds.

Most recently, a partnership of organizations signed up to the Learning Outside the Classroom Manifesto (LOtC) to campaign for real-world experiences that take place outside the classroom, in museums, historic houses, theatres, field study and outdoor education centres and places of worship. A key aim of this movement is to enable children and young people to develop better personal and social skills through the experience of becoming more aware of their environment and cultural heritage. Initiatives such as these illustrate ways in which the school environment can be enhanced so as to counteract bullying and other forms of antisocial behaviour by building on children's natural curiosity and willingness to engage with the critical issues of the day.

Developing a partnership with parents and carers, and the community

Anti-bullying work is greatly enhanced too if the school involves the active participation of parents/carers and the local community. Parents and carers often notice the signs and symptoms of a bullied child's distress long before teachers do. As Cooper and Tiknaz (2007) point out, there are some potential barriers that can too easily act against the formation of a productive working partnership between home and school. Some parents/carers may feel intimidated by the school or feel alienated on the basis of their own experiences as children. They may also feel disempowered in terms of their own capacity to help the school, especially in situations where their children are involved in bullying, whether as victims, bullies or bystanders. It may be that the origins of the bullying behaviour lie in the family itself since bullying is positively correlated with authoritarian, punitive child-rearing methods and violence within the family setting (Mooij 1998) and some adults are unable or unwilling to model the authoritative adult–child interaction, emotionally warm climate and clear rules that Olweus (1993) deemed to be at the heart of effective anti-bullying interventions.

Skiba et al. (2006) found that parents/carers and communities become very critical of schools if they perceive that punitive zero tolerance disciplinary methods and sanctions pose a threat to the rights of certain children to be educated. This can be all the more contentious if particular ethnic groups appear to be targeted by the policies. Therefore, it is essential for the professionals in the school setting to communicate with the parents/carers as partners in educating children to relate to one another in respectful, caring and supportive ways. Cooper (2006: 73) advises a systemic approach that takes account of the contexts within which aggressive behaviour happens. His approach in addressing any form of social emotional and behavioural difficulty is to view the young person involved less as an 'object to be treated' than as a 'partner in the search for a solution to a problem that affects many people'. Cooper's own work with nurture groups confirms that the involvement of parents/carers leads to their greater confidence in relating to their children, a strengthening of the parent-child relationship and consequently a reduction in the behavioural and interpersonal difficulties. Examples of successful anti-bullying programmes that include the parents/carers as partners involve focused talks with the parents/carers of children who bully (Olweus 1993) and resource packs for all parents/carers (O'Moore and Minton 2004). An essential component lies in positive, open communication from school to home to ensure that parents/carers fully understand the rationale that underpins the school's anti-bullying policy so that they can see ways in which their contribution as carers is valued by the school.

Pepler, Craig et al. (2004) recommend the use of the media as an important way to reach out to the wider community, including alienated parents/carers with little involvement in the school. Smith, Pepler et al. (2004) note in their evaluation that a number of the successful programmes (e.g. Alsaker 2004; Hanewinkel 2004) benefited from national campaigns to promote their work. Others benefited from outreach work into the community through newsletters and meetings for interested parents/carers (Limber et al. 2004; Pepler, Craig et al. 2004). They argue that as networks are established within these communities, so the support for parents/carers and children involved in bullying will increase.

In Box 8.1, we describe an evaluation of a large-scale intervention designed to prevent violence in schools and the community (Aber et al. 2003).

Box 8.1   The Resolving Conflict Creatively Program (RCCP): an Evaluation

The RCCP is a school-based violence-prevention curriculum that promotes positive conflict resolution in order to create a more caring and peaceful school environment. RCCP aims to increase children's knowledge about how to approach conflict situations, to give them the skills to deal with conflict and, in general, to help them to develop positive interpersonal and inter-group relationships. RCCP also aims to promote tolerance and respect for cultural differences and to transform the school ethos into one that consistently demonstrates non-violence and acceptance of diversity. The lessons centre on: communication skills; expression of emotions; managing anger; conflict resolution; cooperative groupwork; respecting diversity; counteracting prejudice. Skills are taught experientially through such methods as role play, interviewing, brainstorming and small group discussions. RCCP is introduced to a school gradually. Initially, only highly motivated teachers participate voluntarily but over time increasing numbers of teachers are encouraged to participate and, in addition, pupils in participating schools are trained in peer mediation skills.

Aber et al. (2003) studied the effects of RCCP on 11,160 elementary schoolchildren in inner-city areas. The data were gathered at 4 time points from 15 New York schools over a period of 3 years. The schools were divided into four categories: (1) non-intervention (control group schools); (2) beginning stage of RCCP; (3) integration of some components of RCCP; and (4) integrations of all components of RCCP. The findings are highly relevant to the issue of bullying. The main effects of RCCP were:

- the higher the levels of instruction in RCCP, the lower the levels of aggression in the children who participated;
- children who experienced the highest levels of teaching in RCCP showed steady increases in pro-social behaviour over time;
- the intervention effects of RCCP were consistent across ethnicity and gender;
- the programme was effective for those from poorer as well as for those from better-off families.

(adapted from Aber et al. 2003)

The evaluation by Aber et al. (2003) has been on the whole extremely positive about RCCP, with only a few reservations based on the evidence that the intervention was slightly less successful with high-risk children who were more likely than their peers to have experienced violence in their families and communities.

We can link these findings back to our discussion of risk and protective factors in Chapter 1. If the number of risks to which a child is exposed is high, then bullying behaviour is more likely to emerge. However, if protective factors are present then the risks may be diminished. Schools, parents/carers and the community are in a much stronger position to counteract bullying if they are able to work constructively together in a responsible way for the best interests of the children in their care. As we saw in Chapter 7, parents/carers have a critical part to play by engaging their children regularly in conversation about their experiences and by providing opportunities for the sharing of narratives of everyday life. Authentic communication with trusted adults and peers, whether at school, in the family or in the community, is essential for all children, but especially for those who are experiencing difficulties with peer relationships or aggressive, bullying behaviour.

Listening to the voices of children and young people

In order to address the issue of bullying, parents/carers and teachers must be sensitive to what the children are actually trying to say. This means that they should listen to them and be vigilant to the symptoms of a young person's distress. They should also be responsive to the solutions that young people themselves have to offer. Aynsley-Green (2006), in his role as Children's Commissioner, found through his consultations with children and young people that many were very critical of schools' anti-bullying work on the grounds that it is often superficial and unrelated to their everyday experiences. A major complaint was that teachers are often too busy to facilitate in-depth discussions about bullying and could not always be trusted to handle personal information with tact and sensitivity. These young people asked for more opportunities to be actively involved in designing the school's anti-bullying policies and practices, and in evaluating their effectiveness.

Fortunately, we are in the midst of an evolution in the ways in which children in our culture are perceived. This can be seen through national and international initiatives to enhance the rights of the child, as evidenced by the UN Convention on the Rights of the Child (United Nations 1989) and the UK Children Act legislation and *Every Child Matters* agenda (DfES 2004). These documents acknowledge that children are people, that they should be consulted on decisions that affect them and that they play an active part in the creation of their social worlds. Recent legislation arising from the *Every Child Matters* agenda has placed significantly more emphasis on the active participation of young people in the movement to find solutions to bullying; for example through the widespread development of peer support systems and through greater opportunities for young people to be democratically involved in the school's structures, for example through participation in School Councils. Furthermore, researchers are becoming more aware of child-centred participatory methods (Cowie and Jennifer 2007); Punch 2002; Thomas and O'Kane 2000) which can be adapted and used in a variety of ways, both independently and alongside more traditional methods, to facilitate children's voice so that we can learn more from them about their experiences of bullying, as we see in Box 8.3.

Box 8.2 Listening to children's voices

Jennifer (2007) devised a study that explored children's understanding of the role of the social group context in which school bullying takes place. Her design involved one-to-one interviews with 64 10- to 11-year-olds (47 per cent boys and 53 per cent girls) in Year 6 classes in two London primary schools, combined with a structured classroom activity. The overall aim of this approach was to engage children meaningfully as active participants in the research process in order to explore their understanding of school bullying in their own voices.

Interviews were conducted during lesson time, each lasting approximately 20 minutes, using a semi-structured interview schedule facilitated by the use of a series of 14 A4 pictorial vignettes depicting a hypothetical story of peer bullying. The first 10 vignettes were laid out on a table one by one, in a pre-ordered sequence. Participants were asked a series of questions to explore: how they interpreted the hypothetical story represented in the vignettes; what kind of causes they attributed to bullying; what kind of emotional experiences they attributed to the story's protagonists; what type of coping strategies and emotional release strategies they would choose to address bullying; and what type of ending they would select as the anticipated conclusion to the story. The final stage of the interview required the presentation of the four story out- comes: (1) optimistic end; (2) pessimistic end; (3) peer social support end; and (4) adult social support end. A detailed analysis of six of the participant interviews was conducted using an adapted version of the voice-centred relational method (Brown and Gilligan 1992).

The analysis revealed that participants used moral language in their explana- tions and justifications for school bullying, making rich and insightful com- ments about the complexity of interpersonal relationships and peer processes in relation to involvement in bullying others. Central to the task of exploring these understandings of school bullying was the distinction between two relational perspectives or moral orientations, that is, concerns of care (attachment/detachment, connection/disconnection) and justice (equality, reci- procity, fairness). For example, reading Freema's account reflects support for the presence of two moral voices and, at times, certain phrases can provide evidence for either perspective: 'Um I think that the little one there is worried because she's not really doing much she's just laughing and stuff and I think that she thinks like I'm not going to really get involved in it that much I'm just going to laugh about it and say things to her because she's not that big herself" can either refer to the assistant's lack of involvement and disconnection from the bullying behaviour (care orientation) or to justification for bullying behaviour in terms of limited involvement (justice orientation). Reading for care, Freema's account mainly reflects concern for relationships and the welfare of others within the bully group. Furthermore, reading from a justice perspective, Freema's statements indicate a concern for fairness of treatment in terms of justification for the bullying behaviour.

Jennifer (2007) concludes that the findings have important implications for school-based interventions to address bullying. It may be prudent for interven- tions to focus on fostering emotionally healthy interpersonal relationships that include components such as understanding moral values, understanding emotional states and strategies for building empathy. It is apparent that researchers and practitioners need to take into account the perspectives of children if anti-bullying work is to prove effective.

(adapted from Jennifer 2007)

The ways in which researchers see children has a powerful impact on how they study them, for example, in the methods they choose, the research population under investigation and the interpretation of the data gathered. Traditionally, adults as experts in child development gathered evidence about children 'objectively'. More recently, researchers have seen the need to record children's own perspectives on the grounds that children themselves are the most important source of evidence on how they experience their lives (Aynsley-Green 2006; James and Prout 1997). This is especially relevant to our understanding of how children experience school bullying and how they perceive attempts on the part of adults to prevent or reduce bullying. Such evaluation should, it is hoped, give insights into the impact of a relational approach to resolving the problem and to achieving fair and just schools where young people can learn and work together in a supportive, friendly community. What better lesson can we give them to prepare them for their future lives as citizens?

We end with a message of hope from the contribution that positive psychology offers a message of hope. There are strategies that we can use to enhance the quality of relationships and ways of being towards one another (see Box 8.3).

Box 8.3 The contribution of positive psychology

Research by Seligman and his colleagues (Seligman 2002) indicates that the people who are most satisfied with their lives are those who engage with three critical aspects of life: the cultivation of *positive emotions*, *engagement* and *meaningfulness*, with the greatest weight carried by engagement and meaning. For example, Park et al. (2005) found that strengths of the heart, including zest, gratitude, hope and love, were more strongly associated with life satisfaction among adolescents and adults than the more cognitive characteristics of curiosity and love of learning. They also found that interventions which build happiness bring many more benefits than simply feeling good since happy people are more likely to be healthier and more socially engaged. In the study reported by Seligman et al. (2005) individuals were asked to carry out happiness exercises that aimed to increase awareness of positive strengths within the self and build consistently on those strengths in everyday contexts. Beneficial effects were evident from the beginning and were maintained six months later. In comparison with controls, participants in this study expressed greater happiness in their lives and reported significantly fewer depressive symptoms. The researchers reported that the participants who continued to benefit from the exercises were those who carried on doing them after the required one-week period of the study. In other words, the participants found the interventions empowering and fun, and the more they built on their own strengths, the more they found that there were positive improvements in their lives. The researchers conclude that these positive qualities can be maintained and strengthened through practice so that they become an integral part of a person's way of being in relation to others.

The pioneering work of Seligman and his colleagues is highly relevant to all those who are engaging with the task of achieving fair and just schools where young people can work and learn in harmony in a supportive, friendly community. The ideas that we have proposed in this book essentially concern the quality of relationships. We can all play a part in achieving this vision by beginning the enterprise with those who are closest to us and working outwards from that point. This is a process that each one of us can start to do from today in order to address the issue of bullying. The power is in each person's hands to develop new, creative, empathic and responsible ways of relating to self, to others and to the community with integrity.

Resources

Blatchford, P. and Sharp, S. (eds.) (1994) *Breaktime in the School: Understanding and Changing Playground Behaviour*. London: Routledge.

Blatchford, P. and Sumpner, C. (1998) What do we know about breaktime? Results from a national survey of breaktime and lunchtime in primary and secondary schools, *British Educational Research Journal*, 24: 79–94.

Diego, M. A., Field, T., Hernandez-Reif, M., Shaw, J. A., Rothe, E. M., Castellanos, D. and Mesner, L. (2002) Aggressive adolescents benefit from massage therapy, *Adolescence*, 37: 597–607.

Field, T. (1999) American adolescents touch each other less and are more aggressive toward their peers as compared with French adolescents, *Adolescence*, 34: 753–58.

Field, T., Quintino, O., Hernandez-Reif, M. and Koslovsly, G. (1998) Adolescents with Attention Deficit Hyperactivity Disorder benefit from massage therapy, *Adolescence*, 33: 103–08.

Higgins, C. (1994) How to improve the school ground environment as an anti-bullying strategy, in S. Sharp and P. K. Smith, (1994) *Tackling Bullying in your School: A Practical Handbook for Teachers* (pp. 133–173). London. Routledge.

O'Moore and Minton (2004) *Dealing with Bullying in Schools: A Training Manual for Teachers, Parents and Other Professionals*. London: Sage Publications.

Ross, C. and Ryan, A. (1990) *"Can I stay in today Miss?" Improving the School Playground*. Staffordshire: Trentham Books.

Smith, N. (2002) Transition to the school playground: an intervention programme for nursery children, *Early Years: An International Journal of Research and Development*, 22: 129–46.

Warren, C. and Williams, S. (2007) *Restoring the Balance* 2. Changing Culture Through Restorative Approaches: The Experience of Lewisham Schools. London: Lewisham Council Restorative Approaches to Partnership.

Web sites

A Box Full of Feelings (www.smallwood.co.uk).

Antidote (UK) (www.antidote.org.uk).

Collaborative for Academic, Social, and Emotional Learning (CASEL) (www.casel.org/home/index.php).

Committee for Children (UK) (www.cfchildren.org.uk/).

Department of Health (www.wiredforhealth.gov.uk/).

Incredible Years (US) (www.incredibleyears.com/).

Kids EQ (www.kidseq.com).

Learning through Landscapes (www.teachernet.gov.uk/teachingandlearning/resource materials/outsideclassroom/).

Massage in Schools (www.massageinschools.com).

Miss Dorothy.com (UK) (www.missdorothy.com/).

National Emotional Literacy Interest Group (www.nelig.com).

Nurture groups (www.nurturegroups.org).

Promoting Alternative Thinking Strategies (PATHS) (US) (www.channing-bete.com/positiveyouth/pages/PATHS/PATHS.html).

School of Emotional Literacy (www.schoolofemotional-literacy.com).

Second Step (UK) (www.cfchildren.org.uk/).

Social and Emotional Aspects of Learning (SEAL) (www.teachernet.gov.uk).

UK Observatory for the Promotion of Non-Violence (www.ukobservatory.com/).

20 practical ways to a friendlier playground (www.kidscape.org.uk/assets/downloads/ks20wayssaferplayground.pdf).

References

Aber, J., Lawrence, J. L. and Jones, S. M. (2003) Developmental trajectories toward violence in middle childhood: course, demographic differences, and response to school-based intervention, *Developmental Psychology*, 39(2): 324–48.

Alderson, P. (1999) *Civil Rights in Schools 1996–1998. Final Report to ESRC March 1999* (www.ioe.ac.uk/ssru/reports/Civil_rights_in_schools_end_project_report_1999.pdf: accessed 29 February 2008).

Alderson, P. (2000) School students' views on school councils and daily life at school, *Children and Society*, 14: 121–34.

Alsaker, F. (2004) Bernese programme against victimization in kindergarten and elementary school, in P. K. Smith, D. Pepler and K. Rigby (eds.) *Bullying in Schools: How Successful Can Interventions Be?* (pp. 289–306). Cambridge: Cambridge University Press.

Andershed, H., Kerr, M. and Stattin, H. (2001) Bullying in school and violence on the streets: are the same people involved? *Journal of Scandinavian Studies in Criminology and Crime Prevention,* 2(1): 31–49.

Andrés, S. (2007) Los sistemas de ayuda entre iguales como instrumentos de mejora de la convivencia en la escuela: evaluacion de una intervención, [Peer support systems as instruments for increasing *convivencia* in schools: an evaluation] Unpublished PhD thesis, Universidad Autonoma, Madrid.

Andrés, S. and Barrios, A. (2006) El modelo del alumno ayudante a discusión: la opinión de los alumnos participantes y sus beneficiarios [The model of the student helping in discussion: the opinion of participating students and their beneficiaries], En F. Justicia y J.L. Benítez (coords). Monográfico: Maltrato entre iguales y problemas de convivencia escolar [Bullying and problems in *convivencia* at school], *Revista de Investigación Psicoeducativa*, 4(2): 160–74. Versión impresa y electrónica en español e inglés. (www.investigacion-psicopedagogica.org/revista/articulos/9/espannol/Art_9_129.pdf: accessed 29 February 2008).

Andrés, S., Gaymard, S. and Martín, E. (2005) Evaluación de la competencia social en el contexto escolar: la experiencia de un programa de ayuda entre iguales en adolescentes de secundaria [Evaluation of social competence in the school context: the experience of a programme of peer support in secondary school students], en J. A.

Del Barrio e I. Fajardo (comps.) *Nuevos contextos psicológicos y sociales en educación. Buscando respuestas* [New Psychological and Social Contexts in Education]: (pp. 17–32). Santander: INFAD, Psicoex.

Angelides, P. and Ainscow, M. (2000) Making sense of the role of culture in school improvement, *School Effectiveness and School Improvement*, 11(2): 145–63.

Aronson, E. (1978) *The Jigsaw Classroom*. Beverley Hills, CA: Sage Publications.

Arora, C. M. J. (1996) Defining bullying, *School Psychology International*, 17: 317–29.

Arora, C. M. J. and Thompson, D. A. (1999) 'My Life in School Checklist', in N. Frederickson and R. J. Cameron (series eds.) and S. Sharp (vol. ed.), *Bullying Behaviour in Schools: Psychology in Education Portfolio*. Windsor: NFER NELSON.

Arsenault, L., Walsh, E., Trzesniewski, K., Newcombe, R., Caspi, A. and Moffitt, T. (2006) Bullying victimization uniquely contributes to adjustment problems in young children: a nationally representative cohort study, *Pediatrics*, 118: 130–38.

Askew, S. (1989) Aggressive behaviour in boys: to what extent is it institutionalized? In D. P. Tattum and D. A. Lane (eds.) *Bullying in Schools*, (pp. 59–71). Stoke-on-Trent: Trentham Books.

Aylett, R. S., Louchart, S., Dias, J., Paiva, A. and Vala, M. (2005) FearNot!: an experiment in emergent narrative, in T. Panayiotopoulos, J. Gratch, R. Aylett, D. Ballin, P. Olivier and T. Rist (eds.) *Proceedings of Intelligent Virtual Agents (IVA) 2005 Conference*: (pp. 305–16). Hamburg: Springer.

Aynsley-Green, A. (2006) *Bullying Today*. London: Office of the Children's Commissioner.

Baines, E., Blatchford, P. and Kutnick, P. with Chowne, A., Ota, C. and Berdondini, L. (2008) *Promoting Effective Group Work in the Classroom: Developing Relationships to Enhance Learning and Inclusion*. London: Routledge.

Baldry, A. and Farrington, D. P. (2000) Bullies and delinquents: personal characteristics and parental styles, *Journal of Community and Applied Psychology,* 10: 17–31.

Baldry, A. and Farrington, D. P. (2007) Effectiveness of programs to prevent school bullying, *Victims and Offenders*, 2: 183–204.

Bauman, S. and Del Rio, A. (2006) Preservice teachers' responses to bullying scenarios: comparing physical, verbal and relational bullying, *Journal of Educational Psychology*, 98: 219–31.

Baumeister, R. F., Smart, L. and Boden, J. M. (1996) Relation of threatened egotism to violence and aggression: the dark side of high self-esteem, *Psychological Review*, 103: 5–33.

Beinart, S., Anderson, B., Lee, S. and Utting, D. (2002) *Youth at Risk? A National Survey of Risk Factors, Protective Factors and Problem Behaviour Among Young People in England, Scotland and Wales*. London: Joseph Rowntree Foundation.

Bennathan, M. and Boxall, M. (1998) *The Boxall Profile: A Guide to Effective Intervention in the Education of Pupils with Emotional and Behavioural Difficulties.* Maidstone: AWCEBD.

Bennathan, M. and Boxall, M. (2000) *Effective Intervention in Primary Schools: Nurture Groups* (2nd ed.). London: David Fulton.

Besag, V. (2006) *Understanding Girls' Friendships: Friendships, Fights and Feuds.* Maidenhead: Open University Press.

Bettelheim, B. (1976) *The Uses of Enchantment.* London: Thames & Hudson.

Björkqvist, K. and Österman, K. (1998) *Scales for Research on Interpersonal Relations.* Vasa, Finland: Åbo Akademi University.

Björkqvist, K., Lagerspetz, K. M. J. and Kaukiainen, A. (1992) Do girls manipulate and boys fight? Developmental trends in regard to direct and indirect aggression, *Aggressive Behavior,* 18: 117–27.

Björkqvist, K., Lagerspetz, K. M. J. and Österman, K. (1992) *Direct and Indirect Aggression Scales (DIAS).* Vasa, Finland: Åbo Akademi University.

Blatchford, P. (1998) *Social Life in School: Pupils' Experiences of Breaktime and Recess from 7 to 16 Years.* London: Falmer.

Blatchford, P. and Sumpner, C. (1998) What do we know about breaktime and lunchtime in primary and secondary schools. *British Educational Research Journal,* 24: 79–94.

Blatchford, P. and Sharp, S. (1994) (eds.) *Breaktime and the School: Understanding and Changing Playground Behaviour.* London: Routledge.

Blatchford, P., Baines, E., Rubie-Davies, C., Bassett, P. and Chowne, A. (2006) The effect of a new approach to group work on pupil–pupil and teacher–pupil interactions, *Journal of Educational Psychology,* 98(4): 750–65.

Bliss, T. and Tetley, J. (2006) *Circle Time.* Bristol: Lucky Duck Publishing.

Boal, A. (1999) *Legislative Theatre: Using Performance to Make Politics.* London: Routledge.

Bosacki, S. L., Marini, Z. A. and Dane, A. V. (2006) Voices from the classroom: pictorial and narrative representations of children's bullying, *Journal of Moral Education,* 35(2): 231–45.

Bosacki, S., Dane, A., Marini, Z. and YLC-CURA (2007) Peer relationships and internalizing problems in adolescents: mediating role of self-esteem, *Emotional and Behavioural Difficulties,* 121(4): 261–82.

Bossert, S. T. (1988) Cooperative activities in the classroom, *Review of Research on Education,* 15: 225–52.

Boulton, M. J. (1997) Teachers' views on bullying: definitions, attitudes and ability to cope, *British Journal of Educational Psychology*, 67(2): 223–33.

Boulton, M. and Underwood, K. (1992) Bully/victim problems among middle school children, *British Journal of Educational Psychology*, 62: 73–87.

Bowers, L., Smith, P. K. and Binney, V. (1994) Perceived family relationships of bullies, victims and bully victims in middle childhood, *Journal of Social and Personal Relationships*, 11: 215–32.

Braverman, M. (1999) *Preventing Workplace Violence: A Guide for Employers and Practitioners*. London: Sage Publications.

Bretherton, I. (1990) Open communication and internal working models: their role in attachment relationships, in R. Thompson (ed.) *Nebraska Symposium on Motivation: Vol 36, Socioemotional Development*: (pp. 59–113). Lincoln: University of Nebraska Press.

Brown, L. M. and Gilligan, C. (1992) *Meeting at the Crossroads: Women's Psychology and Girls' Development*. Cambridge, MA: Harvard University Press.

Brun, B., Pedersen, E.W. and Runberg, M. (1993) *Symbols of the soul: therapy and guidance through fairy tales*. London: Jessica Kingsley.

Bruner, J. S. (1986) *Actual Minds, Possible Worlds*. Cambridge, MA: Harvard University Press.

Bruner, J. S. (1990) *Acts of Meaning*. Cambridge, MA: Harvard University Press.

Burns, G. W. (2005) *101 Healing Stories for Kids and Teens*. Hoboken, NJ: John Wiley and Sons, Inc.

Byron, T. (2008) *Safer Children in a Digital World* (www.dcsf.gov.uk/byronreview/).

Cairns, R. B., Cairns, B. D., Neckerman, H. J., Gest, S. D. and Gariépy, J-L. (1988) Social networks and aggressive behavior: peer support or peer rejection? *Developmental Psychology*, 24(6): 815–23.

Cairns, R. B., Cairns, B. D., Neckerman, H. J., Ferguson, L. L. and Gariépy, J.-L. (1989) Growth and aggression: 1. Childhood to early adolescence, *Developmental Psychology*, 25: 320–30.

Cameron, L. and Thorsborne, M. (2000) Restorative justice and school discipline: mutually exclusive? in H. Strang and J. Braithwaite (eds.) *Restorative Justice and Civil Society* (pp. 180–194). Cambridge: Cambridge University Press.

Candela, A. (2005) Students' participation as co-authoring of school institutional practices, *Culture Psychology*, 11: 321–37.

Carlsson-Paige, N. and Levin, D. (1990) *Who's Calling the Shots? How to Respond Effectively to Children's Fascination with War-Play and War Toys?* Philadelphia, PA: New Society Publishers.

Carter, C. (2002). Schools ethos and the construction of masculine identity: do schools create, condone and sustain aggression? *Educational Review*, 54(1): 27–36.

Cartwright, N. (1996) Combatting bullying in school: the role of peer helpers, in H. Cowie and S. Sharp (eds.) *Peer Counselling in Schools: A Time to Listen* (pp. 97–105). London: David Fulton.

Cartwright, N. (2005) Setting up and sustaining peer support systems in a range of schools over 20 years, *Pastoral Care in Education*, 23: 45–50.

Cattanach, A. (1997) *Children's stories in play therapy*. London: Jessica Kingsley.

ChildLine (2005) *ChildLine Annual Review 2005*. London: Author.

Coie, J. D. and Dodge, K. A. (1998) Aggression and anti-social behavior, in W. Damon and N. Eisenberg (eds.) *Handbook of Child Psychology: Vol. 3. Social, Emotional and Personality Development* (5th ed.) (pp. 779–862). New York: John Wiley and Sons, Inc.

Conn, C. (1997) Dramatherapy and schools, *Young Minds Magazine*, 30: 14–17.

Cooper, P. (2004) Learning from nurture groups, *Education 3–13*, October: 59–64.

Cooper, P. (2006) *Promoting Positive Engagement*. Luqa, Malta: Agenda Publications.

Cooper, P. and Tiknaz, Y. (2007) *Nurture Groups in School and at Home*. London: Jessica Kingsley.

Cooper, P. and Whitebread, D. (2007) The effectiveness of nurture groups on student progress: evidence from a national research study, *Emotional and Behavioural Difficulties*, 12(3): 171–90.

Cooper, P., Arnold, R. and Boyd, E. (2001) The effectiveness of nurture groups: preliminary research findings, *British Journal of Special Education*, 28(4): 160–66.

Costabile, A., Genta, M. L.., Zucchini, E., Smith, P. K. and Harper, R. (1992) Attitudes of parents towards war play in young children, *Early Education and Development*, 3: 356–69.

Council of Europe (2004) *European Charter for Democratic Schools without Violence*: Project Report. Strasbourg: Author. (www.coe.int/t/e/integrated_projects/democracy/02_activities/15_European_school_charter

Cowie, H. (1998) Perspective of teachers and pupils on the experience of peer support against bullying, *Educational Research and Evaluation*, 4: 108–25.

Cowie, H. and Sharp, S. (1992) Students themselves tackle the problem of bullying, *Pastoral Care in Education*, 10(4): 31–37.

Cowie, H. and Sharp, S. (1994) How to tackle bullying through the curriculum, in S. Sharp and P. Smith (eds.), *Tackling Bullying in Your School* (pp. 41–65). London: Routledge.

Cowie, H., and Sharp, S. (1996) *Peer Counselling in Schools: A Time to Listen*. London: David Fulton.

Cowie, H. and Wallace, P. (2000) *Peer Support in Action: From Bystanding to Standing By.* London: Sage Publications.

Cowie, H. and Berdondini, L. (2001) Children's reactions to cooperative group work: A strategy for enhancing peer relationships among bullies, victims and bystanders, *Learning and Instruction*, 11: 517–530.

Cowie, H., and Olafsson, R. (2001) The role of peer support in helping the victims of bullying in a school with high levels of aggression, *School Psychology International*, 21: 79–95.

Cowie, H. and Hutson, N. (2005) Peer support: a strategy to help bystanders challenge school bullying, *Pastoral Care in Education*, 23: 40–44.

Cowie, H. and Jennifer, D. (2007) *Managing Violence in Schools: A Whole-School Approach to Best Practice*. London: Sage Publications.

Cowie, H. and Oztug, O. (2008) Pupils' perceptions of safety at school, *Pastoral Care in Education*, 26: 59–67

Cowie, H. and Smith, P. K. (2008) Peer support as a means of improving school safety and reducing bullying and violence, in B. Doll, J. Charvat, J. Baker and G. Stoner (eds.) *Handbook of Prevention Research*. Upper Saddle River, NJ: Lawrence Erlbaum.

Cowie, H., Smith, P. K., Boulton, M. J. and Laver, R. (1994) *Co-operation in the Multi-ethnic Classroom*. London: David Fulton.

Cowie, H., Naylor, P., Talamelli, L., Chauhan, P. and Smith, P. K. (2002) Knowledge, use of and attitudes towards peer support, *Journal of Adolescence*, 25: 453–67.

Cowie, H., Boardman, C., Dawkins, J. and Jennifer, D. (2004) *Emotional Health and Well-being: A Practical Guide for Schools*. London: Sage Publications.

Cowie, H., Hutson, N., Oztug, O. and Myers, C. (2008) The impact of peer support schemes on pupils' perceptions of bullying, aggression and safety at school, *Emotional and Behavioural Difficulties*, 13(1): 63–71.

Cremin, H. (2007) *Peer Mediation*. London: Open University Press.

Crick, N. R. and Dodge, K. A. (1996) Social information-processing mechanisms in reactive and proactive aggression, *Child Development*, 67: 993–1002.

Crick, N. R. and Grotpeter, J. K. (1995) Relational aggression, gender, and social-psychological adjustment, *Child Development*, 66: 710–22.

Cunningham, C., Cunningham, L., Martorelli, V., Tran, A., Young, J. and Zacharias, R. (1998) The effects of primary division, student-mediated conflict resolution programs on playground aggression, *Journal of Child Psychology and Psychiatry*, 39: 653–62.

Daly, A. L. (2006) Bullying, victimisation, self-esteem, and narcissism in adolescents. Unpublished PhD thesis, Flinders University School of Education, South Australia.

Demetriades, A. (1996) Children of the Storm: peer partnership, in H. Cowie and S. Sharp (eds.) *Peer Counselling in Schools: A Time to Listen* (pp. 64–72). London: David Fulton.

Departments for Children Schools and Families (DCSF) (2000) *Bullying: Don't Suffer in Silence: An anti-bullying pack for schools* (second edition) London: HMSO.

Department for Children, Schools and Families (2004) *Every Child Matters: Change for Children in Schools.* (www.publications.teachernet.gov.uk/: accessed 29 February 2008)

Department for Children, Schools and Families (2007a) *Cyber bullying. Safe to Learn: Embedding Anti-bullying Work in Schools.* London: Author.

Department for Children, Schools and Families (2007b) *Safe to Learn: Embedding Anti-bullying Work in Schools.* London: Author.

DeRosier, M. E., Cillessen, A. H. N., Coie, J. D. and Dodge, K A. (1994) Group social context and children's aggressive behavior, *Child Development*, 65: 1068–79.

Derrington, C. (2005) Perceptions of behaviour and patterns of exclusion: gypsy traveller students in English secondary schools, *Journal of Research in Special Educational Needs*, 5(2): 55–61.

Diego, M. A., Field, T., Hernandez-Reif, M., Shaw, J. A., Roethe, E. M., Castellanos, D. and Mesner, L. (2002) Aggresive adolescents benefit from massage therapy. *Adolescence*, 37: 597–607.

Duncan, N. (1998) Sexual bullying in secondary schools, *Pastoral Care in Education*, June: 27–31.

Duncan, N. (2004) It's important to be nice, but it's nicer to be important: girls, popularity and sexual competition, *Sex Education*, 4(2): 137–52.

Duncan, N. (2006) Homophobia, misogyny and school bullying. Paper presented at the British Educational Research Association Annual Conference, University of Warwick, 6–9 September.

Dunn, J. (2004) *Children's Friendships: The Beginnings of Intimacy.* Oxford: Blackwell Publishing.

Dunn, J., Brown, J. and Beardsall, L. (1991) Family talk about feeling states and children's later understanding of others' emotions, *Developmental Psychology*, 27: 448–55.

Dusenbury, L., Falco, M., Lake, A., Brannigan, R. and Bosworth, K. (1997) Nine critical elements of promising violence prevention programs, *Journal of School Health*, 67(10): 409–14.

Egan, S. K. and Perry, D. G. (1998) Does low self-regard invite victimization? *Developmental Psychology*, 34: 299–309.

Elias, M. J. and Clabby, J. F. (1992) *Building Social Problem Solving Skills: Guidelines From a School Based Program.* New York: Institute for Rational Living.

Ellis, A. A. and Shute, R. (2007) Teacher responses to bullying in relation to moral orientation and seriousness of bullying, *British Journal of Educational Psychology*, 77: 649–63.

Engel, S. (1995) *The Stories Children Tell*. New York: W. H. Freeman and Company.

Engström, K., Hallqvist, J., Möller, J. and Laflamme, L. (2005) Do episodes of peer victimization trigger physical injury? A case-cross-over study of Swedish school children, *Scandinavian Journal of Public Health*, 33(19): 19–25.

Escobar, M. (2008) *Aceptación sociométrica e inadaptación socioemocional en la infancia: modelos predictivos* [Peer acceptance and socioemotional maladjustment in children: predictive models]. Unpublished PhD thesis, University of Malaga.

Eslea, M. and Smith, P. K. (2000) Pupil and parent attitudes towards bullying in primary schools, *European Journal of Psychology of Education*, 15(2): 207–19.

Farrington, D. P. (1993) Understanding and preventing bullying, *Crime and Justice*, 17: 381–458.

Farrington, D. P. (1995) The development of offending and antisocial behaviour from childhood: key findings from the Cambridge Study in Delinquent Development, *Journal of Child Psychology and Psychiatry*, 360(6): 929–64.

Farrington, D. P. (1996) *Understanding and Preventing Youth Crime*. York: York Publishing Services for the Joseph Rowntree Foundation.

Fernandez, I., Villaoslada, E. and Funes, S. (2002) *Conflicto en el Centro Escolar [Conflict in Schools]*. Madrid: Catarata.

Ferrazzuolo, S. (2004) *Relationships among patterns of family interaction, participant roles in bullying and case study profiles*. Unpublished MPhil thesis, School of Psychology, Roehampton University.

Field, T. (1999) American adolescents touch each other less and are more aggressive towards their peers as compared with French adolescents. *Adolescence*, 34: 753–758.

Fonagy, P., Twenlow, S., Vernberg, E., Sacco, F. and Little, T. (2005) Creating a peaceful school learning environment: the impact of an anti-bullying environment: an educational attainment in elementary schools, *Medical Science Monitor*, 11(7): 317–25.

France, A. and Utting, D. (2005) The paradigm of 'Risk and Protection-focused Prevention' and its impact on services for children and families, *Children and Society*, 19: 77–90.

Freeman, J., Epson, D., and Lobovits, D. (1997). *Playful approaches to serious problems*. New York: W. W. Norton.

Frey, K. S., Nolen, S. B., Van Schoiack Edstrom, L. and Hirschstein, M. K. (2005) Effects of a school-based social-emotional competence program: linking children's goals, attributions, and behavior, *Applied Developmental Psychology*, 26: 171–200.

Frosh, S., Phoenix, A. and Pattman, R. (2002) *Young Masculinities*. Basingstoke: Palgrave.

Galloway, D. and Roland, E. (2004) Is the direct approach to reducing bullying always the best?, in P. K. Smith, D. Pepler and K. Rigby (eds.) *Bullying in Schools: How Successful Can Interventions Be?* (pp. 37–53). Cambridge: Cambridge University Press.

Galvin, P. (2006) The role of a school audit in preventing and minimizing violence, in C. Gittins (ed.), *Violence Reduction in Schools: How to Make a Difference*: (pp. 23–38). Strasbourg: Council of Europe Publishing.

Gersie, A. (1997) *Reflections on Therapeutic Storymaking*. London: Jessica Kingsley.

Gittins (ed.) (2006) *Violence Reduction in Schools – How to make a Difference*. 23–38. Strasbourg: Council of Europe Publishing.

Glover, D., Gough, G. and Johnson, M. (2000) Bullying in 25 secondary schools: incidence, impact and intervention, *Educational Research,* 42(2): 141–56.

Goleman, E. (1995) *Emotional Intelligence: Why it Can Matter More than IQ.* New York: Bantam.

Greenberg, M. T., Kusche, C. A., Cooke, E. T. and Quamma, J. P. (1995) Promoting emotional competence in school aged children: the effects of the PATHS curriculum, *Development and Psychopathology,* 7: 7–16.

Greene, S. and Hogan, S. (eds.) (2005) *Researching Children's Experience*. London: Sage Publications.

Griffin, R. S. and Gross, A. M. (2004) Childhood bullying: current empirical findings and future directions for research, *Aggression and Violent Behavior,* 9: 379–400.

Grossman, C. D., Neckerman, H. J., Koepsell, T. D., Liu, P. Y., Ashere, K., Beland, K., Frey, K. and Rivara, F. P. (1997). Effectiveness of a violence prevention curriculum among children in elementary school: a randomized controlled trial, *Journal of the American Medical Association,* 277: 1605–11.

Guerin, S. and Hennessy, E. (2002) Pupils' definitions of bullying, *European Journal of Psychology of Education,* 17(3): 249–61.

Guggenbhul, A. (1991) Tales and fiction, *School Psychology International,* 12: 7–16.

Gunter, B. and McAleer, J. (1997) *Children and Television: The One-eyed Monster* (2nd ed.). London: Routledge.

Hall, L., Woods, S., Dautenhahn, D., Sobral, A., Paiva, A., Wolke, D. and Newall, L. (2006) Designing empathic agents: adults versus kids. Paper presented at the Intelligent Tutoring Systems 7th International Conference, ITS, 2004, Maceio, Brazil.

Hanewinkel, R. (2004) Prevention of bullying in German schools: an evaluation of an anti-bullying approach, in P. K. Smith, D. Pepler and K. Rigby (eds.) *Bullying in Schools: How Successful Can Interventions Be?* (pp. 81–98). Cambridge: Cambridge University Press.

Harachi, T. W., Catalano, R. F. and Hawkins, J. D. (1999) Canada, in P. K. Smith, Y. Morita, J. Junger-Tas, D. Olweus, R. Catalano and P. Slee (eds.) *The Nature of School Bullying*: (pp. 296–306). London: Routledge.

Harris, P. L. (2000) Understanding emotion, in M. Lewis and J. Haviland-Jones (eds.) *Handbook of Emotions*: (pp. 281–92). New York: Guilford Press.

Hartup, W. W. (1996) The company they keep: friendships and their developmental significance, *Child Development*, 67: 1–13.

Hawker, D. S. J. and Boulton, M. J. (2000) Twenty years' research on peer victimization and psychosocial maladjustment: a meta-analytic review of cross-sectional studies, *Journal of Child Psychology and Psychiatry*, 41(4): 441–55.

Hazler, R. J. (1996a) *Breaking the Cycle of Violence: Interventions for Bullying and Victimization*. Washington, DC: Accelerated Development/Taylor & Francis.

Hazler, R. J. (1996b) Bystanders: an overlooked factor in peer on peer abuse, *Journal for the Professional Counselor*, 11(2): 11–21.

Hazler, R.J., Miller, D.L., Carney, J.L. and Green, S. (2001) Adult recognition of school bullying situations, *Educational Research*, 43: 133–46.

Higgins, C. (1994) How to improve the school ground environment as an anti-bullying strategy. In S. Sharp and P. K. Smith (1994) *Tackling bullying in your school: a practical handbook for teachers*. London: Routledge.

Holmes, S. R. and Brandenburg-Ayres, S. J. (1998) Bullying behaviour in school: a predictor of later gang involvement, *Journal of Gang Research*, 5(2): 1–6.

Hopkins, B. (2004) *Just Schools: A Whole-school Approach to Restorative Justice*. London: Jessica Kingsley (www.coe.int/t/e/integrated_projects/democracy/02_activities/15_european_school_charter/04_Charter.asp#TopOfPage).

Hurst, T. (2001) An evaluation of an anti-bullying peer support programme in a (British) secondary school, *Pastoral Care in Education*, 19: 10–14.

Hutson, N. and Cowie, H. (2007) Setting up an e-mail peer support scheme, *Pastoral Care in Education*, 25: 12–16.

James, A. and Prout, A. (1997) *Constructing and Reconstructing Childhood: Contemporary Issues in the Sociological Study of Childhood*. London: Falmer Press.

Jennifer, D. (2000) Bullying at work: the role of work environment quality, in M. Sheehan, S. Ramsey and J. Patrick (eds.), *Transcending Boundaries: Integrating People, Processes and Systems*: (pp. 194–200). Brisbane, Australia: Griffith University.

Jennifer, D. (2007) Understanding bullying in primary school: listening to children's voices, Unpublished PhD thesis, University of Surrey.

Jennifer, D. and Shaughnessy, J. (2005) Promoting non-violence in schools: the role of cultural, organizational and managerial factors, *Educational and Child Psychology*, 22(3): 58–66.

Jennifer, H., Cowie, H. and Bray, D. (2006) 'Bully Dance': animation as a tool for conflict resolution, *Pastoral Care in Education*, March: 27–32 .

Johnson, D. W. and Johnson, R. T. (1987) *Learning Together and Alone*. Englewood Cliffs, NJ: Prentice Hall.

Johnson, D. W., Johnson, R. T. and Holubec, E. J. (1994a) *Cooperative Learning in the Classroom*. Alexandria, VA: Association for Supervision and Curriculum Development.

Johnson, D. W., Johnson, R. T. and Holubec, E. J. (1994b) *The New Circles of Learning: Co-operation in the Classroom and School*. Alexandria, VA: Association for Supervision and Curriculum Development.

Kagan, S. (1986) *Beyond Language: Social and Cultural Factors in Schooling Language Minority Students*. California: Evaluation, Dissemination and Assessment Center, California State University.

Kaltiala-Heino, R., Rimpela, M., Marttunen, M., Rimpela, A. and Rantenan, P. (1999) Bullying, depression, and suicidal ideation in Finnish adolescents: school survey, *British Medical Journal*, 319: 348–51.

Kaltiala-Heino, R., Rimpela, M., Rantanen, P. and Rimpela, A. (2000) Bullying at school: an indicator of adolescents at risk for mental disorders, *Journal of Adolescence*, 23, 661–74.

Kaukiainen, A., Salmivalli, C., Largerspetz, K., Taminen, M., Vaura, H., and Poskiparta, E. (2002) Learning difficulties, social intelligence, and self-concept: connections to bully-victim problems, *Scandinavian Journal of Psychology*, 43, 269–78.

Kumpulainen, K. and Räsänen, E. (2000) Children involved in bullying at elementary school age: their psychiatric symptoms and deviance in adolescence: An epidemiological sample, *Child Abuse and Neglect*, 12, 24, 1567–77.

Laflamme, K., Engström, K., Möller, J. and Hallqvist, J. (2002) Bullying in the school environment: an injury risk factor? *Acta Psychiatrica Scandinavica*, 106(412): 20–25.

Lagerspetz, K. M. J., Björkqvist, K., Berts, M. and King, E. (1982) Group aggression among school children in three schools, *Scandinavian Journal of Psychology*, 23: 45–52.

LaGreca, A. and Harrison, H. (2005) Adolescent peer relations, friendships and romantic relationships: do they predict social anxiety and depression? *Journal of Clinical Child and Adolescent Psychology*, 34: 49–61.

Lahelma, E. (2004) Tolerance and understanding? Students and teachers reflect on differences at school, *Educational Research and Evaluation*, 10(1): 3–19.

Lane-Garon, P. and Richardson, T. (2003) Mediator mentors: improving school climate – nurturing student disposition, *Conflict Resolution Quarterly*, 21: 47–69.

Leather, P., Lawrence, C., Beale, D., Cox, T. and Brady, C. (1999) Managing work-related violence: the way forward, in P. Leather, C. Brady, C. Lawrence, D. Beale and T. Cox (Eds.), *Work-related Violence Assessment and Intervention*: (pp. 84–88) London: Routledge.

Li, Q. (2006) Cyber bullying in schools: a research of gender differences, *School Psychology International*, 27: 157–70.

Limber, S. P., Nation, M., Allison, J.T., Melton, G. B. and Flerx, V. (2004) Implementation of the Olweus Bullying Prevention Programme in the Southeastern United States. In P. K. Smith, D. Pepler and K. Rigby (eds.) *Bullying in Schools: How Successful Can Interventions Be?* (pp. 55–80). Cambridge: Cambridge University Press.

Livingston, S. and Bober, M. (2005) *UK Children Go Online: Final Report of Key Project Findings*. London: London School of Economics and Political Science (www.children-go-online.net).

Lloyd, G. and Stead, J. (2001) 'The boys and girls not calling me names and the teachers to believe me': Name-calling and the experiences of travellers in school, *Children and Society*, 15: 361–74.

Louchart, S., Aylett, R., Dias, J. and Paiva, A. (2005) Unscripted narrative for affectively driven characters. Proceedings of the International Conference on Virtual Storytelling (AIIDE) 2005: 81–86.

Lucas, T. (2004) Homophobia: an issue for every pupil? *Education Review, 17*(2). (www.lgbthistorymonth.org.uk/aboutus/schools.htm).

Ma, X. (2004) Who are the victims?, in C. Sanders and G. D. Phye (eds.) *Bullying: Implications for the Classroom*: (pp. 20–31). San Diego, CA: Elsevier Press.

Maines, B. and Robinson, G. (1997) *Crying for Help: The No Blame Approach to Bullying*. Bristol: Lucky Duck Publishing.

Malley, J., Beck, M. and Adorno, D. (2001) Building an ecology for non-violence in schools, *International Journal of Reality Therapy*, XX1(1): 22–26.

Marini, Z. A., Dane, A., Bosacki, S. and YLC-CURA (2006) Direct and indirect bully-victims: differential psychosocial risk factors associated with adolescents involved in bullying and victimization, *Aggressive Behavior*, 32: 551–69.

Martlew, M. and Hodson, J. (1991) Children with mild learning difficulties in an integrated and in a special needs school: comparisons of behaviour, teasing and teachers' attitudes, *British Journal of Educational Psychology*, 61: 355–72.

Mavroveli, S., Petrides, K. V., Rieffe, C. and Bakker, F. (2007) Trait emotional intelligence, psychological well-being, and peer-rated social competence in adolescence, *British Journal of Developmental Psychology*, 25: 263–75.

McKenna, K. Y. A. and Bargh, J. A. (2000) Plan 9 from cyberspace: the implications of the internet for personality and social psychology, *Personality and Social Psychology Review*, 4(1): 57–75.

Mencap (2007) *Don't Stick It Stop It!* London: Author.

Menesini, E., Codecasa, E., Benelli, B. and Cowie, H. (2003) Enhancing children's responsibility to take action against bullying: evaluation of a befriending intervention in Italian middle schools, *Aggressive Behavior*, 29: 1–14.

Menesini, E., Sanchez, V., Fonzi, A., Ortega, R., Costabile, A. and Lo Feudo, G. (2003) Moral emotions and bullying: a cross-national comparison of differences between bullies, victims and outsiders, *Aggressive Behavior,* 29: 515–30.

Mental Health Foundation (2002) Peer support: someone to turn to. An evaluation report of the Mental Health Foundation Peer Support Programme. London and Glasgow, Mental Health Foundation.

Meuret, D. and Morlaix, S. (2003) Conditions of success of a school's self-evaluation: some lessons of an European experience, *School Effectiveness and School Improvement,* 14(1): 53–71.

Mooij, T. (1998) Pupil-class determinants of aggressive and victim behavior in pupils, *British Journal of Educational Psychology,* 68: 373–85.

Mooney, A., Creeser, R. and Blatchford, P. (1991) Children's views on teasing and fighting in junior schools, *Educational Research,* 33(2): 103–12.

Moran, S., Smith, P. K., Thompson, D. and Whitney, I. (1993) Ethnic differences in experiences of bullying: Asian and White children, *British Journal of Educational Psychology,* 63(3): 431–40.

Morrison, B. (2003) Regulating safe school communities: being responsive and restorative, *Journal of Educational Administration,* 41(6): 689–704.

Morrison, B. (2007) *Restoring Safe School Communities: A Whole School Response to Bullying, Violence and Alienation.* Sydney: The Federation Press.

Morrison, L. and Matthews, B. (2006) How pupils can be helped to develop socially and emotionally in science lessons, *Pastoral Care in Education,* 24(1): 10–19.

Murray-Close, D., Crick, N. R. and Galotti, K. M. (2006) Children's moral reasoning regarding physical and relational aggression, *Social Development,* 15(3): 345–72.

Nabuzoka, D. and Smith, P. K. (1993) Sociometric status and social behaviour of children with and without learning difficulties, *Journal of Child Psychology,* 34(8): 1435–48.

Nangle, D., Erdley, C., Newman, J., Mason, C. and Carpenter, E. (2003) Popularity, friendship quantity, and friendship quality: interactive influences on children's loneliness and depression, *Journal of Clinical Child and Adolescent Psychology,* 32: 546–55.

Naylor, P. and Cowie, H. (1999) The effectiveness of peer support systems in challenging school bullying: the perspectives and experiences of teachers and pupils, *Journal of Adolescence,* 22: 467–79.

Naylor, P., Cowie, H., Cossin, F., de Bettencourt, R. and Lemme, F. (2006) Teachers' and pupils' definitions of bullying, *British Journal of Educational Psychology,* 76: 553–76.

Newson, E. (1994) Video violence and the protection of children, *The Psychologist,* 7: 272–74.

Nicolaides, S., Toda, Y. and Smith, P.K. (2002) Knowledge and attitudes about school bullying in trainee teachers, *British Journal of Educational Psychology,* 72: 105–18.

Noret, N. and Rivers, I. (2006) The prevalence of bullying by text message and email: results of a four year study. Poster session presented at the BPS Annual Conference, Cardiff, UK, March.

Norwich, B. and Kelly, N. (2004) Pupils' views on inclusion: moderate learning difficulties and bullying in mainstream and special schools, *British Educational Research Journal,* 30(1): 43–65.

O'Connell, P., Pepler, D. and Craig, W. (1999) Peer involvement in bullying: insights and challenges for intervention, *Journal of Adolescence,* 22: 437–52.

Office of the Children's Commissioner (2006) *Bullying Today: A Report by the Office of the Children's Commissioner, with Recommendations and Links to Practitioner Tools.* London: Author.

Olweus, D. (1980) Familial and temperamental determinants of aggressive behaviour in adolescent boys: a causal analysis, *Developmental Psychology,* 16(6): 644–60.

Olweus, D. (1991) Bully/victim problems among schoolchildren: basic facts and effects of a school based intervention program, in D. J. Pepler and K. H. Rubin (eds.), *The Development and Treatment of Childhood Aggression*: (pp. 411–48). Hillsdale, NJ: Lawrence Erlbaum.

Olweus, D. (1978) *Aggression in Schools: Bullies and Whipping Boys.* Washington, DC: Hemisphere.

Olweus, D. (1993) *Bullying: What We Know and What We Can Do.* Oxford: Basil Blackwell.

Olweus, D. (1994) Annotation: bullying at school: basic facts and effects of a school based intervention program, *Journal of Child Psychology and Psychiatry,* 35: 1171–90.

Olweus, D. (1996) *The Revised Olweus Bully/Victim Questionnaire.* Bergen, Norway: Research Center for Health Promotion (HEMIL Center), University of Bergen.

Olweus, D. (1997) Bully/victim problems in school: knowledge base and an effective intervention program, *The Irish Journal of Psychology,* 18(2): 170–90.

Olweus, D. (1999) Sweden, in P. K. Smith, Y. Morita, J. Junger-Tas, D. Olweus, R. Catalano and P. Slee (eds.), *The Nature of School Bullying*: (pp. 7–27). London: Routledge.

Olweus, D. (2004) The Olweus Bullying Prevention Programme: design and implementation issues and a new national initiative in Norway, in P. K. Smith, D. Pepler and K. Rigby (eds.) *Bullying in Schools: How Successful Can Interventions Be?* (pp. 13–36). Cambridge: Cambridge University Press.

O'Moore, M. (2006) *Silent Witnesses.* Ireland: Trinity College Dublin Anti-Bullying Research and Resource Centre (www.abc.tcd.ie).

O'Moore, A. M. and Minton, S. J. (2001) Tackling violence in schools: a report from Ireland, in P. K. Smith (ed.) *Violence in Schools: The Response in Europe* (pp. 282–97). London: RoutledgeFalmer.

O'Moore, A. M. and Minton, S. J. (2004) Ireland: the Donegal Primary Schools' anti-bullying project, in P. K. Smith, D. Pepler and K. Rigby (eds.) *Bullying in Schools: How Successful Can Interventions Be?* (pp. 275–87). Cambridge: Cambridge University Press.

O'Moore, A. M., Kirkham, C. and Smith, M. (1997) Bullying behaviour in Irish schools: a nationwide study, *Irish Journal of Psychology*, 18(2): 141–69.

O'Moore, M. (2000) Critical issues for teacher training to counter bullying and victimization in Ireland, *Aggressive Behavior*, 26: 99–111.

O'Moore, M. and Minton, S. J. (2004) *Dealing with Bullying in Schools: A Training Manual for Teachers, Parents and Other Professionals*. London: Sage Publishers.

Opie, I. and Opie, P. (1969) *Children's Games in Street and Playground*. Oxford: Clarendon Press.

Oppenheim, D., Nir, A., Warren, S. and Emde, R. (1997) Emotion regulation in other-child narrative co-construction: associations with children's narratives and adaptation, *Developmental Psychology*, 33(2): 284–94.

Ortega, R. and Lera, M. J. (2000) The Seville anti-bullying in school project, *Aggressive Behavior*, 26: 113–23.

Ortega, R., Fox, T. and del Rey, R. (2003) Working in cooperative groups to destabilize the school's violence roles. Paper presented at the *Xth Biennial Conference EARLI*, Padova, 26–30 August.

Ortega, R., del Rey, R. and Mora-Merchán, J. A. (2004) SAVE model: an anti-bullying intervention in Spain, in P. K. Smith, D. Pepler and K. Rigby (eds.) *Bullying in Schools: How Successful Can Interventions Be?* (pp. 167–85). Cambridge: Cambridge University Press.

Osborn, R. (2007) Bullying as a relationship problem. (www.rtime.info/initatives.htm).

Owens, L., Shute, R. and Slee, P. (2000) "Guess what I just heard!" indirect aggression among teenage girls in Australia, *Aggressive Behavior*, 26: 67–83.

Park, N., Peterson, C. and Seligman, M. E. P. (2005) Character strengths in forty nations and fifty states. Unpublished manuscript, University of Rhode Island.

Patchin, J. W. and Hinduja, S. (2006) Bullies move beyond the schoolyard: a preliminary look at cyber bullying, *Youth Violence and Juvenile Justice*, 4: 148–69.

Paterson, H., Bentley, M., Singer, F. and O'Hear, P. (1996) The anti-bullying campaign (ABC) at Acland Burgley, in H. Cowie and S. Sharp (eds.) *Peer Counselling in Schools: A Time to Listen*: (pp. 114–23). London: David Fulton.

Pellegrini, A. D., Bartini, M. and Brooks, F. (1999) School bullies, victims, and aggressive victims: factors relating to group affiliation and victimization in early adolescence, *Journal of Educational Psychology,* 91(2): 216–24.

Pepler, D., Craig, W. M. and O'Connell, P. (1999) Understanding bullying from a dynamic systems perspective, in A. Slater and D. Muir (eds.), *The Blackwell Reader in Developmental Psychology*: (440–51). Oxford: Blackwell.

Pepler, D., Craig, W. M., O'Connell, P., Atlas, R. and Charach, A. (2004) Making a difference in bullying: evaluation of a systemic school-based programme in Canada. In P. K. Smith, D. Pepler and K. Rigby (eds.) *Bullying in Schools: How Successful Can Interventions Be?* (pp. 125–40). Cambridge: Cambridge University Press.

Pepler, D., Smith, P. K. and Rigby, K. (2004) Looking back and looking forward: implications for making interventions work effectively, in P. K. Smith, D. Pepler and K. Rigby (eds.) *Bullying in Schools: How Successful Can Interventions Be?* (pp. 307–24). Cambridge: Cambridge University Press.

Percy-Smith, B. and Matthews, H. (2001) Tyrannical spaces: young people, bullying and urban neighbourhoods, *Local Environment*, 6(1): 49–63.

Perlman, J. (2000) Bully Dance (La Danse des Brutes). Canada: National Film Board of Canada (www.bullfrogfilms.com/catalog/bully.html).

Perry, D. G., Kusel, S. J. and Perry, L. C. (1988) Victims of peer agression, *Developmental Psychology*. 24(6), 807–814.

Petrides, K. V., Chamorro-Premuzic, T., Frederickson, N. and Furnham, A. (2005) Explaining individual differences in scholastic behaviour and achievement, *British Journal of Educational Psychology*, 75: 239–55.

Petrides, K. V. Sangareau, Y. Furnham, A. Frederickson, N. (2006) Trait emotional intelligence and children's peer relations at school, *Social Development*, 3: 537–47.

Pikas, A. (2002) New developments in the shared concern method, *School Psychology International*, 23(3): 307–26.

Protherough, R. (1983) *Developing Response to Fiction*. Milton Keynes: Open University Press.

Punch, S. (2002) Research with children: the same or different from research with adults? *Childhood*, 9(3): 321–41.

Raskin, R. and Novacek, J. (1989) An MMPI description of the narcissistic personality. *Journal of Personality Assessment, 53*, 66–80.

Ray, V. and Gregory, R. (2001) School experiences of the children of lesbian and gay parents, *Family Matters*, 59: 28–34.

Regnolds, S. and Kearney, M. (2007) Nurture groups: the answer to everything? Paper presented at the British Psychological Society Division of Educational and Child Psychology Conference, Glasgow, February.

Rigby, K. (2003) Consequences of bullying in schools, *Canadian Journal of Psychiatry*, 48(9): 583–90.

Riley, P. L. and Segal, E. C. (2002) Preparing to evaluate a school violence prevention program: Students against violence everywhere, *Journal of School Violence*, 1(2): 73–86.

Rivers, I. (2000) Social exclusion, absenteeism and sexual minority youth. *Support for Learning*, 15(1): 13–8.

Rivers, I. and Cowie, H. (2006) Bullying and homophobia in UK schools: a perspective on factors affecting resilience and recovery, *Journal of Gay and Lesbian Issues in Education*, 3(4), 11–43.

Robinson, G. and Maines, B. (2007) *Bullying*. London: Sage Publications.

Roffey, S. (2000) Addressing bullying in schools: organisational factors from policy to practice, *Educational and Child Psychology*, 17(1): 6–19.

Roland, E. (2000) Bullying in schools: three national innovations in Norwegian schools in 15 years, *Aggressive Behavior*, 26(1): 135–43.

Roland. E. and Munthe, E. (1997) The 1996 Norwegian program for preventing and managing bullying in schools, *Irish Journal of Psychology*, 18: 233–47.

Rustin, M. and Rustin, M. (1987) *Narratives of Love and Loss*. London: Verso.

Salmivalli, C. (1999) Participant role approach to bullying: implications for interventions, *Journal of Adolescence*, 22: 453–59.

Salmivalli, C. (2001a) Group view on victimization: empirical findings and their implications, in J. Juvonen and S. Graham (eds.) *Peer Harassment in School: The Plight of the Vulnerable and Victimized:* (pp. 398–419). New York, Guilford Press.

Salmivalli, C. (2001b) Peer-led intervention campaign against school bullying: who considered it useful, who benefited? *Educational Research*, 43: 263–78.

Salmivalli, C., Huttunen, A. and Lagerspetz, K. M. J. (1997) Peer networks and bullying in school, *Scandinavian Journal of Psychology*, 38: 305–12.

Salmivalli, C., Lagerspetz, K., Björkqvist, K., Österman, K. and Kaukiainen, A. (1996) Bullying as a group process: participant roles and their relations to social status within the group, *Aggressive Behavior*, 22: 1–15.

Salmivalli, C., Lappalainen, M. and Lagerspetz, K. M. J. (1998) Stability and change of behavior in connection with bullying in schools: a two-year follow-up. *Aggressive Behavior, 24*: 205–18.

Salmivalli, C., Kaukiainen, A., Kaistaniemi, L. and Lagerspetz, K. M. J. (1999) Self-evaluated self-esteem, peer-evaluated self-esteem, and defensive egotism as predictors of adolescents' participation in bullying situations, *Personality and Social Psychology Bulletin, 25*: 1268–78.

Salmivalli, C. and Nieminen, E. (2002) Proactive and reactive aggression among school bullies, victims, and bully-victims, *Aggressive Behavior,* 28: 30–44.

Salovey, P. and Mayer, J. D. (1990) Emotional intelligence, *Imagination, Cognition and Personality*, 9: 185–211.

Scarlett, G. and Wolf, D. (1979) When it's only make-believe: the construction of a boundary between fantasy and reality in story-telling, in E. Winner and H. Gardner (eds.) *Fact, Fiction and Fantasy in Childhood*: (pp. 29–40) San Francisco: Jossey-Bass.

Seligman, M. (2002) *Authentic Happiness*. New York: Free Press.

Seligman, M. E. P., Steen, T. A., Park, N. and Peterson, C. (2005) Positive psychology progress: empirical validation of interventions, *American Psychologist*, 60(5): 410–21.

Sharan, S. (1985) Cooperative learning and the multi-ethnic classroom, in R. Slavin, S. Sharan, R. Hertz-Lazarowitz, N. Webb and R. Schmuck (eds.) *Learning to Cooperate: Cooperating to Learn*: (pp. 1–4). New York: Plenum Press.

Sharp, A., Sellors, A. and Cowie, H. (1994) Time to listen: setting up a peer counselling service to help tackle the problem of bullying in schools, *Pastoral Care in Education*, 12(2): 3–6.

Sharp, S. and Cowie, H. (1998) *Counselling and Supporting Children in Distress*. London: Sage Publications.

Shaughnessy, J. and Jennifer, D. (2004) *Report to Birmingham LEA: Evaluation of Checkpoints for Schools*. Roehampton University, Froebel College.

Shaughnessy, J. and Jennifer, D. (2007) *Mapping the Statistics: Moving Towards a Shared Understanding of the Scale and Nature of Bullying and Violence in Schools Across Birmingham LEA*. Roehampton University, Froebel College.

Skiba, R., Reynolds, C. R., Graham, S., Sheras, P., Conoley, J. C. and Garcia-Vasquez, E. (2006) *Are Zero Tolerance Policies Effective in the Schools? An Evidentiary Review and Recommendations*. A Report by the American Psychological Association Zero Tolerance Taskforce (www.apa.org/ed/cpse/zttfreport.pdf).

Slavin, R. (1987) Developmental and motivational perspectives on cooperative learning, *Child Development*, 58: 1161–167.

Slavin, R. E. (1995) *Cooperative Learning: Theory, Research, and Practice* (2nd ed.). Massachusetts: Allyn and Bacon.

Slee, P. T. (1995) Bullying: health concerns of Australian secondary school students, *International Journal of Adolescence and Youth*, 5: 215–24.

Slee, P. T. (2003) Violence in schools: an Australian commentary, in P. K. Smith (ed.) *Violence in Schools: The Response in Europe*: (pp. 301–16). London: RoutledgeFalmer.

Smith, P. K. (2004) Bullying: recent developments, *Child and Adolescent Mental Health*, 9(3): 98–103.

Smith, P. K. and Levan, S. (1995) Perceptions and experiences of bullying in younger pupils, *British Journal of Educational Psychology,* 65(4): 489–500.

Smith, P. K. and Morita, Y. (1999) Introduction, in P. K. Smith, Y. Morita, J. Junger-Tas, D. Olweus, R. Catalano and P. Slee (eds.), *The Nature of School Bullying*: (pp. 1–4). London: Routledge.

Smith, P. K. and Sharp, S. (1994) *School Bullying.* London: Routledge.

Smith, P.K. and Watson, D. (2004) Evaluation of the CHIPS (ChildLine in Partnership with Schools) programme. Research report RR570, DfES publications.

Smith, P. K., Cowie, H. and Berdondini, L. (1994) Co-operation and bullying, in P. Kutnick and C. Rogers (eds.) *Groups in Schools:* 195–210. London: Cassell.

Smith, P. K., Madsen, K. C. and Moody, J. C. (1999) What causes the age decline in reports of being bullied at school? Towards a developmental analysis of risks of being bullied, *Educational Research,* 14(3): 267–85.

Smith, P. K., Cowie, H., Olafsson, R. F. and Liefooghe, A. P. D. (2002) Definitions of bullying: a comparison of terms used, and age and gender differences, in a fourteen-country international comparison, *Child Development,* 73: 1119–133.

Smith, P. K., Pepler, D. and Rigby, K. (2004) (eds.) *Bullying in Schools: How Successful Can Schools Be?* Cambridge: Cambridge University Press.

Smith, P. K., Talamelli, L., Cowie, H., Naylor, P. and Chauhan, P. (2004) Profiles of non-victims, escaped victims, continuing victims and new victims in school bullying, *British Journal of Educational Psychology,* 24: 565–81.

Spears, B., Heading, D., McVeity, M., Webber, J., Harris, P. and Ormond, B. (2007) Yards ahead for boys: a lunch-time intervention to reduce aggression and bullying in a South Australian primary school. Paper presented at the *Department of Education and Children's Services, School of Education, University of South Australia, Adelaide, Australia.*

Stacey, H. and Robinson, P. (2003) *Let's Mediate: A Teacher's Guide to Peer Support and Conflict Resolution Skills for All Ages.* Bristol: Lucky Duck Publications.

Steiner, M. (1993) *Learning from Experience: World Studies in the Primary Curriculum.* Stoke-on-Trent: Trentham Books.

Stephenson, P. and Smith, D. (1989) Bullying in the junior school, in D. P. Tattum and D. A. Lane (eds.) *Bullying in Schools*: (pp. 45–57). Stoke-on-Trent: Trentham Books.

Sullivan, K. (2000) *The Anti-bullying Handbook.* Oxford: Oxford University Press.

Sutton, J. and Smith, P. K. (1999) Bullying as a group process: an adaptation of the participant role approach, *Aggressive Behavior,* 25: 97–111.

Sutton, J., Smith, P. K. and Swettenham, J. (1999) Bullying and theory of mind: a critique of the 'social skills deficit' view of anti-social behaviour, *Social Development,* 8: 117–27.

Sutton-Smith, B. (1988) War-toys and childhood aggression, *Aggression, Play and Culture*, 1: 57–69.

Terranova, A. M., Sheffield Morris, A. and Boxer, P. (2008) Fear reactivity and effortful control in overt and relational bullying: a six-month longitudinal study, *Aggressive Behavior*, 34(1): 104–15.

Thomas, N., and O'Kane, C. (2000). Discovering what children think: connections between research and practice, *British Journal of Social Work*, 30: 819–35.

Titman, W (1994) *Special People, Special Places*. Winchester: Learning through Land-scapes.

Toda, Y. (2005) International comparison of peer support in Japan, in M. Tsuchiya, P. K. Smith, K. Soeda and K. Oride (eds.), *Ijime/Bullying: Responses and Measures to the Issues on Ijime/Bullying in Schools in Japan and the World*. Kyoto, Japan: Minerva Publishing.

Tuckman, B. W. (1965) Developmental sequences in small groups, *Psychological Bulletin*, 63: 384–89.

Tulloch, M. (1998) Australian school children's perceptions of television representation of bullying and victimization, in P. Slee and K. Rigby (eds.), *Children's Peer Relations:* (pp. 215–16). London: Routledge.

Underwood, M. K., Galen, B. R. and Paquette, J. A. (2001) Top ten challenges for understanding gender and aggression in children: why can't we all just get along? *Social Development,* 10(2): 248–66.

United Nations (1989) *Convention on the Rights of the Child*. Geneva, Switzerland: Office of the United Nations High Commissioner for Human Rights. (www.unicef.org/crc: assessed 9 March 2207).

Van Schoiack Edstrom, L., Frey, K. S. and Beland, K. (2002) Changing adolescents' attitudes about relational and physical aggression: an early evaluation of a school-based intervention, *School Psychology Review*, 31(2): 201–16.

Varma-Joshi, M., Baker, C. J. and Tanaka, C. (2004) Names will never hurt me? *Harvard Educational Review*, 74(2): 175–208.

Varnava, G. (2000) *Towards a Non-violent Society: Checkpoints for Schools*. London: National Children's Bureau.

Varnava, G. (2002) *Towards a Non-Violent Society: Checkpoints for Young People*. London: National Children's Bureau.

Veale, A. (2005) Creative methodologies in participatory research with children, in S. Greene and D. Hogan (eds.), *Researching Children's Experience*: (pp. 253–72). London: Sage Publications.

Verkuyten, M. and Thijs, J. (2001). Peer victimization and self-esteem of ethnic minority group children, *Journal of Community and Applied Social Psychology*, 11: 227–34.

Vicars, M. (2006) Who are you calling queer? Sticks and stones can break my bones but names will always hurt me, *British Education Research Journal*, 32(3): 347–61.

Wachtel, T. and McCold, T. (2001) Restorative justice in everyday life: beyond the formal ritual, in H. Strang and J. Braithwaite (eds.), *Restorative Justice and Civil Society:* (pp. 114–29). Cambridge: Cambridge University Press.

Warden, D. and Christie, D. (1997) *Teaching Social Behaviour*. London: David Fulton.

Warren, C. and Williams, S. (2007) *Restoring the Balance 2. Changing Culture Through Restorative Approaches: The Experience of Lewisham Schools*. London: Lewisham Council Restorative Approaches Partnership.

Watkins, C., Mauthner, M., Hewitt, R., Epstein, D. and Leonard, D. (2007) School violence, school differences and school discourses, *British Educational Research Journal*, 33(1): 61–74.

Watson, S., Vannini, N., Davis, M., Woods, S., Hall, M. and Dautenhahn, K. (2007) FearNot! an anti-bullying intervention: evaluation of an interactive virtual learning environment (www.e-circus.org).

Weare, K. (2004) *Developing the Emotionally Literate School*. London: Paul Chapman Publishing.

Wegerif, R. and Mercer, N. (1997) Using computer-based text analysis to integrate quantitative and qualitative methods in the investigation of collaborative learning, *Language and Education*, 11(4): 271–86.

White, M. and Epston, D. (1990) *Narrative Means to Therapeutic Ends*. New York: W. W. Norton.

Whitney, I. and Smith, P. K. (1993) A survey of the nature and extent of bully/victim problems in junior/middle and secondary schools, *Educational Research*, 35: 3–25.

Whitney, I., Smith, P. K. and Thompson, D. (1994) Bullying and children with special educational needs, in P. K. Smith and S. Sharp (eds.), *School Bullying: Insights and Perspectives*: (pp. 213–40). London: Routledge.

Whittle, S., Turner, L. and Al-Alami, M. (2007) *Engendered Penalties: Transgender and Transsexual People's Experiences of Inequality and Discrimination*. Crown Copyright: Equalities Review.

Winslade, J. and Monk, G. (1999) *Narrative Counseling in Schools: Powerful and Brief.* Thousand Oaks, CA: Sage Publications.

WOMANKIND Worldwide (2007) *Challenging Violence Changing Lives. Gender on the UK Education Agenda: Findings and Recommendations 2004–2007*. London: Author.

World Health Organization (WHO) (1999) *Violence Prevention: An Important Element of a Health-promoting School. WHO Information Series on School Health*. Geneva Author.

World Health Organization (WHO) (2002) *World Report on Violence and Health*. Geneva Author.

Young, S. (1998) The support group approach to bullying in schools, *Educational Psychology in Practice*, 14: 32–9.

Youth Justice Board (YJB) (2004) *National Evaluation of the Restorative Justice in Schools Programme*. London: Author (www.youth-justice-board.gov.uk).

Youth Justice Board. (2005) *Risk and Protective Factors*. London: Author.

Zehr, H. (2002) *The Little Book of Restorative Justice* Intercourse, PA: Good Books Publications.

Zoll, C., Enz, S., Schaub, H., Aylet, R. and Paiva, A. (2006) Fighting bullying with the help of autonomous agents in a virtual school environment. Proceedings of the 7th International Conference on Cognitive Modelling (ICCM-06), Trieste, Italy: Lawrence Erlbaum.

INDEX

ABC Training and Support 89–90
Aber, J. 124, 126–127
Aggression
    Proactive 4–5
    Reactive 4–5
Aggressive behaviour 4, 25
Ainscow, M. 29
Alderson, P. 30–31
Alsaker, F. 126
Andershed, H. 4, 25
Andrès, S. 88, 91, 92, 97, 99–100
Angelides, P. 29
Anti-Bullying Alliance 73
Aronson, E. 69
Arora, T. 1, 95,
Arsenault, L. 42, 46
Askew, S. 20
Attachment theory 63–66, 106–107
Aylett, R. S. 109, 112
Aynsley-Green, A. 128, 130
Baldry, A. 19, 119,
Bargh, J. A. 92
Barrios, A. 99
Bauman, S. 3
Baumeister, R. F. 57–58
Befriending 43, 88–91
Beinart, S. 20–21
Bennathan, M. 63, 64, 65
Berdondini, L. 71, 73
Besag, V. 57, 62,
Bettelheim, B. 108
Blatchford, P. 74–75, 124–125, 131
Björkqvist, K. 3, 7
Boal, A. 109
Bober, M. 11
Bosacki, S. L. 5, 43, 110
Bossert, S. T. 69
Boulton, M. J. 1, 4, 42
Boxall, M. 63, 64, 65
Brandenburg-Ayres, S. J. 4, 25
Braverman, M. 28

Bretherton, I. 106
Brown, L. M. 129
Brun, B. 116
Bruner, J. S. 108
Buddying 88–91
Bullied children 41–53, 54–66, 68–84
    Relationships 42–53
Bullies 54–66,
    Assistants 55,
    Reinforcers 55,
    Relationships 54–66,
Bully-victims 8, 42, 54, 55–57
Bullying
    Behaviours
    Causes 11–12, 18–21
    Context 18–21
    Cyber 10–12, 24, 33
    Definitions of 1–2, 3–16
    Direct 3
    Disablist 12–13
    Gender 15–16
    Gender differences 3
    Homophobic 15, 26
    Incidence of 5, 26–27
    Indirect 3
    Injury risk factor 16–18
    Negative consequences of 3–4, 16–18,
        25
    Neighbourhood 13–15
    Participant roles in 7–9
    Physical 2–10, 57,
    Psychological 2–10, 57
    Racist 12
    Relational 2–10, 41–52, 54–66, 68–84
    Risk and protective factors 18–21
    Scale and nature of 6–7
    Sexual 15–16
    Social group context 7–10
    Verbal 2–10
    Victims of 42, 43–44, 62–63
Burns, G. W. 115–116, 117

Byron, T. 112–113
Bystanders 118, 125
Cairns, R. B. 19
Cameron, L. 46
Candela, A. 69
Carlsson-Paige, N. 111
Carter, C. 20
Cartoons 111–112,
Cartwright, N. 87–88, 91
Cattanach, A. 117
Checkpoints for Schools 29
Checkpoints for Young People 94–95
ChildLine 27
ChildLine in Partnership with Schools
    103
Christie, D. 69
Circle time 77, 93
Civil rights 31
Clabby, J. F. 124
Coie, J. D. 3, 25
Cole, T. 52, 103,
Conferencing 50–51
Conflict resolution 47–51, 92–93,
    126–127
Context 18–21
    Individual 18–19
    Interpersonal 19–20
    Community 19–20
    Wider society 20
Convivença 98–103
Cooper, P. 63, 64, 65–66, 125–126
Cooperative group learning 68–85
    Buzz groups 76–77
    Circle time 77
    Developing effective groups 76
    Discussion groups 77
    Duration of 84
    Essential aspects of 68–76
    Group membership 84
    Problem-solving circles 77
    Production activities 81–82
    Quality circles 77–81
    Role play 82–83
    Simulations 82
    Successful 83–84
    Task 84
Costabile, A. 111
Council of Europe 93–94
Cowie, H. 4, 10–11, 15, 27–29, 38–39, 46,
    49, 52, 55–57, 62, 66, 68–69, 71–76,
    77–81, 83–84, 86, 87, 88, 91–96,
    97–98, 100–104, 124, 128
Cremin, H. 48, 92, 93, 96, 98
Crick, N. R. 3, 4, 5, 25

Cunningham, C. 92, 93
Culture change 29–30, 38
Cyber peer support 91–92
Daly, A. 58, 59
Defensive egotism 57–58
Del Rio, A. 3
Demetriades, A. 124
Department for Children, Schools and
    Families 10, 24, 26, 32, 104, 121, 123,
    128
Depression 42–45
DeRosier, M. E. 7
Derrington, C. 12
Diego, M. A. 131
Dodge, K. A. 4, 5, 25
Donegal Project 69
Drama 109
Duncan, N. 11, 15–16
Dunn, J. 41–42, 106, 107, 125
Dusenbury, L. 69
Ecological framework 33–34
Ecological model 18–21
Education Act 2002 26
Education and Inspections Act 2006 26
Egan, S. K. 44,
Elias, M. J. 124
Ellis, A. A. 3
Emotional literacy 81–82, 122–124
Engel, S. 106
Engeström, K. 16, 118–18, 120
Epston, D. 114–116
Escobar, M. 44
Evaluation 38–39
Every Child Matters 24–26, 37
Farrington, D.P. 4, 19, 20–21, 119
Fernandez, I. 92
Ferrazzuolo, S. 8, 45,
Fiction 73, 107–108
Field, T. 131
Fonagy, P. 110
France, A. 20
Freeman, J. 107
Frey, K. S. 124
Friendship 41, 43, 62–63, 121
Frosh, S. 59
Galloway, D. 69
Galvin, P. 32
Gang membership 4, 25
Gender 15–16,
Glover, D. 87
Gersie, A. 116, 117
Gilligan, C. 124
Glover, D. 5, 25
Goleman, E. 66, 122

Greene, S. 95,
Greenberg, M. T. 124
Gregory, R. 15
Griffin, R. S. 8
Gross, A. M. 8
Grossman, C. D. 37, 124
Grotpeter, J. K. 3, 4, 25
Guerin, S. 2
Gunter, B. 110
Hall, L. 109, 112, 113–114
Hanewinkel, R. 126
Happiness 41
Harachi, T. W. 4
Harris, P. L. 123
Harrison, H. 42
Hartup, W. W. 42, 66
Hawker, D. S. J. 3, 42
Hazler, R. J. 3, 25, 52, 60–61, 66, 124
Hennessy, E. 2
Higgins, C. 131
Hinduja, S. 11
Hodson, J. 13
Hogan, S. 95
Holmes, S. R. 4, 25
Hopkins, B. 47, 52
Hurst, T. 98
Hutson, N. 87, 91–92, 95–96
Interpersonal Process Recall 72–73
James, A. 95
Jennifer, D. 4, 6–10, 11–12, 26, 27–28, 29,
    46, 49, 62, 66, 95, 111–112, 124, 128,
    128–130
Johnson, D. W. 68, 69, 83
Johnson, R. T. 69
Kagan, S. 69
Kaltiala-Heino, R. 25, 54
Kaukiainen, A. 57
Kelly, N. 13
Kumpulainen, K. 54
La Greca, A. 42,
Laflamme, L. 16–17, 119
Lagerspetz, K. M. J. 7
Lahelma, E. 11
Lane-Garon, P. 98
Learning through Landscapes 124–125
Leather, P. 27, 32
Lera, M. J. 69
Levan, S. 2
Levin, D. 111
Li, Q. 10
Limber, S. P. 126
Livingston, S. 11
Lloyd, G. 12
Local Government Act 2000 26

Loneliness 42–43
Louchart, S. 109
Lucas, T. 16
Ma, X. 42,
Maines, B. 52, 61–62, 67, 122
Malley, J. 25, 33–34, 37
Marini, Z. A. 42, 66
Martlew, M. 13
Matthews, B. 81–82
Matthews, H. 13–15
Mavroveli, S. 123–124
Mayer, J. D. 122–123
McAleer, J. 110
McCold, T. 46
McKenna, E. 92
McLaughlin, E. 52
Mediation 48–51, 96
Mencap 11
Menesini, E. 19, 91
Mercer, N. 69
Method of Shared Concern 46, 61–62, 66,
    122
Meuret, D. 30
Minton, S. J. 69, 119, 126, 131
Monk, G. 115
Morlaix, S. 30
Mooij, T. 126
Mooney, A. 12
Moran, S. 11, 12
Morita, Y. 1
Morrison, B. 46
Morrison, L. 81–82
Munthe, E. 69
Murray-Close, D. 4
Nabuzoka, D. 13
Nangle, D. 42,
Narcissism 57–59,
Narrative 105–117
    Representations of bullying 5, 11–12
    Tasks 70, 71–73
    Therapy 114–116
Naylor, P. 1, 2, 5, 97, 98
Needs analysis 27–39
    Acceptance of the existence of school
        bullying 27
    Relational approach 33–37
    Senior Management Team 28–30
    Systematic and impartial
        implementation 32–33
    Working group 30–32
    Training in policy and practice 37–38
Nicolaides, S. 4
Nieminen, E. 4, 5
Noret, N. 11

Norwich, B. 13
Novacek, J. 57
Nurture groups 63–66, 125–126
O'Connell, P. 7
Office of the Children's Commissioner 27
Olweus, D. 1, 2, 4, 7, 9, 18, 19, 42, 119, 126
O'Kane, C. 128
O'Moore, A. M. 20, 69, 73, 119, 126, 131
Olafsson, R. 97–98
Opie, I. 125
Opie, P. 125
Oppenheim, D. 107
Ortega, R. 69, 71
Osborne, R. 74
Ostracism 59,
Owens, L. 5, 55
Oztug, O. 100–103
Parents/carers 63–66, 125–126
Park, N.130
Participant Roles 7–9
    Assistants 7–8, 55
    Bullies 7–8, 54–66
    Bully-victims 8, 42, 54, 55–57
    Bystanders 118, 125
    Defenders 7–8
    Outsiders 7–8
    Reinforcers 7–8, 55
    Victims 7–8
Participant Role Scale 7, 8, 70–71
Patchin, J. W. 11
Paterson, H. 88
Peer counselling 87–88, 90
Peer mediation 48
Peer support 86–104
Pellegrini, A. D. 19
Pepler, D. 5, 119, 126
Percy-Smith, B. 13–15
Perlman, J. 73, 117
Perry, D. G. 42, 44,
Petch, B. 52, 104
Petrides, K. V. 123–124
Pikas, A. 46, 61, 66, 122
Play 106, 124–125
Positive psychology 130–131
Promoting Issues in Common 60–61
Protherough, R. 107
Prout, A. 95, 130
Punch, S. 128
PSHCE 48
Räsänen, E. 54
Raskin, R. 54
Ray, V. 15
Relational approach 33–37, 41–52

Group support level 34–35
    Individual support level 35
    Whole-school support level 34
Relationship difficulties 41–42
Resilience 43–45
Restorative approach 35–36, 46–51
Restorative conferences 50–51
Restorative practice 46–51, 118–119
Review and evaluation 38–39
Revised Olweus Bully/Victim Questionnaire 6, 33
Richardson, T. 98
Rigby, K. 3
Riley, P. L. 38
Rivers, I. 11, 15, 26
Risk and protective factors 18–19, 120–122, 127–128
Robinson, G. 52, 61–62, 67, 122
Roffey, S. 29–30
Rogaland Project 69
Roland, E. 69
Role play 82–83, 109
Ross, C. 131
R Time 73–74
Rustin, Margaret 108
Rustin, Michael 108
Safe to Learn: Embedding Anti-bullying Work in Schools 26, 32
Salmivalli, C. 4, 5, 7, 8, 9, 58, 70, 73, 98, 99, 110
Salovey, P. 122–123
Salter, K. 52, 104
Scarlett, G. 106
Scherer-Thompson, J. 104
School councils 30–31
School environment/ethos 98–103, 118–132
School Standards Framework Act 1998 26
Second Step Programme 37
Segal, E. C. 39
Self-esteem 3, 25, 43–45, 59–60
Seville Anti-bullying Project 69, 70–71
Sharan, S. 69
Sharp, S. 46, 52, 62, 67, 68, 76, 77–81, 83–84, 88, 98, 119, 124–125, 131
Shaughnessy, J. 6–7, 26, 28, 29, 94
Sheffield Anti-Bullying Project 69
Shute, R. 3
Slavin, R. 69
Slee, P. T. 2
Skiba, R. 37, 60, 118–119, 126
Smith, D. 2
Smith, N. 131

Smith, P. K. 1, 2, 4, 5, 7, 8, 13, 43, 71, 87, 88, 97, 98, 119, 126
Social anxiety 43–45
Social and Emotional Aspects of Learning (SEAL) 48, 119, 123–124
Social Pedagogic Research into Grouping (SPRinG) 75
Stacey, H. 92
Stead, J. 12
Steiner, M. 68–69, 83, 84
Stephenson, P. 2
Student councils 93–94, 95
Sullivan, K. 46, 62, 67
Sutton, J. 7, 55
Support Group Method 61–62, 66
Talamelli, L. 43,
Terranova, A. M. 57, 58
Thijs, J. 44,
Thomas, N. 128
Thompson, D. 93
Thorsborne, M. 46
Tiknaz, Y., 125
Titman, W. 124
Toda, Y. 92
Tuckman, B. W. 75–76
Tulloch, M. 111
Twidle, R. 52, 104
UK Observatory 53,
Underwood, M. K. 1, 2, 5
United Nations Convention on the Rights of the Child 24, 30, 37, 128
Utting, D. 20
Van Schoiack Edstrom, L. 124
Varnava, G. 29, 94–95
Varma-Joshi, M. 11, 12
Veale, A. 95
Verkuyten, M. 44

Vicars, M. 11
Victims
    Continuing 8, 43–44
    Defenders of 62–63
    Escaped 8
    Passive 18
    Provocative 8, 18, 42
Virtual reality 107, 112–114,
Voice of the child 128–130
Wachtel, T. 46,
Wallace, P. 29, 86, 88, 104
Warden, D. 69
Warren, C. 36, 47, 48, 51, 52, 119, 132
Watkins, C. 34
Watson, D. 86, 88, 97, 98, 112, 113–114
Weare, K. 66
Wegerif, R. 69
White, M. 114–116
Whitebread, D. 63, 65–66
Whitney, I. 5, 13
Whittle, S. 16
Whole-school approach 24–40, 119–122
Williams, S. 36, 47, 48, 51, 52, 119, 132
Winslade, J. 115
Withers, T. 52, 104
Wolf, D. 106
WOMANKIND Worldwide 16
World Health Organization 18, 19, 27
World Report on Violence and Health 27
    Four-stage process for reducing and preventing violence 27
Youth Justice Board 19–21, 46–47
Youth Offending Teams 47
Zehr, H. 52
Zero tolerance 36–37, 60, 118–119, 126
Zoll, C., 113

UNDERSTANDING GIRLS' FRIENDSHIPS, FIGHTS AND FEUDS

A Practical Approach to Girls' Bullying

Val Besag

Girls' bullying is more subtle and less physical than that perpetrated by boys; however, it can be just as powerful, and the emotional repercussions of bullying among girls can be more destructive and longer lasting than the effects of more obvious forms of bullying. Teachers report that quarrels between girls are far more time-consuming and difficult to resolve than the disputes of boys, yet not enough information is available to guide them on dealing with girls' fighting and unhappiness caused by their relationships with other girls, many of whom may have been their closest friends.

Understanding Girls' Friendships, Fights and Feuds illuminates the issue of girls' bullying – an issue that can cause a great deal of distress but which is sometimes ignored or dismissed by adults. Drawing on close observations of girls' behaviour, Val Besag provides an in-depth understanding of girls' bullying, exploring the mechanisms and language that girls use to entice some into their groups and exclude others.

The book offers detailed practical advice for dealing with girls' bullying, which will help both students and teachers to understand and combat different kinds of bullying, as well as comprehensive guidance for preventing or reducing bullying activities among girls, including:

- Whole school approaches
- Programmes for developing emotional literacy and resilience
- Approaches for dealing with gangs
- Using methods such as art and drama
- Developing conflict resolution skills
- Student – parent programmes
- Peer support programmes

This is key reading for teachers, trainee teachers, educational psychologists and social workers, academics and researchers in the field, and others who have an interest in creating bully-free schools and societies.

Contents: *Acknowledgements – Preface – Section 1 Exploring the problem – She's my best friend, but I hate her! – The activity club – Section 2 Gender differences in children's social behaviour – The power of the peer group: Affiliation and differentiation – Toys for boys: Gossip for girls? – Girls cooperate – but boys compete? – When things go sour – Bullying – Mirror, mirror on the wall: Cruel comparisons – Section 3 Groups – Cliques, groups and gangs – Dyads, triads and lover's quarrels – Little miss popular – Madam machiavelli – Section 4 The language of conflict – The language of conflict – Grassing – Insult – Gossip and rumour – Section 5 Emotional issues – The more deadly of the species? – The green eyed god – Section 6 Case studies – Case studies – Section 7 Remediation, reparation and resolution – Strategies for supporting individual girls – What can the school do? – References.*

2006 217pp

978-0-335-21982-7 (Paperback) 978-0-335-21983-4 (Hardback)

IMPROVING BEHAVIOUR AND ATTENDANCE AT SCHOOL

Susan Hallam and Lynne Rogers

Behaviour remains a huge issue of concern at all levels of education. This book draws together research and practice to uncover the complexities of improving behaviour and attendance in school and offers a range of practical solutions aimed at tackling behavioural issues and its prevention for schools, teachers, non-teaching staff, and those working to support them in Local Authorities.

It considers current concerns relating to the behaviour of children and young people, the theoretical underpinnings of possible approaches to improving behaviour and attendance, as well as what we know about the causes of disaffection. In exploring ways that behaviour and attendance can be improved, the authors examine a range of perspectives including school management and whole school policies, and behaviour in and around the school, in the classroom, and of individual pupils, particularly those at risk of exclusion from school.

It discusses the work of Behaviour and Educational Support Teams, teacher coaches, learning mentors and nurture groups as ways of supporting children and young people, particularly those identified as being 'at risk'. It also outlines ways of improving relationships between the school and home, as well as the ways that parents can be supported to assist in changing their children's behaviour and attendance. Alternatives to exclusion and new curricula are discussed in relation to their success in maintaining students in education.

The final chapters focus on attendance and what can be done to improve it in the general school population and those students who are persistent absentees. Throughout the book case studies are used to illustrate examples of good practice and the impact on children, parents and teachers. The book concludes with an overview of key issues emerging for practice.

Contents: *Section 1: The context – Background – Theoretical underpinnings and the causes of poor behaviour – Section 2: Improving behaviour – Management and whole school policies – Behaviour in and around school – Home-school relationships – Supporting parents through the use of parenting programmes – Behaviour in the classroom – Alternative curricula – Supporting at risk children – Approaches to exclusion – Section 3: Improving attendance – Whole school approaches to attendance – Working with persistent absentees – Section 4: Overview – Overview.*

2008 312pp

978-0-335-22242-1 (Paperback) 978-0-335-22241-4 (Hardback)

BEHAVIOUR IN SCHOOLS 2/e

Theory and Practice for Teachers

Louise Porter

Behaviour management in the classroom and playground is one of the most challenging aspects of teaching. The new edition of *Behaviour in Schools* offers a comprehensive overview of the major theories of behaviour management in primary and secondary schools, illustrated with detailed case studies.

The theories covered range from teacher-dominated methods to more democratic approaches. They include assertive discipline, applied behaviour analysis, the new cognitive behavioural approaches, neo-Adlerian theory, humanism, Glasser's control theory and systems theory. The emphasis is on proactive approaches to discipline which allow teachers to achieve their educational and social goals for their students and themselves. Porter also shows how to enhance students' motivation and help students become confident and independent learners.

Maintaining the balance of theory and practice, the new edition has been fully updated in light of recent research, including a strengthened discussion of inclusion and anti-bias curricula, and sections on motivation and self-esteem. References have been also been updated, making fuller use of UK research.

Behaviour in Schools is a textbook for education students and a reference for experienced teachers who want to improve their ability to cope with disruptive behaviour.

Contents: *Part one: The theories – Introduction – The limit-setting approaches – Applied behaviour analysis – Cognitive-behaviourism – Neo-Adlerian theory – Choice theory – Systems theory – Critique of the theories – Part two: Motivating students – Safeguarding students – Meeting students' need for autonomy – Fostering competence – Meeting students' social needs – Part three: Beyond the classroom – Collaborating with parents – Formulating a discipline policy – Bibliography – Index.*

2006 368pp

978-0-335-22001-4 (Paperback)